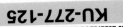

Other Titles in this Series

Mike Bartlett
BULL
GAME
AN INTERVENTION
KING CHARLES III
WILD

Tom Basden
THE CROCODILE
HOLES
JOSEPH K
THERE IS A WAR

Deborah Bruce
THE DISTANCE
GODCHILD
SAME

Jez Butterworth
JERUSALEM
JEZ BUTTERWORTH PLAYS: ONE
MOJO
THE NIGHT HERON
PARLOUR SONG
THE RIVER
THE WINTERLING

Caryl Churchill
BLUE HEART
CHURCHILL PLAYS: THREE
CHURCHILL PLAYS: FOUR
CHURCHILL: SHORTS
CLOUD NINE
DING DONG THE WICKED
A DREAM PLAY *after* Strindberg
DRUNK ENOUGH TO SAY
    I LOVE YOU?
ESCAPED ALONE
FAR AWAY
HERE WE GO
HOTEL
ICECREAM
LIGHT SHINING IN
    BUCKINGHAMSHIRE
LOVE AND INFORMATION
MAD FOREST
A NUMBER
SEVEN JEWISH CHILDREN
THE SKRIKER
THIS IS A CHAIR
THYESTES *after* Seneca
TRAPS

Vivienne Franzmann
MOGADISHU
PESTS
THE WITNESS

debbie tucker green
BORN BAD
DIRTY BUTTERFLY
HANG
NUT
RANDOM
STONING MARY
TRADE & GENERATIONS
TRUTH AND RECONCILIATION

Stacey Gregg
LAGAN
OVERRIDE
PERVE
SHIBBOLETH
WHEN COWS GO BOOM

Sam Holcroft
COCKROACH
DANCING BEARS
EDGAR & ANNABEL
PINK
RULES FOR LIVING
THE WARDROBE
WHILE YOU LIE

Vicky Jones
THE ONE

Lucy Kirkwood
BEAUTY AND THE BEAST
    with Katie Mitchell
BLOODY WIMMIN
CHIMERICA
HEDDA *after* Ibsen
IT FELT EMPTY WHEN THE
    HEART WENT AT FIRST BUT
    IT IS ALRIGHT NOW
NSFW
TINDERBOX

Cordelia Lynn
LELA & CO.

Evan Placey
CONSENSUAL
GIRLS LIKE THAT
PRONOUN

James Rushbrooke
TOMCAT

Stef Smith
HUMAN ANIMALS
REMOTE
SWALLOW

Jack Thorne
2ND MAY 1997
BUNNY
BURYING YOUR BROTHER IN
    THE PAVEMENT
HOPE
JACK THORNE PLAYS: ONE
LET THE RIGHT ONE IN
    after John Ajvide Lindqvist
MYDIDAE
THE SOLID LIFE OF SUGAR WATER
STACY & FANNY AND FAGGOT
WHEN YOU CURE ME

Phoebe Waller-Bridge
FLEABAG

Tom Wells
FOLK
JUMPERS FOR GOALPOSTS
THE KITCHEN SINK
ME, AS A PENGUIN

Evan Placey

GIRLS LIKE THAT
and other plays for teenagers

Banana Boys
Holloway Jones
Girls Like That
Pronoun

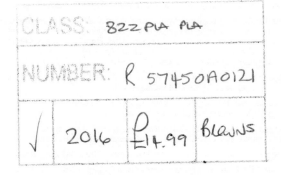

CLASS: 822 PLA PLA

NUMBER: R 57450A0121

| ✓ | 2016 | £14.99 | BLAWNS |

NICK HERN BOOKS
London
www.nickhernbooks.co.uk

A Nick Hern Book

Girls Like That & Other Plays for Teenagers first published in Great Britain
as a paperback original in 2016 by Nick Hern Books Limited, The Glasshouse,
49a Goldhawk Road, London W12 8QP

Cover image, clockwise from top left: photograph by Matthew Hargraves, image
design by John McAreavy for West Yorkshire Playhouse; © iStock.com/ Flamingo_
Photography; John McAreavy for West Yorkshire Playhouse; shutterstock.com/iatlo

Designed and typeset by Nick Hern Books, London
Printed in Great Britain by CPI Books (UK) Ltd

A CIP catalogue record for this book is available from the British Library

ISBN 978 1 84842 515 6

Contents

Introduction

About eight years ago, I was on the South Bank of the Thames for New Year's Eve, watching the fireworks. When the clock struck midnight, like the other couples that surrounded us, my boyfriend and I kissed. And then a woman nearby with her two kids calmly said to us: 'There are kids around.' I said nothing. If she'd used a homophobic slur or sworn or been angry I quickly would have had a retort. But what she calmly said floored me so much that I didn't have a response. I've unpacked this moment many times over the past eight years. I've also replayed it over and over with the aim of replying with what I should have said. But in truth, I still don't know what I should have said to her, or her kids for that matter. But that woman, whoever and wherever you are, know that I think about you a lot, even though I was probably a barely passing blip in your life. And know also – and this is going to sound weird, particularly as we don't know each other, and particularly as you've only ever said one thing to me, and I haven't actually ever said anything to you, even when given the chance – that you are part of the reason I write plays for young people. Or more specifically, your kids are. I think about them a lot and wonder – *hope* – that they're incidentally in the audience of one of my plays. If I had a better sense of humour I would have dedicated this collection to you. Because you made me realise why we need theatre for young audiences. Adults, for the most part, have made up their mind about the world around them. But young people are still questioning it and making up their own minds. But, and I say this as a parent myself, we can't always trust our parents to foster these questions, and encourage us to see the world in new ways. And that's why we need plays for young people. To ask the questions that no one else is asking. To challenge the world as we think we know it. To help us make sense of the moment we see two blokes kissing by the river and our mum thinks she should shield our eyes.

Fast-forward several years...

'But how did you know?' It was after a readthrough for the first draft of *Girls Like That* with a group of young people to elicit their feedback. The boy asking stared at me with genuine curiosity. He wanted to know how I, a fully grown man, had penetrated the secret world of teenagers. And the answer is simple: I was a teenager once too. The world has changed, the clothes, the language, the technology, the social attitudes, but the fundamental shape of the teenage experience has remained the same for decades. It's the details that make each of our experiences unique during those formative years, but deep down at its roots, we've all lived the same experience, the one that teens will continue living until the end of time: a collection of moments and choices in which we begin forming the person we want to be. (And spoiler for young readers: it really is just the beginning. You never stop trying to figure out who you want to be. I'm certainly still trying.) When people say 'Write what you know', I very much agree. But perhaps not in the conventional sense. Not in a write-about-a-world-or-story-you-*literally*-know way. For me it's about what you know emotionally, and in your heart. I know about feeling like I don't fit in; I know about heartbreak; I know about not living up to family's expectations, about losing friends, about not standing up to the group, about regret, and loss, and lust, and love. I am not and have never been captain of the football team, or part of a gang of girls. I've not had a parent in prison, and I'm not transgender. But I am Cameron from *Banana Boys*, and the Girls in *Girls Like That*, and *Pronoun*'s Dean, and I am Holloway Jones. Their experience is one I know: the outsider.

Whilst I was doing my MA, we had a guest workshop with Kate Leys, a film script editor. She talked about the story structure as 'A stranger came to town'. I don't remember what kinds of stories she was talking about or how widely she was applying it. I don't remember anything about how she elucidated this, but 'A stranger came to town' stuck. And it's the same play I've been writing and rewriting over and over one way or another. Perhaps because I have always felt like a stranger. As an immigrant, as a gay man, as a Jew. And I think that maybe we all feel like strangers when we're teenagers – to the parents and friends who don't understand us; to our changing bodies which aren't doing what we want them to; to ourselves as we try to understand why we do the things we do. To be a young person is to be a stranger to the wider world who never quite gets you. All of the plays in this collection are about the stranger who came to town. Cameron, Holloway, Scarlett and Dean are all strangers: because of their sexuality, gender identity, or family background.

When writing for young people I think a lot about the characters I wish I'd seen as a kid. And those characters and stories are still the ones I'm not seeing on stage. It's my desire to bring those people to life that inspired these four plays. No, it's the *responsibility* I feel to tell the stories that has pulled me to table and chair and forced me to write them. For the other strangers in the audience. Since becoming a dad, it's a responsibility I feel more acutely than ever. My son is a child of colour, with two dads, and the sad truth is there will come a day when he too feels like a stranger in the country he calls home. What plays do I want him to see? Because art has a responsibility to reflect the world of its audiences. But also it *should* go one step further. It should show them the world they don't know, tell them the stories they haven't heard, and ask them the questions they haven't thought of. I don't write just for the strangers in the audience, I write for the town.

My favourite films and plays as a kid were worlds and stories run by children, void of adults. And this has permeated not only the worlds of the plays I write for young audiences, but the way I approach writing them too. I ignore the adults: the parents and the teachers. I'm not writing for the gatekeepers, but for the young people in the audience, and the young people performing in the play. The main characters in my plays are always young people, but beyond that there is no difference in how I approach writing a play for young people versus how I write plays for adults. Because unlike that woman on the South Bank eight years ago, I don't censor the world for young people. They encounter it in their daily lives, so why shouldn't they encounter it in the theatre?

There isn't a moral or message in these plays, so don't try to find one. There aren't any answers either. I don't have them. But maybe these plays can act as provocations for young people to find the answers. It's they who must find them. It's their future.

* * *

Banana Boys came about because of a lovely man named Neil Grutchfield from that lovely breed of people writers depend on – the silent partner, the dramaturg. He was the literary manager at Hampstead Theatre and we were having a chat about another play of mine, and I'd mentioned that my job – since at the time I was not making any money from playwriting – was running educational theatre projects for young people. But I'd never combined my two passions. So he put me up for a commission to write for heat&light, the theatre's youth theatre, for which young people decide upon the selected writer. Which luckily was me. Once I'd landed the gig to write for a big cast of teenagers, I didn't have any idea what to write. So I read the back catalogue of plays they'd done and noticed that not a single one mentioned sex. At all. Which I'd found odd since when I was sixteen that was pretty much all I thought about. And none of the plays had a single gay character. So I decided to bring both to the forefront of the play.

Growing up queer there weren't many young gay role models to look up to. So instead I looked up to music divas. I'm not sure what it was, but there was something about their power, their confidence, and their absolutely being at ease in their own skin that left me in awe. And so the opportunity to create my very own group of divas, The Banana Girls, was irresistible. My favourite films as a teen were the romcoms, except the queer characters didn't exist in them, never mind being forefront. So it was my chance to rectify the past.

But as is often the case when I write a play, I start off writing one thing and end up writing something else. I think I started thinking I would write a coming-out story. And then that I'd write a love story. But that's not really what I wrote in the end. Instead I wrote a play about friendship. With maybe a little coming-out and love story on the side.

* * *

In the midst of *Banana Boys* rehearsals, Neil moved to Synergy Theatre Company and introduced my work to Esther Baker, the artistic director. And Synergy, in many ways, has become a home away from home for me. They do work across the criminal justice system, and their attitude and outlook – which is no bullshit, and all about the art – is very inspiring. They asked me to write a play for a schools' tour. To discover what I wanted to write about, I worked with people who were parents while in prison, young people in prison, young people at risk of offending, and young people in care. I was interested in how young people are set up to do bad and how difficult it is to break away from what people expect of you. 'Snitches get stitches,' said a young man to me as I was running a workshop in a school. When I questioned the statement further, it became clear the class was united on this law, and I was the ignorant outsider who had somehow gone through life without an understanding of the code. A code which was more than about loyalty, about friendship, about right and wrong – a code which is simply an unquestioned tenet of life. It just is.

My induction into 'snitches get stitches' fuelled my desire to write a play about choices: the choices of what we wear, of who we're friends with, of who we love. The choice to ask questions or to stay silent. The choice to help or merely be an onlooker. The choice to accept the life we're given, or to pave our own future.

During my research there were two stories in particular which were a driving force in creating Holloway Jones's journey. First, there was a young woman I spoke to who was in prison for joint criminal enterprise. Having gone along with her boyfriend's mate, she was present when he was involved in an attack. As she clearly explained to me, she didn't actually have anything to do with it; she didn't do anything. But it was this very doing nothing that had her put in jail. Rather than stay and call the police, she ran off with the culprit, which under joint enterprise, made her as culpable. This got me thinking about those instant decisions we make which can change our lives completely, and how our inactions are as much decisions as our actions. When do we become responsible for what happens to others? This same young woman also talked about the world in which she lived before going to prison: one in which boys bought her expensive things, drove around in the coolest cars – but how none of it was worth it when faced with prison.

The second was a mother, who had been in prison for the majority of the time while her children were growing up. I was struck by the idea of writing a mother/daughter relationship whose development was confined to a prison visiting room. How much is their relationship a product of the space in which it takes place? This also fitted into wider themes of how much are we the products of the places where we grow up. Meanwhile, I was seeing young people estranged from the 2012 London Olympics coming to their own city. So a seed was planted of how a girl born in prison goes on to become an Olympian. The Olympic idea led on to my wanting to explore a Greek chorus and what this would be like in a modern context. But because it's a play about a girl who challenges her destiny, they had to be an unreliable and biased chorus.

The reality of writing *Holloway Jones* for a schools' tour, before its run at the Unicorn Theatre in London, was that there wouldn't necessarily be any access to lights or anything technical in some schools, so I needed to find a way to keep the play 'alive' without anything to help me – and the bikes, screen and chorus allowed that. Also, I can't ride a bike (I have disproven the expression 'It's like riding a bike'), so this play allowed me to pretend like I can.

The original production had a cast of six actors, but it's a totally flexible cast size, as the chorus can be as big or small as you like, and an entire class could certainly perform the play. I encourage you to use the physicality of the chorus in how you tell the story and also embrace the use of bikes. While the play works without them, there is something supremely theatrical and exciting about seeing people on bikes on stage.

* * *

My interest in the chorus continued when writing *Girls Like That*. I'd been co-commissioned by Birmingham Rep, West Yorkshire Playhouse and Theatre Royal Plymouth to write a play that each of their youth theatres could perform. As each was a different size, the cast numbers needed to have some sort of flexibility. I decided I'd worry about how to do that last. First, I had to find the play to write.

I was doing workshops with each youth theatre exploring different themes I was interested in to see what struck a chord. I came to feminism and the group quickly told me feminism wasn't relevant any more. And I found myself arguing with a bunch of teenage girls as to why we needed it. I was the only feminist in the room. And precisely because they weren't interested in it, I realised I needed to write a play about it. Meanwhile, Amanda Todd, a girl in Canada, made a YouTube video that went viral after she killed herself. In it she explains how a photo of her topless was circulated at school and how her classmates bullied her relentlessly for it – same thing happened when she switched schools. At one point it escalated to the point that a group of girls beat her up and left her in a ditch. When the media covered the story, it quickly became a game of 'blame the man who coerced her into taking the photo'. Obviously he's a key player in the story. But no one was talking about the gap between him sending the photo to her classmates and her killing herself – because then we'd have to talk about our own complicity. We'd have to talk about all the young people who made her life hell, their seemingly ignorant parents, and the teachers who looked the other way. And so after starting to write a play about Scarlett, the girl whose photo goes round, I quickly realised it wasn't working. Because it wasn't Scarlett's story. It was the story of the girls who destroy her life; it needed to be from their point of view. It was as simple as these girls telling us the story of what happened, of making us, the audience, complicit in their actions.

For me it's a play which is about a lot more than just sexting. It's about the messages young people are absorbing from an early age, the pressures of being part of a group, and, like *Holloway Jones*, how inaction is sometimes as violent as action. I think I was very angry when writing the play, and re-reading it I think that comes through the writing. It's there in the viciousness of the comedy. Behind the writing was a question I had: why were young women using the same misogynistic language and tools that men use to oppress women in order to oppress each other? Why are young women calling each other 'sluts'? I don't think there's anything intrinsically wrong in sending a naked photo of yourself. I'm certainly not encouraging it, but for me this is not the real problem. The real problem is a society that judges young women for any form of sexual expression on the one hand, and pressures them to be sexual on the other. The real problem is how we react when we see that photo. The problem is *us*, not the sender or the photo. And I think that's what I wrote a play about.

As an artistic exercise, and a practical one to suit the flexible cast sizes, I didn't allocate any of the lines. The characters therefore emerge in part from the group of lines given to (or taken by) each actor. Each of the youth theatres had fifteen to twenty-five in the cast. It was later produced professionally by Synergy and the Unicorn for a schools' tour and run at the theatre. For that it had a cast of six. Having seen both, I really think it works either way, with a small cast or a large one. And we, the audience, are none the wiser.

The play is fast-moving, so don't worry about getting too literal with your staging. Trust the simple power of a group of young women on stage telling us a story. It's totally possible to include boys in your casting of it. But when writing it I was imagining a cast of all women. When I used to teach youth theatre, I'd be looking for a play to do and I'd find that all the big-cast plays were for mostly men, and yet all my youth theatres were mostly women. So I wanted to write for a big cast of women. But by all means include boys in the cast if you like.

* * *

Pronoun felt a bit like coming full circle. I came back to the romcom world of *Banana Boys*. Anthony Banks at the National Theatre and I had a chat about my writing a play for the NT's annual Connections scheme. I didn't start writing the play with a story idea, I wrote the play because I wasn't seeing trans or gender-nonconforming characters on our stages, and certainly not in plays for young people. I wrote it because I was tired of hearing our government calling for a 'tolerant' society, when, in the words of Dean, 'tolerance is horseshit'. I wrote it because I want to live in a society that embraces difference, loves people, appreciates their contributions – not one that merely *tolerates* them.

While Dean's transition provides the structural spine for the story, it's really a story about Dean and Josh. It's a love story. It's a romantic comedy. For a play about gender, I felt the play's form had to somehow play with gender too. When researching the play I ran a workshop with a youth theatre in Ipswich. I went in wearing make-up just to see what would happen. Nothing happened. When I asked the group halfway through if anyone noticed my make-up, about half had but hadn't thought much more about it. Which was really refreshing. Perhaps contradictorily, they were less open to the idea of one of their friends being transgender. They didn't care if I didn't conform to gender norms because I was some random guy doing a drama workshop. But they cared if it was someone closer to home. And so that's when I decided the play had to be a love story. And I hope, by the end of the play, we're all rooting for Dean and Josh to get back together.

Gender is a social construct, and the play's form tries to play with this. For the characters of the mum and dad in the play, don't worry about playing their gender – their costumes, the signifiers, are there – just play the truth of what they're saying. I'm not sure at what point I landed on James Dean as the fairy-godmother figure. But I've always loved James Dean, or the idea of James Dean, and if someone was going to appear in my bedroom to offer guidance I'd want it to be him.

I worked briefly with a lovely group called Gendered Intelligence when writing the play. The young people there were far more articulate about gender than I can ever be, and I was terribly intimidated by the cleverness of people half my age. Lots of their insights helped when writing the play. But I should say this is only Dean's story. It can't, won't – and like any character, should not – represent a whole community. Dean's experience isn't meant to represent *the* trans experience, only *his* experience.

To enable different group sizes to perform the play, there's again a flexibility in cast size. It could be done with a minimum of seven up to infinite numbers as there can be as many doctors or members of the Senior Management Team as needed. I was amazed that forty different groups across the country chose to perform the play during the Connections scheme. In most cases it was groups where the young people participating had been allowed to choose what play to perform. And that they chose to perform this story gives me great hope for the future.

* * *

That's the context as I remember it for each play. And now that you know it, you can forget it. Because all that matters for you – the director, the actor, the teacher, the student – is the story on the page. What I intended probably doesn't matter any more. These plays are now yours. So take ownership of them as you bring them to life. I'll still be there, like James Dean or The Banana Girls, as a fairy godmother in the rehearsal room. My words can give you guidance, but you've got to make the actual decisions.

And like the fairy godmother sending you off to the ball I must say, 'Remember to have fun.' I certainly had loads of fun writing them.

Evan Placey
November 2015

BANANA BOYS

For Danny

Acknowledgements

Neil Grutchfield for the faith, support, and astute dramaturgy.

Debra Glazer, and the company of young people in heat&light at the Hampstead Theatre. The most joyous time I've ever had in rehearsal, and doing research.

All the girl groups mentioned, quoted and used in the play, and the writers of their songs. And my parents, for forcing me to listen to them all throughout my childhood.

E.P.

Banana Boys was commissioned by the heat&light company and first performed at Hampstead Theatre, London, on 9 December 2011. The cast was as follows:

THE SCHOOLBOYS
CAMERON   Myles Howard
CALUM   Caleb Hughes
RILEY   Cavell O'Sullivan
MAX   Awaab El-Essawy
ZACH   Edmund Ludlow
BEN   Tom McDermott

THE SCHOOLGIRLS
PIPPA   Skye Stuart
ETTA   Jimena Meza Mitcher
ALISHA   Ellie Horne
TANISHA   Francesca Green
FALISHA   Nyaueth Riam

OTHERS AT SCHOOL
DJ   Ricardo Benavides
MIRANDA   Jean Mackay

THE SIBLINGS
RACHEL   Marlie H-C
JORDAN   Jesse Gassongo
NAT   Ellie O'Donnell

THE BANANA GIRLS
SANDRA   Akuc Bol
GEORGIA   Chantè Joseph
MANDY   Chloe Evans

Director   Debra Glazer
Set & Costume Designer Robbie Sinnott
Lighting Designer   George Bishop
Sound Designer   Cressida Klaces
Dramaturgs   Neil Grutchfield
                         Debra Glazer

Characters

THE SCHOOLBOYS, *all sixteen years old*
CAMERON
CALUM
RILEY
MAX
ZACH
BEN

THE SCHOOLGIRLS, *all sixteen years old*
PIPPA
ETTA
ALISHA
TANISHA
FALISHA

OTHERS AT SCHOOL
DJ, *nineteen years old*
MIRANDA, *eighteen years old*

THE SIBLINGS
RACHEL, *thirteen years old, Cameron's sister*
JORDAN, *eighteen years old, Calum's brother*
NAT, *eighteen years old, Jordan's girlfriend*

THE BANANA GIRLS, *early twenties*
SANDRA
GEORGIA
MANDY

Author's Note

As much as possible, The Banana Girls should assist with scene changes/transitions – orchestrating changes and/or performing in changes as indicated. It is expected that The Banana Girls will lip-sync to their songs, and while they are women playing women, there should be something a bit drag about their huge theatricality.

Ideally the play should run straight through; however, if it's necessary to have an interval this should go between Scene Nine and Scene Ten.

A Note on Punctuation

A dash (–) is a cut-off, sometimes of one's own thought with a different thought (not a pause or beat).

An ellipsis (…) is a loss or search for words.

Words in square brackets [ ] are not spoken, but there to clarify a line's meaning.

A lack of punctuation at the end of a line means the next line comes right in.

Scene One

Hampstead Heath, overlooking water. CAMERON *and* CALUM *hold hands.*

CALUM. On three.

CAMERON. Do we jump on three or after three?

CALUM. I don't know.

CAMERON. Well you have to decide.

CALUM. Oh just jump whenever. One, two –

CALUM *turns to the 'audience', speaks to them as if he's pitching a film. Throughout the rest of the scene, the boys go back and forth between pitching to the audience, and speaking to each other.*

That's how it opens.

CAMERON. That's how it would start.

CALUM. The movie of our lives. Who's gonna play us?

CAMERON. Casting later.

On the edge of a cliff, water crashing below.

CALUM. It's not a cliff

CAMERON. It's like a cliff

CALUM. It's Hampstead Heath

CAMERON. But they're eight and it seems like a cliff.

CALUM. Danger.

CAMERON. Risk.

Calum and Cameron.

CALUM. Cam and Cal.

CAMERON. Zoom in on the edge of a cliff

CALUM. A Heath.

CAMERON. A summer that's so hot you feel like a runaway

CALUM. A pioneer

CAMERON. The summer Cameron learns to ride his bike.

CALUM. Though you're not very good.

> The summer Calum learns to spit over a metre in front of himself.

CAMERON. The summer they discover this spot here, the cliff, their secret spot on the Heath.

CALUM. They can be anything.

CAMERON. They can talk about anything.

CALUM. Why the latest Batman movie was crap.

CAMERON. Whether Playstation 2 or Xbox is better.

CALUM. Why Pepsi is far superior to Coca-Cola, despite widespread public opinion to the contrary.

CAMERON. Cal and Cam

CALUM. Cam and Cal.

CAMERON. Think *Stand by Me* but without the crazy murderous dog that they spend all summer avoiding.

CALUM. Cameron, that's *The Sandlot*.

CAMERON. No.

CALUM. *Stand by Me* they go looking for the body of a missing boy in the woods. *Sandlot*'s the dog.

CAMERON. Right. Yeah.

CALUM. I'm right.

CAMERON. You're right. Okay.

CALUM. Point to me.

CAMERON. Our film. It's a summer so hot car alarms start going off for no reason.

CALUM. Teenagers restlessly wander the streets smashing beer bottles.

CAMERON. It stinks. North London stinks of car fumes, and dead grass, and cigarettes.

CALUM. It stinks of summer.

CAMERON. And we love it.

CALUM. They love it.

CAMERON. They discover home-made ice lollies

CALUM. They discover porn.

CAMERON. Thinking they've put in *Spy Kids*.

CALUM. What is in fact *Spy Jizz*.

CAMERON. And they laugh.

CALUM. Because the woman is moaning.

CAMERON. And the guy with the moustache kind of looks like Cal's dad.

CALUM. And what does the word 'jizz' mean?

CAMERON. And it's that summer they discover:

CALUM. They discover:

BOTH. The Banana Girls.

THE BANANA GIRLS *appear, posed for a show, their backs to us.*

CAMERON. Sandra, Georgia, and Mandy.

CALUM. They were fit.

CAMERON. A film. Three girls, three black girls, different classes, different everything, run off together from... Alabama? Atlanta?

CALUM. Really fit.

CAMERON. They run off together, away from their lives, from the prejudices of their towns, from the men they're engaged to be married to who none of them like, who put them down because they're girls, and they form a singing group, the three of them – travel from city to city, road-trip across the USA singing covers of famous girl-group songs: The Shirelles.

CALUM. The Chiffons.

CAMERON. The Supremes.

CALUM. The Exciters.

CAMERON. Well they lip-synced. But Cam and Cal don't care.

THE BANANA GIRLS *sing a line or two from 'My Boyfriend's Back' by The Chiffons. But they perform with their backs to us, as though the audience were on the other side.*

CALUM. We were kind of obsessed with it, weren't we?

CAMERON. Cal and Cam are obsessed with it. The film.

CALUM. And the girls have three things that bond them together:

As THE BANANA GIRLS *say and act out the following (again with their backs to us) – a clip from the film – the boys mouth the words to the dialogue and act out the scene exactly the same as the girls, move for move.*

GEORGIA. Honesty with ourselves.

MANDY. Honesty with each other.

SANDRA. And above all…

ALL THREE. LOVE!

CAMERON. Those are the rules.

CALUM. And we're in love with them.

CAMERON. Cal and Cam are in love with them.

CALUM. We wanted to have sex with all three of them at once.

CAMERON. Calum, we were eight.

CALUM. Cam –

CAMERON. And Cal.

CALUM. No I just meant Cam. Like I'm talking to you.

CAMERON. Oh. What?

CALUM. Well it's made me think… Just when do you think is the perfect time to… you know… do it?

CAMERON. Do what?

CALUM. Pippa and I. Like, was just thinking when should I… you know. The location's gotta be perfect so she feels – and I keep getting mixed signals from her 'bout it. Is she saying she wants to?

CAMERON. How should I know? What does this have to do with –

CALUM. Just what do you think?

CAMERON. Pippa's not in the film. You didn't meet her till we were twelve.

CALUM. Just the other night, right, she was wearing this really short skirt and I thought is she trying to you know… signal? Like they do in movies, right?

The opening chords of 'Tell Him' by The Exciters is heard. Only CAMERON *can hear it.*

D'you think?

CAMERON. I don't – … (*To audience.*) They find themselves lost on the edge of this cliff with water. The Banana Girls. Their car's broken down, they're in their performance outfits – right? – and they're stuck on this cliff. Right, Calum? Right?

CALUM (*slowly joining back in*). Yeah.

CAMERON. There were no mobiles back then. And so what do you think they do?

CALUM. They jump. The Banana Girls.

CAMERON. Just hold hands and jump into the water, off the cliff fully clothed.

CALUM. Start laughing hysterically when they hit the water.

CAMERON. Because they're free.

CALUM. So we hold hands.

CAMERON. Cam and Cal hold hands.

Holds out hand… CALUM *doesn't take it.*

Well come on.

CALUM. What?

CAMERON. You know what.

Beat. CALUM *hesitates, then takes it.*

CALUM. On three.

CAMERON. Do we jump on three or after three?

CALUM. I don't know.

CAMERON. Well you have to decide.

CALUM. Oh just jump whenever. One, two, three!

CAMERON. As we're in the air holding hands

CALUM. Star-jump in the air.

CAMERON. We're flying

CALUM. We're dying

CAMERON. We're Indiana Jones

CALUM. Spider-Man

CAMERON. The Banana Girls.

We're

CALUM. Cam breaks his hand, hits a rock at a funny angle.
Your mum bollocked me for like an hour. How was it my
fault? 'No more jumping in the water, no more watching
Banana Girls, and no more going to… where is this secret
spot of yours?'

CAMERON. They don't tell her.

CALUM. It's a secret.

CAMERON. They promise not to go any more.

CALUM. But we do. Course we do. Even now.

CAMERON. Took almost a year for my hand to heal properly.
Had to learn to write with my left hand that year.

CALUM. Why Cam's ambidextrous now. Which hand do you use to wank off?

CAMERON. We're eight right now, Cal.

CALUM (*receiving text message*). Whoa. Look at the pic Pippa just sent me of her. This is what I mean. One moment I get the feeling she wants to wait. She's all coy like. It's all cuddles. Next minute she sends me this. (*Hands him phone.*) What do you think?

The opening chords of 'Tell Him' are heard again.

Cam?

CAMERON (*to audience again*). It's a summer like how they show it in the movies. It's all so...

CALUM. Simple?

CAMERON. And it stays like that for many summers after.

CALUM. The pic on my phone.

CAMERON. A montage sequence. Kids running. Riding bikes.

CALUM. Winning the game?

CAMERON. Maybe in slow motion. Set to a soundtrack of some old-school song by The Supremes.

CALUM. We'll see.

CAMERON. Cal and Cam.

CALUM (*of pic on phone*). My phone. What do you think?

CAMERON. Not sure she'd want you showing me this.

CALUM. Nah she knows I tell you everything. Cam and Cal.

CAMERON (*to audience*). Cam and Cal. It was Cam and Cal.

Until...

CALUM. Until...?

Beat.

BANANA GIRLS (*turn around to audience*). Sex.

A sudden burst of music, and a group of boys and girls enter in various stages of undress.

Boys: MAX, ZACH, RILEY – *with* CAMERON *and* CALUM *joining them.*

Girls: ALISHA, TANISHA, FALISHA, ETTA *and* PIPPA.

THE BANANA GIRLS *exit, and the boys and girls on stage stand facing the other gender – threateningly, daringly, something could explode…*

CAMERON. And we cut to opening credits.

The music continues for a moment. Then:

Lights change and we're in:

Scene Two (a)

Boys' changing room/girls' changing room.

The boys and girls are actually in two different rooms and what looks like them facing one another is actually a mirror between them. CALUM *exits to the showers.*

RILEY. Seeeexxxyy.

MAX. That was dead sick.

ZACH. The way you took the ball off him.

MAX. Like you owned it.

RILEY. Like it was your bitch.

MAX. You were the man.

RILEY. The pimp.

ZACH. The Prince of fucking Denmark.

MAX. Moving across the field like you were on ice.

ZACH. On butter.

RILEY. On I Can't Believe It's Not Butter.

CAMERON. Thanks, guys. I was there.

ZACH. You were fucking more than there.

MAX. Bloody Superman.

RILEY. Spider-Man.

MAX. The Road Runner!

ZACH. What do you mean Road Runner?

MAX. The Looney Tunes bird.

ZACH. Who wants to be the Road Runner?

MAX. Cos he's so fast, he's kicking the ball like –

ZACH. You're so gay. The Road Runner. A peacock. You're saying Cameron's a peacock?

MAX. It's not a peacock. It's a ground cuckoo.

ZACH. You're so gay.

RILEY. Captain Cam!

ZACH. Captain Cam!

Chanting, they pick up and carry him around the room – he desperately wants to be put down.

ZACH/RILEY/MAX (*sing*). We love you, Cameron... oh yes we do... We love you, Cameron...

CAMERON. Put me down.

MAX. Did you see the way Etta was looking at you? That goal will definitely get you head.

CAMERON. What?

MAX. Etta was staring at you the whole game.

ZACH. And maybe if you'd been watching the ball instead of Etta the whole game, you would've stopped that goal.

MAX. I have a lazy eye, okay? I can't help it.

ZACH. You're a moron.

MAX. He's using my medical condition against me. That is low, bro.

CALUM *enters from the showers.*

RILEY. You so busy eyin' out there, you busy dyin' out there.

CAMERON. 'Get busy living'

CAMERON/CALUM. 'Or get busy dying.'

CAMERON. Point to me.

ZACH. What movie crap is that?

MAX (*to* CAMERON). Just saying. Take advantage of the opportunity. Ask Etta out.

CALUM. You didn't tell me you were in to Etta?

CAMERON. I didn't say –

CALUM. You want me to ask Pippa to hook it up? Why didn't you ask?

CAMERON. Uhh…

CALUM. We could double.

RILEY. Gang bang.

CALUM. Double date, you moron.

RILEY. 'Date'? You're like from the eighteenth century. You like a Shakespeare character.

MAX. Shakespeare wasn't in the eighteenth century.

ZACH. I saw a porno where they were all dressed up in Shakespeare costumes. Corsets and bonnets and the like. And they totally had an orgy. Why doesn't Miss teach us that in English class?

CALUM. So what do you say? Do you want me to hook you up?

Enter THE BANANA GIRLS.

CAMERON *covers up, self-consciously.*

CAMERON. Uh this is the boys' changing room.

SANDRA. We've seen it all before, honey.

CAMERON. Girls aren't meant to be in here.

GEORGIA. Haven't you heard of equal rights?

MANDY. Besides we ain't really here.

CALUM. Cam, do you want to?

SANDRA. He's asking you a question.

GEORGIA. He's pretty cute.

CAMERON. Are you like my fairy godmothers?

GEORGIA. I ain't no fairy.

MANDY. And I ain't mother to nobody.

SANDRA. Besides, how many Disney films you seen with a black fairy godmother?

CAMERON. I guess…

Pocahontas?

SANDRA. Pocahontas? She ain't a fairy. And she ain't black.

GEORGIA. She's one of them Indians.

MANDY. Don't think you're meant to use that word any more. She was a Native-American.

GEORGIA. Really?

MANDY. Times have changed.

CAMERON. Who are you?

SANDRA. You know exactly who we are.

CAMERON. This… this isn't really the best time.

SANDRA. Time waits for nobody. And neither will he.

CALUM. Cam?

CAMERON. It's just…

MANDY. What's the hold-up?

GEORGIA. She's the most popular girl in school.

MANDY. You're captain of the football team.

SANDRA. This is the way it's supposed to go.

GEORGIA. It's even in the Bible.

MANDY. And you don't wanna be messin' with that shit.

SANDRA. Unless… unless you're one of them…

GEORGIA/MANDY. One of them what?

SANDRA.…Homo sapiens!

All three gasp.

CAMERON. We're all… Homo sapiens.

SANDRA. Well then what's the problem? You want it all to end, don't you – the spots and awkwardness and hard-ons in the middle of science when you're dissecting frogs and waking up in the morning to discover you've gotta ask Mum to wash your sheets; well here's your answer: goodbye teens, hello life.

CALUM. Do you want me to hook you up with Etta or what?

Beat.

CAMERON. Yeah.

Course.

Scene Two (b)

FALISHA. Does anyone have a tampon?

PIPPA. You never buy your own.

FALISHA. Yes I do.

ETTA. Here.

PIPPA. They're expensive you know. That's eight pence that.

FALISHA (*to* ETTA). I'll give you eight pence tomorrow.

PIPPA. Charge VAT on that you know. Luxury tax. Cos that's, like, a fucking luxury.

TANISHA. It's a luxury not to bleed all over the floor during maths lesson.

ALISHA. Can you imagine Mr Simons' face?

FALISHA (*imitation of Mr Simons*). It would seem to me that there's some vaginal liquid on the floor? Has anyone lost some? Tanisha?

ALISHA. Ew. Can you not say that? Vaginal.

FALISHA. Vaginal?

ALISHA. I don't like it. It sounds… awful.

FALISHA. You're such a twelve-year-old.

TANISHA. You're a twelve-year-old, Alisha.

ALISHA. You're the one not wearing a bra.

PIPPA. Who's not wearing a bra?

FALISHA. Tanisha.

TANISHA. They make me uncomfortable. Leave marks on my back.

PIPPA. You know if you don't wear one your tits'll like be on the floor by the time you hit twenty.

TANISHA. Shut up.

FALISHA. I know why she's not wearing one. For Riley.

PIPPA. Oooohhhh. 'Do you want me to pick up your book for you, Riley?' (*Bends over.*)

TANISHA. Shut up. You don't know what you're talking about.

FALISHA. You so fancy him.

TANISHA. No I don't.

ALISHA. Yes you do.

TANISHA. So?

FALISHA. He's a moron.

ALISHA. And he's demeaning to women.

TANISHA. What do you mean he's demeaning to women? You've hardly never spoken to him.

ALISHA. I'm telling you. I'd stay away.

TANISHA. You're such a feminist.

ALISHA. I heard him say once to his mate: women only have one purpose: cleaning. Cleaning the kitchen and cleaning his tool.

PIPPA. Thank you for that anecdote, Virginia Woolf.

ALISHA. Look, Riley only sees breasts. That's all he sees. Nothing else.

FALISHA. That's all any boy sees.

PIPPA. Not Calum. He loves me for my mind.

TANISHA. Really?

PIPPA. As we're doing it, we have the most fantastic discussions.

They all laugh.

ETTA. Shut up. You haven't even done it.

PIPPA. My lips are sealed.

FALISHA. Saw Cameron looking at you, Etta.

ETTA. Really?

FALISHA. Well you were looking at him anyhow. Drooling.

ETTA. I was not.

PIPPA. Cameron? Really? He's so…

ETTA. What?

PIPPA. Quiet.

ETTA. He's just shy.

ALISHA. I think it's quite charming.

PIPPA. No one asked you, Alisha.

I like my men loud. Like them calling out my name.

FALISHA. 'Pippa! Pippa! Ow, teeth, Pippa!'

PIPPA. Yeah yeah shut up.

(*To* ETTA.) Calum and I are going to the movies tonight I think. If you want to come, we could like see if we could get Cameron along too.

ALISHA. You're going to the movies on a school night?

PIPPA. This is why you will never have a boyfriend, Alisha. You are such a prude.

TANISHA. Can I come?

ALISHA. No. You guys are coming to my house remember. To make the decorations.

PIPPA. Oh is this the Valentine's Day social committee?

ALISHA. You could have been on it, Pippa. You chose not to.

PIPPA. Because I don't want to be on some dumb dance-planning committee.

ALISHA. It's not a dance. It's a ball.

TANISHA. I want to go to the movies.

ALISHA. You have to come over tonight. I promised Mr Lamb I'd make it look nice – only reason he let me organise it.

FALISHA. He let you organise it cos he wants to put his hand down your pants.

PIPPA. He is such a paedo.

ALISHA. That is not true. He has a wife. I've seen a picture of her on his desk.

PIPPA. Probably a photo he got off the net or something. So he can fool stupid girls like you.

ALISHA. Well whatever. The ball is going to look amazing.

ETTA. I can't wait.

ALISHA. You can help too if you want.

FALISHA. I'm already the vice president.

TANISHA. I'm deputy vice president.

ALISHA. You can't officially be on the committee but you can be like an honorary member or something.

PIPPA. Sorry, Etta can't. Her hands will be otherwise occupied tonight.

FALISHA. Nasty.

PIPPA. I hear Cameron's got a big one.

ETTA. How do you know?

FALISHA. Ew. I bet he does.

PIPPA. The quiet ones always do.

'Oh Etta. Catch my football, will you?' (*Takes out a tampon, pretends it's a penis, thrusts it against* ETTA.) 'Oh Etta. Etta.'

ALISHA. Can I ask you something, Pippa?

PIPPA. No, I will not sleep with you.

Speaking of which, I heard that girl Miranda, in Year 11, you know the really ginge one – well I heard she's a total lesbo.

TANISHA. Like a real one?

PIPPA. Total muff-diver.

ETTA. Really?

FALISHA. No way. She's too pretty.

PIPPA. Anyway, watch yourself, that's all I'm saying. But aside from whether or not I'd stick my tongue down your throat, what were you going to ask me, Alisha?

ALISHA. Do you love him? Calum? Are you in love?

PIPPA. Only you would ask that.

ALISHA. I want to know.

PIPPA. I don't know. I guess so.

FALISHA. I don't believe in love.

ALISHA. How can you not believe in love? That was totally a prerequisite to being on the Valentine's committee.

FALISHA. You're talking to the girl whose parents have each been divorced three times.

Anyway we're too young to fall in love. If it even exists.

ALISHA. Romeo and Juliet were like twelve.

FALISHA. Well they're not real, are they? They were in a play. And I don't remember the part when Juliet was having to deal with period pains.

Scene Two (c)

RILEY. So you and Pippa done the pushy-pushy yet?

ZACH. Prolly just told her he loved her and they have cuddles and shit.

RILEY. You done it though?

CALUM. I don't kiss and tell.

ZACH. What? You a girl?

RILEY. He hasn't.

ZACH. He definitely hasn't.

CALUM. And how would you know?

ZACH. He'd be shoutin' it from the football field. (*Grabs CALUM's bag, throws it to someone.*) He shoots, he scores.

During the following, the boys playfully pass the bag to one another, a sort of piggy in the middle, which CALUM enjoys.

RILEY. Is it cos Kiddy Cal's too small?

ZACH. Pippa couldn't find it.

CAMERON. They're just joking around.

ZACH. Yeah listen to your boyfriend, we're just joking, right. It's not your fault. Some of us were born with bananas, others with baby carrots. It's natural.

CALUM. Luckily your mum loves baby carrots.

ZACH (*laughs*). That is so Year 9.

CALUM. Honestly, just shut up.

ZACH. Or what? You gonna smack me with your little veggie?

CAMERON. Come on, guys, we just won a game.

ZACH (*tosses bag back to CALUM*). We're just joking around, right, Cal?

CALUM. Yeah. Yeah.

ZACH. I only said it cos Max said so.

MAX. I said what?

ZACH. How Cal's dick is teeny. Saw you in the shower.

RILEY. Why you lookin' at his dick for?

ZACH. Wasn't much to look at, from what I hear.

CALUM. You a batty boy?

ZACH. Not Max's fault you got mini-eggs.

CALUM. Max can't even see in the shower without his goggles
on. Can't even see his own teeny dick. That's why he's gotta
wear those Sherlock Holmes magnifying glasses on his face.

MAX. Nerd-chic is in, alright. My sister saw it on *Loose Women*.

CALUM. The only loose woman you'll be getting.

ZACH. You totally wank off to Denise Welch.

MAX. And you wank off to Justin Beiber.

RILEY (*to* ZACH). You kind of look like Justin Beiber.

ZACH. I do not look like Justin Beiber.

MAX. You so do.

CAMERON. They're right.

ZACH. So I wank off thinking about myself then, do I? I do not
look like Justin Beiber.

CALUM. Yeah you got that prepubescent androgynous look
about you.

RILEY. You're androgynous.

ZACH. You don't even fucking know what that means.

RILEY. So? You are anyway.

ZACH. I am fucking as male and pubescent as they come, okay?

CALUM. Look at you. You've got the body of an eight-year-
old. There's barely anything under your arms. We can only
imagine the barren field below, home to the little worm.

ZACH. I'm a fucking monkey down there. A fucking rainforest.
Girls get lost in all that hedge. Need a fucking lawnmower. A
tractor. A tour guide. Need fucking David Attenborough to
take you around my pubes.

Enter BEN *in his football kit. He wears a bit of make-up.*
(Maybe eyeliner and some sparkles; black nail polish.) No
one acknowledges he's entered.

CALUM. Show us then.

Go on.

MAX. Yeah go on, Bieber. Show us.

RILEY. Show us the Bieber beaver.

MAX. The Bieber bush.

ZACH. I'm not showing you anything, paedos. (*To* BEN.) Yo,
bum boy.

Hey, faggot, I'm talking to you.

Bent Ben, you deaf or something?

Didn't your parents teach you it's rude to ignore someone
when they're talking to you? Ben?

BEN. What?

ZACH. What, *sir.* What. *Sir.*

BEN. Whatever.

ZACH. Say it. What, sir.

BEN. What sir.

ZACH. We're all wondering what you're doing here. Think
you've made a mistake. The girls' changing room is next door.

CALUM. No girls or gays in here.

ZACH. We haven't finished changing, have we, boys?

MAX. No, sir.

ZACH. And we don't want you in here perving on us.

RILEY. Dropping soap and stuff.

ZACH. Tryin' to sneak a peek, are you?

Pause. BEN *goes to leave.* ZACH *grabs his bag.* BEN *stops.*

BEN. Can I have my bag please?

ZACH *tosses it to someone else.*

ZACH. What bag?

A short game ensues in which the boys throw around the bag as before, BEN *trying to get it back.*

RILEY. Piggy in the middle. Or more like poof in the middle.

The bag lands in CAMERON*'s hands.*

CALUM. Cameron! Here.

Pause. He purposefully throws it badly so it accidentally lands at BEN*'s feet. But* CALUM *gets in there first and grabs it.*

That was so yours, Max. This is why you're always on the bench.

MAX. It was a crap throw.

CALUM *throws it back to* CAMERON.

CALUM. What's in the precious bag?

RILEY. Yeah, what's in the queer's bag?

ZACH. Open it.

CAMERON *looks to* THE BANANA GIRLS. *They shrug. Hesitantly* CAMERON *does.*

What's in it?

CAMERON. Nothing… just change of clothes… books.

ZACH. Take 'em out.

CAMERON. Why?

ZACH. It's funny.

He does.

Holy shit! What is that? Tighty whiteys. He wears tighty whiteys.

RILEY. Gay pants!

CALUM. Don't touch 'em. You'll get Aids or something. (*To* BEN.) Go get your stuff, Batty Boy.

Slowly BEN *takes his things from* CAMERON. *Goes to leave.*

What do you say?

Someone blocks the door.

What do you say to Cameron?

Pause.

ZACH. I think the words you're looking for are Thank You.

BEN. Thank you.

(*Mumbles.*) Arsehole.

ZACH. What he just call you?

They grab him. Hold him up against a locker.

You hear what this faggot just called you, Cameron. An arsehole.

You gonna take that?

He's all yours.

Cameron.

Beat.

BEN. I wasn't calling him an arsehole. I was calling you an arsehole.

ZACH. You what?

CALUM. The gay boy's always thinking about arseholes.

ZACH *punches him in the stomach.* BEN *falls to the floor.* ZACH *pins him down, his arms above his head, sitting on his waist.*

ZACH. This the way you like it, bitch boy.

Up close you do look absolutely beautiful. You should wear more make-up.

Riley, find me his make-up.

RILEY *retrieves eyeliner pencil or lipstick from* BEN's *bag.*

Hands to ZACH. *The boys all gather round so we can't see what's happening. Save* CAMERON *who stays back. He looks to* THE BANANA GIRLS *for advice, help. They just shrug.*

SANDRA. All we do is sing.

Beat.

They begin to sing 'Mama Said' by The Shirelles. It continues under the rest of the dialogue of the scene.

Ad libbing from boys: 'Ohhh…', laughing, etc.

ZACH. Now you look really beautiful.

CALUM. A princess.

RILEY. A fairy.

CALUM. Cam, you gotta see this.

The boys get off BEN. *On his forehead they've written 'BATTY BOY'.*

A school bell rings. The music stops.

ZACH. Laterz.

MAX. Heath after school.

ZACH. Yeah. Maybe.

RILEY. I got detention with Tillwoods first.

MAX. Tight Tillwoods.

CALUM. You done the maths stuff?

CAMERON. What? No. Yeah. Some.

All have exited, except THE BANANA GIRLS, BEN – *who's still on the floor – and* CAMERON. CAMERON *walks over to where* BEN *is, they stare at one another.* CAMERON *is about to say something.*

Beat.

He doesn't. He exits. THE BANANA GIRLS *begin singing again from where they left off.*

Scene Three

CAMERON*'s bedroom*/CALUM *and* JORDAN*'s bedroom.*

CAMERON *and* RACHEL *are in* CAMERON*'s bedroom.*
CALUM, JORDAN *and* NATALIE *are in* CALUM *and*
JORDAN*'s.*

CAMERON. Why are you in my room?

RACHEL. You have a date or something?

CAMERON. Why would you say that?

RACHEL. You're wearing your best outfit.

CAMERON. It's not an outfit. It's only a jumper.

RACHEL. It's the jumper you save for special occasions.

CAMERON. Shut up.

RACHEL. Your Zac Efron jumper.

CAMERON. What you on about?

RACHEL. You look like Zac Efron when you wear it.

CAMERON. How does a jumper make me like Zac Efron?

RACHEL. You make a Zac Efron face when you wear it. When
you look at yourself in the mirror. There. See.

CAMERON. Shut up.

RACHEL. You only make the face when you're wearing that
jumper.

CAMERON. I don't make a face.

RACHEL. You do. A poofy kind of face. A Zac Efron face.

CAMERON. Zac Efron isn't a poof.

RACHEL. Zac Efron's hot.

CAMERON. Would you get out of my room?

JORDAN. Can't you knock before you enter my room?

CALUM. No. Cos it's *our* room.

RACHEL. Where are you going?

CALUM. To the movies. Grab some food. Double date.

NATALIE. Aw, that's sweet. Isn't that sweet, Jordan?

JORDAN. Yeah.

NATALIE. What you seeing?

CALUM. A romantic comedy. From the nineties. They play new classics sometimes.

NATALIE. I wish Jordan would take me to a romantic comedy. He hates them.

RACHEL. Who's going? Can I come?

CAMERON. No.

RACHEL. Is she your girlfriend?

CAMERON. Who?

RACHEL. Whoever you're going out with?

CAMERON. No.

RACHEL. So can I come?

CAMERON. No. It's… a date… I guess.

RACHEL. You never go on dates. Who is she?

CALUM. Etta.

NATALIE. What kind of name's Etta?

CALUM. Think it's actually Ethel.

NATALIE. That's a nan name.

RACHEL. That's a granny name.

CALUM. Which is why she changed it to Etta I'm guessing. Her and Cameron are hooking up.

NATALIE. Cam? I love Cameron. He's adorable.

Do you remember that time I was over and you guys were watching that DVD. And he paused it so he could get me a drink.

JORDAN. Yeah. So what?

NATALIE. I'm just saying.

JORDAN. I get you drinks, don't I? Don't you have hands?

NATALIE. He's just nice. A gentleman.

JORDAN. But does he know how to treat a woman in bed like I do?

NATALIE. Jordan!

JORDAN. What?

NATALIE. Your brother's here.

JORDAN. So?

NATALIE. So it's embarrassing.

JORDAN. He knows. Runs in the Reese family. I bet Pippa knows too. Right, bro?

CALUM. Yeah, yeah.

RACHEL. Did you get her anything?

CAMERON. It's only the first date.

RACHEL. You need to make her feel special. Not anything big. Just something that tells her you're thinking of her. That you appreciate her.

JORDAN. That you been thinking ahead, you get me?

RACHEL. Like on our first date, Ryan brought me this little teddy bear. And it was just, you know?

CAMERON. Who's Ryan?

RACHEL. My boyfriend.

CAMERON. You have a boyfriend?

RACHEL. Uh, yeah.

CAMERON. Since when? I didn't know you have a boyfriend.

RACHEL. Why would you? You just come home every day and lock yourself in your room like some stereotype of a moody teenager.

CAMERON. You're only thirteen. I don't think you're meant to have a boyfriend.

RACHEL. You're so weird.

CAMERON. I don't know that I like that. You having a boyfriend. Is he… nice?

RACHEL. I'm not talking to you about him.

CAMERON. I'm your older brother. I'm supposed to ask these things.

JORDAN. Here. Bring this. (*Hands condom.*) And one for Cameron. And that fine fine Etta.

NATALIE. What did you say?

JORDAN. What?

NATALIE. Who you calling fine?

JORDAN. I was just saying –

NATALIE. Well don't be saying anything about some girl.

JORDAN. You said Cam was hot.

NATALIE. No no no. That is not the same.

JORDAN. Why not?

NATALIE. Because… it's not. Right, Calum?

CALUM. Uh.

JORDAN. Back me up here, bro. That is what you call a double standard.

NATALIE. I am going to Facebook this girl. And if she is prettier than me, I swear to God, Jordan. (*Exits.*)

CALUM. She okay?

JORDAN. It's how the relationship works.

RACHEL. And don't say anything about other girls. Like even famous ones in the movies. Okay?

CAMERON. Is he… you like him then? Ryan?

RACHEL. He's my boyfriend. Of course I like him.

CAMERON. You're not… are you?

RACHEL. Ew. I am so not talking about that with you, Cam.

She goes to leave.

CAMERON. Rach?

So I look... okay?

RACHEL. You look good. For my brother.

Have fun. Glad you've finally got a date. I was starting to think you were gay.

She exits. He looks around the room. Unplugs a lava lamp.

JORDAN. Oh I almost forgot.

RACHEL (*pops head in*). Don't forget to pay.

JORDAN (*tosses a small packet of lube*). Don't forget lube.

Scene Four

The Heath. CAMERON *and* CALUM *walk ahead of* PIPPA *and* ETTA. ETTA *carries the lava lamp.*

CALUM. What's with the lamp?

CAMERON. Girls like sparkly things, don't they?

CALUM. Oh. Here. (*Hands condom.*) In case. For later.

PIPPA. Would you two wait up! I'm in heels.

CALUM (*putting his arm around* PIPPA). Sorry, babes.

CAMERON. Yeah, sorry.

CAMERON *hesitantly puts his arm around* ETTA, *the condom still in his hand.*

CALUM *notices condom in* CAMERON's *hand. High-fives or something to cover taking the condom, and then slipping it into* CAMERON's *pocket.*

PIPPA. I was just saying I just don't get how they loved each other. They'd never even met.

CALUM. It's romantic.

PIPPA. It's weird. Would you fly all the way to New York to meet some person you didn't even know.

CALUM. Well not from here. But from Seattle it's not that far. It'd be like... going to... Dundee or something.

PIPPA. Who would go to Dundee?

CALUM. I think it's romantic.

PIPPA. People get killed that way. Paedos pretending to be teenagers.

ETTA. It's romantic.

PIPPA. I don't buy it. I don't believe you could love someone you've never spoken to.

ETTA. What do you think?

CAMERON. I think... I think what makes it a contemporary classic is you got these two main characters, both big actors in the nineties, in a love story, but who barely share a scene together, barely talk to each other.

CALUM. And in all the other nineties romcoms, a couple meet at the start and it's all will they won't they finally kiss. Our whole experience hangs on us anticipating that first, and probably only, kiss of the movie. This kind of turns that on its head.

PIPPA. But do you really believe people in real life could actually love someone they'd never even spoken to?

CAMERON. Maybe if it's love, then... then you just know. And it doesn't matter if you've really spoken to them.

PIPPA. Whatever. Where's a good spot to go on the Heath? Anyone know a more secluded spot?

CALUM/CAMERON. No.

ETTA. I'm happy just to walk.

CALUM. You two go ahead. I wanna show Pippa something.

PIPPA. That okay, Etta?

ETTA. Yeah. Yeah.

CALUM. Later, Cameron.

CAMERON. Yeah. Later.

CALUM *and* PIPPA *exit.*

ETTA. It's a bit chilly.

CAMERON. Oh. Do you want to go home?

ETTA. No. I just meant... I'm cold, that's all.

Didn't bring a jacket.

CAMERON. Oh. Right. Bit silly for February.

ETTA. Yeah.

CAMERON. Glad you enjoyed the film.

ETTA. Yeah.

I agree, you know. About sometimes just knowing. Even if you haven't really talked to the person.

I'm glad you finally asked me out.

CAMERON. Well technically it was Calum who asked.

ETTA. You're funny. I like that. Some boys are just... you're not like them.

CAMERON. Okay.

Three HOODIES *start loitering behind them.*

ETTA. I watched your game the other day. You're really good. I don't really know anything about football, but I know that when you get it in the net then obviously that's a goal, and you're really good.

CAMERON. Thanks.

You're shivering.

ETTA. I'm cold.

CAMERON. Oh. Oh. I get it. You want my jacket?

ETTA. No, no, it's fine.

CAMERON. No. Take it. (*Gives it.*)

ETTA. It smells nice. Smells of you.

CAMERON. It's Lynx. They had an offer. Two for one. So my mum bought like a hundred.

She takes his hand.

ETTA. Are you nervous?

CAMERON. Just those guys.

ETTA. They won't bother us.

CAMERON. Okay.

ETTA. You've got goosebumps.

CAMERON. You're wearing my jacket.

ETTA. I can keep you warm.

She puts his arms around her.

The three HOODIES *remove their hoods, it's* THE BANANA GIRLS.

THE BANANA GIRLS *take it in turns to quote a line from 'Love is in the Air' by John Paul Young. When they get to '…when I look in your eyes':*

Why aren't you looking in my eyes?

CAMERON. What?

ETTA. You're avoiding eye contact.

CAMERON. No I'm not.

ETTA. You're shy. It's fine. I like that. You do that in the corridor too.

CAMERON. Do what?

ETTA. When I look at you. Or try to. You look away.

CAMERON. Do I?

She hugs him tight.

THE BANANA GIRLS *sing the beginning of 'And Then He Kissed Me' by The Crystals.*

ETTA *takes her head from his shoulder. Puts it close to his face so he's forced to look at her. Shuts her eyes.*

BANANA GIRLS (*sing*). And then he kissed me.

He doesn't move.

(*Repeating the line, singing.*) And then he kissed me.

Nothing.

(*Repeating again.*) And then he –

CAMERON. I'm not feeling well. I've gotta go.

He runs off, leaving her alone in the woods.

SANDRA. And then he ran away?

GEORGIA. That's not how the song goes.

They put their hoods back on. ETTA *clocks them, hurries away.*

Scene Five

The street.

ALISHA. Why are you ignoring me?

FALISHA. She angry about the balloons.

ALISHA. Well balloons weren't on the list.

TANISHA. Haven't you ever heard of creativity?

ALISHA. Balls don't have balloons. In what fairy tale did you see balloons at the ball? Did you see any balloons in *Cinderella*? In what Disney film do you see balloons?

TANISHA. Dumbo had balloons.

ALISHA. Do you want to be an elephant or a princess?

FALISHA. You know what I never understood about Cinderella. Like she loses the shoe, yeah, and everyone tries it on but it doesn't fit anyone... but like how is that possible?

That no one in the whole world had the same size feet as her? Were her feet like abnormally small or something?

TANISHA. You're an autocratic leader. That's what you are. Learned about that in history.

ALISHA. Well you're still only deputy. I am the president. And I say no balloons.

FALISHA. Not if we give you a vote of no confidence.

ZACH, MAX *and* RILEY *enter drinking from water bottles which contain mixers and alcohol.*

RILEY. Ladies.

ZACH. If it isn't Alisha, Tanisha, and Falisha.

TANISHA. Oh. Hi.

ZACH. And what pray tell are you ladies up to on this fine evening?

TANISHA. We're on the V-Day social committee.

FALISHA. We *are* the social committee.

DJ *strolls past.*

DJ. Hey! Look at all these lovelies
Lookin' all shook up
On a February night
They lookin' to hook up.

ZACH. DJ! Didn't know you were still around?

MAX. I heard you were on some government DIY Business Scheme.

DJ. Exactly, man. D-I-M. Doin' It Myself.
I ain't a fool
Soon my business will be boomin'
At your school.

FALISHA. What's he on about?

DJ. Looks, I got to go, over and out
But talk to you all, give me a shout.

He exits.

FALISHA. Why is everyone who went to our school such a weirdo?

ALISHA. So you guys are coming to the ball, right?

RILEY. Dunno. Don't really like dancing. Bit gay.

TANISHA. Yeah. Really gay.

ALISHA. Tanisha.

RILEY. Bit bric-brac, shack-a-bit-bat, you know.

TANISHA. Totally.

ZACH. We're gonna go to the Heath. You wanna join?

FALISHA. What you gonna do there?

RILEY. Just Heath it, you know.

ALISHA. Yeah. No. We've got a finance meeting.

TANISHA. I can come.

ALISHA. No she can't.

TANISHA. I can make up my own mind.

ALISHA. No you can't. You're the deputy remember.

ZACH. Deputy. Sounds hot. You coming to my party on Friday?

RILEY. It'll be spankin' wankin'.

TANISHA. Sure.

ZACH. Right. We're out.

MAX. Pout.

RILEY. Shakey shakey.

Boys exit.

TANISHA. I think he likes me.

ALISHA. He was staring at your cleavage.

FALISHA. That fool don't even speak English.

Scene Six

The Heath – secret spot.

CAMERON *sits looking out.*

CALUM *stands near, having just arrived.*

CALUM. And close-up on a pensive Cameron staring out. The shot widens and we see Calum standing behind him, finding Cameron exactly where he knew he would.

CAMERON. Cameron was looking for a moment's peace.

CALUM. But he ain't gonna get it.

> CALUM *produces two bottles of WKD, hands one to* CAMERON.

CAMERON. Cameron accepts.

> Seems to get smaller each time I'm here, do you think? The distance between the water and us, the trees, all seems to be getting smaller.

> *Pause.*

CALUM. After a dramatic silence, Calum asks Cameron why he ran away from Etta.

CAMERON. Shuttup. I didn't run away.

CALUM. I thought you were in to her.

CAMERON. I just wasn't feeling well.

CALUM. Cam, this is me you're talking to.

CAMERON. I had food poisoning I think.

CALUM. You hadn't even eaten yet.

CAMERON. From yesterday.

CALUM. No one's forcing you to go out with her. I just thought… well it's not like you're getting any anywhere else, right?

CAMERON. I just got stuff I need to do. Study and stuff. Football. I just don't want to commit to… I don't know if I have time for…

CALUM. Sex?

CAMERON. A girlfriend.

CALUM. Which equals sex. What don't you have time for? Eight minutes? Five in my case.

CAMERON (*laughs*). Shut up. You haven't even done it.

CALUM. Next week.

CAMERON. Scheduled it in, have you?

CALUM. After the Valentine's dance.

CAMERON. Really?

CALUM. Cupid won't be the only one shooting arrows.

CAMERON....right. Aren't you – What about STIs?

CALUM. STIs. What are you talking about, man?

CAMERON. Just. I don't know. Maybe you should... I don't know. Just make sure it's right. That's all.

CALUM. What's this crazy shit you're talking. I thought you'd be happy.

CAMERON. I am. I am happy.

CALUM. It'll happen to you too, mate. That's why I'm saying: Etta. She's in to you, man.

CAMERON. I know.

CALUM. You don't want to marry her, that's cool, I get that. Don't want to do all that dating, and flowers and chocolate shit and get yelled at cos they're from Tesco, so you gotta first pull off the label so she thinks they're from Waitrose or some flower market across town, I get that. But if you just ask her to the Valentine's dance, you could for sure do it after. Or at least get head.

CAMERON. Yeah. Maybe.

CALUM. You're a funny one you know that, Cam. But that's why I love you, man.

CAMERON. I just worry about shit. All the stuff I want to do. The future.

The boys quote the last few lines spoken by Tom Cruise and Penelope Cruz from the film Vanilla Sky, *ending with them re-enacting and/or making sounds for Tom Cruise jumping off a building. They laugh.*

I think a point each.

Beat.

Do you love her?

CALUM. Man. Next you're gonna ask me to brush your hair for you and go to the loo with you too.

CAMERON. You do. Have you told her?

CALUM. Nah.

CAMERON. Why not?

CALUM. Maybe next week.

CAMERON. After you do it.

CALUM. Before we do it. More romantic. Just not sure how to put my feelings for her into words.

Three trees come to life, turn around. It's THE BANANA GIRLS.

SANDRA. This song is dedicated to the one I love.

CAMERON. Oh Jesus Christ.

CALUM. What? You asked.

CAMERON. No, not –

(*To* BANANA GIRLS.) Don't you ever have anywhere else to be?

They begin to sing, 'Dedicated to the One I Love' by The Shirelles.

(*To* CALUM.) I think you should just be honest. Just… tell her. You'll be fine.

CALUM. Yeah. Or if I chicken out I could just write it in a letter, right? Worked in the film.

CAMERON.… Yeah…

CALUM. Hey, don't worry. One day you'll find someone too and you'll know.

CAMERON. How?

CALUM. What?

CAMERON. How will I know? For sure?

CALUM. I dunno. You just know. You get a feeling. And you know.

He lies down looking up at the sky. THE BANANA GIRLS *stop/fade out their singing.*

CAMERON. But what if, I don't know, you ignore it?

CALUM. Why would you do that?

CAMERON. I dunno. Let's just say.

CALUM. You worry too much, man. You've got the whole world ahead of you. All of time. You just gotta grab it by the balls. You'll be fine. Weren't you the one just telling me that?

Just look at the stars.

CAMERON. I don't think those are stars. Think they're just the lights from the Gherkin or the London Eye.

CALUM. See you know everything, man. What have you got to worry about? While the rest of us are staring up at the lights from office buildings you're gonna be off at uni somewhere looking at real stars. Doing real shit.

CAMERON. You'll be doing that too.

CALUM. I'm probably not even gonna pass my GCSEs. Not smart like you.

CAMERON. Well… you'll find something else then.

CALUM. I've found Pippa. And I've got an ace view on the Heath.

CAMERON. And you've got friends… you've got me.

CALUM. Don't be gay, man. Course I have you. And even when you're off being some rich kid somewhere, you'll

come back and we'll sit in this spot. Drinking real booze.
Refined shit. Stella or something.

CAMERON. Yeah.

CALUM. Yeah.

CAMERON. No matter what?

CALUM. What?

CAMERON. No matter what? Even if... right? No matter
what?

CALUM. Unless you go and kill someone.

CAMERON. Yeah. Yeah.

It starts to rain. Pour.

Fuck.

CALUM. I got it. (*Pulls out umbrella.*)

CAMERON. Can't believe you carry an umbrella with you.
That's so – can't believe you...

CALUM. Do you want in or not?

CAMERON *joins him under the umbrella. It's a tight
squeeze so* CALUM *has to put his arm around* CAMERON
so they both fit under.

See look, man. All that. All that world. That's ours, man.
That next generation they're always talking about. That's us.
So we got to take it. We got to take that world. Grab it by the
balls. And fuck it right up the ass.

THE BANANA GIRLS *pull out umbrellas, and begin to sing
'Tell Him' by The Exciters.*

Scene Seven

A busy school corridor. A table with flowers.

CALUM *hands* DJ *a pen, and a pound coin.*

CALUM. Cheers, mate.

DJ. Roses are red
  Violets are blue
  Tell someone you love them
  For a quid or two.

  Just choose a rose
  It ain't really hard
  Put down their name
  And fill out the card.

  We'll deliver it to class
  Make 'em feel fine
  And maybe this rose will
  Make 'em your Valentine.

CAMERON. Hey.

ETTA. Hey.

CAMERON. About yesterday…

ETTA. Don't worry about it.

CAMERON. I was actually just going to ask for my jacket back.

ETTA. Oh. Right. It's at home.

CAMERON. Right. Sorry, though. For running – for briskly
  walking away. It wasn't to do – well it was more of a light
  jog, you know. Sorry. I'm not very good with words. When I
  haven't… prepared.

ETTA. No. You're not.

  You going to Zach's party?

CAMERON. I dunno. Probably.

ETTA. Good. It would be nice to see you there. Less room to
  run away. Jog.

CAMERON. Yeah. Yeah. There is.

The bell rings and all the schoolboys and girls charge onto the stage with bananas.

Scene Eight

A classroom.

MAX, ZACH, RILEY, CAMERON, CALUM, BEN, PIPPA, ETTA, ALISHA, TANISHA *and* FALISHA *are all seated holding a banana.* MIRANDA *stands at the front.*

MIRANDA. I'm Miranda. From Year 12. As part of my A-level project, I have agreed to come in to classes to speak about health. Which includes at this point in my project, at this point in your lives, at this point in the day I am here to discuss sexual health.

MAX. Miss.

MIRANDA. Miranda.

MAX. My banana's wonky.

MIRANDA. That's that's fine.

MAX. How come I got a wonky one?

ZACH. Why do you think?

MIRANDA. I'm running a bit low on… equipment so –

RILEY (*laughing*). His equipment's wonky. Could you help him out?

MIRANDA. So, you'll have to work in pairs.

So I'm, uh, going to give you each one of these. These are… condoms… and we're going to, together, we're going to put them on the banana.

RILEY. Do you like putting condoms on bananas, Miss?

MIRANDA. Miranda.

RILEY. Miranda, I have a question, yeah, cos I was talking to some peeps, and see, you're here teaching us about johnnies on bananas but someone, yeah, not me, but someone said you're a lezzer. And you got one of them dyke haircuts.

MIRANDA. Well that's not… that's not – well that's not really a question. And it doesn't –

MAX. Are you really a lezzer?

MIRANDA. Doesn't have anything to do with –

RILEY. Are you like a real-life lezzer? Like do you make out with your girlfriend and stuff? Cover each other in oil and all that?

ZACH. Is it frustrating cos you can't have sex?

MIRANDA. I'm not sure I [understand]

ZACH. Cos there's no equipment?

RILEY. Is that why you have to use bananas?

CALUM. What are you doing?

MAX. What?

CALUM. You're not supposed to peel the banana.

MAX (*sincere*). Mine's circumcised, innit?

MIRANDA. So if you two can be partners. You two. You two. You two.

CALUM*'s put with* BEN.

CALUM. No way, man. I'm not being partners with him.

MIRANDA. This won't take very long.

CALUM. He'll try and grab my banana or something.

MIRANDA. All we're doing is –

CALUM. Try to put it in my butt or something when I'm not looking.

MIRANDA. I'm just asking –

CALUM. No way!

CAMERON. I'll be his partner.

MIRANDA. Thank you.

CALUM. Watch out, man. That's all I'm saying.

MIRANDA. If everyone takes one of these.

RILEY. Miss –

MIRANDA. Just listen to my instructions.

RILEY. It's about this though, Miss. Miranda.

MIRANDA. Yes?

RILEY. I need an extra-large one.

MIRANDA. It's… we're practising with these.

RILEY. Yeah but I always get the extra-large ones, so it's really better for me to practise with those.

ZACH. He does not.

RILEY. Shuttup, Bieber balls.

ZACH. I am not Justin Bieber.

RILEY (*starts thrusting with the banana, singing the Justin Bieber song, but as if he's having sex*). 'Baby baby oh, like baby baby no.'

ALISHA. We're done.

PIPPA. You weren't meant to start yet.

FALISHA. You did it by yourself. You're meant to share the banana.

ZACH. You can share my banana.

FALISHA. In your dreams.

MIRANDA. So if everyone starts by opening the condom packet.

MAX *takes a bite of his banana*.

CALUM. What are you doing?

MAX. I'm hungry.

CALUM. You just ate a dick. You just ate a dick, man. You are so gay.

Miranda, he just ate the dick.

MIRANDA. Let's see who can do it first. Right. Okay. Then we'll see who's done it right. Oh. And you've got to write down notes on how you did it.

They all get to work.

BEN. You shouldn't use your teeth to open it.

CAMERON. Oh.

BEN. Might accidentally put a hole in the condom.

CAMERON. Right.

BEN *opens it with his fingers.*

Thanks.

CAMERON *self-consciously starts to put condom on banana.*

BEN. And you need to pinch the top.

CAMERON. Oh right. (*Pinches the top of the banana.*)

BEN. Of the condom.

CAMERON. Course. Yeah. (*Pinches the top while* BEN *rolls it down.*)

What happens if you don't pinch it?

BEN. Banana split.

They share a laugh.

Stupid joke.

CAMERON. Really stupid.

ZACH *fires a condom at* ALISHA*'s head.*

ALISHA. Ahhhhhh!!!! Get it off. Get it off!

MIRANDA. It's only a –

ALISHA. It's in my hair!

RILEY *blows his condom up into a balloon. Starts volleying it back and forth with* ZACH.

MIRANDA. Boys, you're meant to put it on the banana.

RILEY. I think our banana has an STI.

ZACH. Banaorrea.

RILEY. Fruitidia.

ZACH. Peel herpes.

MIRANDA. There's a reason we're practising this. If I don't see you do it, I can't give you a tick... which means... this is a required part of your curriculum.

RILEY. Cumiculum.

MIRANDA. You seem to be an expert. Perhaps you'd like to share your expertise with the rest of us.

RILEY. Like this yeah. You got these two, and he's all boom boom yeah, I wanna razzmatazz the zaza and she's all maybe baby seesee, so he's all but love the dove and wanna spread the red of the love, guv, and she's all dispose of the clothes and din the skin of the hype-pipe, so he puts the plastic and the playstick, and then it's all score more to the whore of the amore amour yaya like that sha-tack sha-tack sha-tack sha-POW. And then rewind or the behind or the crawley crawleys or waa-waa, laterz.

MIRANDA. Uhh...

DJ (*entering*). Sorry to interrupt if I mays
But I've got some Valentine deliverays
A rose for Pippa but I can do one betta
An anonymous one, the card says 'To Etta.'

PIPPA. That's so sweet, Calum.

CALUM. Watch the thorns.

PIPPA. And what's this?

CALUM. Have a look.

PIPPA. It's a Travelodge booking. In town. For the night of the V-Day dance.

CALUM. For after. I thought... Happy Valentine's Day.

PIPPA (*genuinely flattered*). Travelodge, aww.

RILEY. Shakey shakey.

CALUM. Somewhere romantic, right. I thought… well it's
     Valentine's Day. And. I.

I… I…

Everyone's looking at him.

I can't wait.

PIPPA. Aww, who's yours from?

ETTA. Doesn't say. (*Glances at* CAMERON.)

ZACH. Read it out then.

ETTA. Etta oh Etta.
     You're so special to me.
     Don't you see.
     Me looking at yo
     But to shy to say hello.

     Could love be true?
     I'll dream of that dance
     In case I've the chance
     To dance with you.

DJ. I almost forgot. I've got one more
     Delivery to help true love soar.
     Nowadays ladies can also give to men.
     I've got a rose here, addressed to Ben.

ZACH. Shit, man. Let me see.

BEN. Can I have it please?

ZACH. Everyone knows you're a batty boy. What dumb girl's
     sending you flowers?

     RILEY *takes the rose*. ZACH *keeps hold of the card*.

     Oh it even rhymes and everything.

     Dear Batty Boy

RILEY. Banana Boy

ZACH. Dear Batty Banana Boy

RILEY. Banana Boy dear
It's too bad… you're such a queer.
We always knew…

ZACH. We always said.

RILEY. This Valentine's Day…

ZACH. We hope you're dead.

ALISHA. That's not what it says.

ZACH. How would you know? Did you send it? Got a little crush on Ben here?

ALISHA. No. I just know that's not what it says. It's a crap rhyme.

ZACH. Shut up.

MAX. Yeah shut up, Specky.

ALISHA. That's original. Especially since you're also wearing glasses.

ETTA. Just give him the card.

Zach.

ZACH. Alright. Alright.

BEN. Can I have my flower please?

By now, RILEY *has covered the rose in a condom.*

RILEY. Look, it's deflowered.

BEN. Can I have it please?

RILEY *puts the stem down his trousers, so it's just the rose sticking out.*

RILEY. Sure you can. Come get it.

Everyone watches.

BEN *moves closer. The two boys stand close to each other, staring each other down.*

Beat.

BEN *yanks the flower out hard*. RILEY *keels over in pain*.

Fuck! The thorns! The little bitch…

TANISHA. You okay?

ETTA. Serves you right.

MAX. You've got herpes now.

RILEY. You can't get herpes from a flower.

MAX. You have.

RILEY. Shut up. (*Throws banana at* MAX's *head*.)

He throws one back. Suddenly a 'food fight' of bananas, condoms and lube occurs. All get involved, ad lib, except for BEN *and* ETTA *who continue to study their cards, and* CAMERON *who watches*.

As the fight continues, THE BANANA GIRLS *appear behind* CAMERON *and begin to sing 'Why Do Fools Fall in Love?' by The Supremes. Instead of microphones, they each have a banana sheathed in a condom, which they use as a microphone*.

Scene Nine

Boys' changing room.

BEN *sits hidden behind a locker*. CAMERON *enters, limping a bit. Spots* BEN *hiding*.

CAMERON. What are you doing here?

BEN. Pretending not to be here.

CAMERON. Huh?

BEN. Pretending to be a locker. Is it working?

CAMERON. Not sure. I've never been very good at drama.

Aren't you meant to be in PE?

BEN. Aren't you?

What happened to your foot?

CAMERON. Nothing.

BEN. Okay.

CAMERON. It just sometimes… it just does this.

BEN. Cos of your fall. When you were eight?

CAMERON. It wasn't a fall. It was a jump.

BEN. Trying to kill yourself?

CAMERON. Trying to re-enact a film with Calum.

BEN. He's a wanker.

CAMERON. You shouldn't say that.

BEN. Why?

CAMERON. He'll beat you up.

BEN. He'll beat me up even if I don't say it.

CAMERON. You shouldn't say it.

BEN. I'm not saying it to him. I'm saying it to you.

CAMERON. Well. He's my best friend.

BEN. Well your best friend's a wanker.

CAMERON. He's still my best friend – Ow. (*His foot.*) I hate
it… it just – out of nowhere. I can go weeks, months, forget
about it, just have a normal fucking foot like everyone else,
have a normal body, and then out of nowhere it comes. [I'll]
Never be a football player.

Ahhh…

BEN. You haven't wrapped it correctly.

CAMERON. I've been doing it since I was eight.

BEN. You've been doing it incorrectly since you were eight then.

CAMERON. How am I meant to do it?

BEN. I can't [explain]… I need to do it.

CAMERON (*looks around*). Go on then.

> BEN *wraps* CAMERON*'s foot.*

> Where'd you learn that?

BEN. My mum used to be a ballet dancer.

CAMERON. Is that why you wear make-up?

BEN. What?

CAMERON. I dunno. Why do you wear it?

BEN. Why do most people wear make-up?

CAMERON. Most people don't. They wouldn't bother you so much if you didn't. It would make it less obvious.

BEN. Make what less obvious?

> *Beat.* CAMERON *breaks eye contact.*

> Gay.

> Make that less obvious?

> It's just a word. You can say it.

CAMERON. I'm not... I know I hang around with – but I'm not like them. I'm not going to insult you.

BEN. It's not an insult. Gay. I'm gay.

CAMERON. You need to – that's what I mean. You say stuff like that it just gives them more to bait you with.

BEN. It's the truth, isn't it? More important to me to be honest with myself than care what a bunch of wankers think.

> SANDRA *pops her head out of a locker. Begins quoting the rules from the film as at the start.*

SANDRA. Be honest with yourself.

BEN. Did you hear something?

> CAMERON *slams the locker door shut.*

CAMERON. No.

> Listen. I'm just trying to... didn't your parents teach you to keep your head down, just get through. Later you can be... you can be...

BEN. Gay.

CAMERON. Later. It's secondary school. You're not supposed to be… in secondary school. If you act normal –

BEN. You think I'm abnormal?

CAMERON. You just have to *act* normal and they'll leave you alone. They're my friends. I'm just trying to help.

BEN. Well I didn't ask for your help.

CAMERON. I'm trying to save your arse getting beaten up.

BEN *gets a wet wipe, smears make-up across his face.*

BEN. There. Am I less gay? Will they leave me alone now?

CAMERON. Ben. I was just trying to…

Whatever. It's your life. (*Goes to leave.*)

BEN. Why did you send me the flower?

CAMERON. I don't know what you mean.

BEN. The rose. (*Pulls it out.*)

CAMERON. Think you're meant to keep that in water.

BEN. Why did you buy it for me?

CAMERON. I don't know what you mean.

BEN. Was it supposed to be a joke? Between you and your friends or…

CAMERON. No.

I didn't. I didn't send it to you.

BEN (*pulls out card*). It's your handwriting.

SANDRA (*poking head out*). Be honest with each other.

CAMERON *slams locker again.*

CAMERON. It's not – how do you know it's my handwriting? It's not.

BEN. Cos it is. The same as the sheet you were writing on in class.

CAMERON. What? Was your mum a graphologist too?

BEN. No. My dad.

CAMERON. Really?

BEN. No.

CAMERON. It's not my handwriting.

BEN. You wrote a love poem.

SANDRA (*poking out*). Love.

CAMERON. Would you butt the fuck out? (*Slams locker shut again.*)

BEN. What?

CAMERON. Not you. I was – look, lots of people have handwriting like that.

BEN. You curl your L's funny.

CAMERON. I don't. It's not.

BEN. Well then prove it.

CAMERON. What do you mean prove it? You prove it.

BEN. Write. Write the same message. And we'll compare the handwriting.

CAMERON. I'm not… what, are you Jessica Fletcher?

BEN. Who's Jessica Fletcher?

SANDRA *pokes her head out and starts singing theme tune to 'Murder She Wrote'. CAMERON shoots her a look and she closes the locker door herself.*

CAMERON. I'm not doing anything.

BEN. Okay.

I'll just ask your friends.

CAMERON. What? You can't… you're not asking my friends.

BEN. Why not? I'll ask Calum or Zach to have a look. Tell them my hypothesis – that you sent gay boy a rose and see what they think.

CAMERON. No.

BEN. Why? It wasn't you. So what are you worried about?

CAMERON. I'll do your stupid test, okay.

BEN *hands him paper and pen.* CAMERON *begins to write.*

BEN. Other hand.

CAMERON. What?

BEN. You're right-handed so why you writing with your left?

CAMERON. Look. I write with this hand.

BEN. No. You *can* write with that hand. Also from your jump when you were eight. But you *do* write with your right.

CAMERON. You are Jessica Fletcher.

CAMERON *copies the poem out. Then reads it.*

'Dearest Ben.

I've to say this lots.
You're often in my thoughts.
Wish you were mine.
Love, your Secret Valentine.'

Bit of a shit poem.

BEN. Yeah. It is. (*Smiles.*)

CAMERON *smiles back.*

Beat. CAMERON *hands him the paper. Only he doesn't let go. It's held between them for a moment.*

CAMERON *kisses* BEN.

Beat.

CAMERON. Fuck. Sorry. Fuck.

BEN. You don't have to be –

CAMERON. I don't know what I'm – shit.

BEN. Relax.

CAMERON. I'm stupid. I'm –

BEN. You're not stupid.

CAMERON. I can't believe I just kissed you.

BEN. Cameron. It's just a kiss.

CAMERON. Shit. What if…

BEN. What if what? … I'm not gonna tell anyone. Is that what you're worried about?

CAMERON. No. I don't know.

BEN. Are you embarrassed?

CAMERON. I'm just. I don't know. It's all just… messed up. Keep your head down. Get through school.

BEN. You're a good kisser.

CAMERON. Am I?

You are. Your lips are…

I mean, I've never –

BEN. I know.

CAMERON. You know everything.

The school bell rings.

You should get out of here. Before everyone –

BEN. Okay.

Thanks for the rose. And the… thanks.

See you later?

CAMERON. Yeah. I mean… yeah.

BEN *exits.*

The locker doors swing open. THE BANANA GIRLS *step out, just as they begin singing 'The Shoop Shoop Song' by Betty Everett. Just as they get to the chorus '…that's where it is', a toilet flushes. They stop singing. Look to the toilets.*

CALUM *comes out from the toilets.* CALUM *and* CAMERON *stare at each other. It's clear* CALUM *heard everything.*

CALUM *exits.*

Scene Ten (a)

ZACH*'s house.*

A house party at ZACH*'s.* ZACH, MAX, RILEY, CALUM, PIPPA, ETTA, ALISHA, TANISHA, FALISHA *are all present. Everyone drinks alcohol, and are visibly already tipsy. People chat, dance.*

CAMERON *enters.*

RILEY. Cam!

MAX. Cam!

ZACH. Caaaaammm!

RILEY. You're late, mate.

MAX. Late mate! That shit rhymes.

ZACH. You gotta catch up. Grab a drink.

> CALUM *is by the drinks.* CAMERON *hesitates, then goes over.*

CAMERON. Hey, Calum.

> CALUM *turns and walks away.*

> *The lamps suddenly pop up – they are* THE BANANA GIRLS *with lamps/lampshades on their heads.*

SANDRA. I do love a party, don't you?

GEORGIA. Pretty boy over there ignoring you, huh?

MANDY. Just talk to him. Doesn't no one talk no more? Like with words. It's all grunts and mmm, and hmm, and uh.

GEORGIA (*agreeing*). Mmm-hmmm.

SANDRA. So how's make-up boy?

CAMERON. Would you shut up?

SANDRA. What? Ain't nobody hearing me but you. Where's the love, honey? You need to show us some love.

GEORGIA. Oh and look, there's that nice girl Etta. You gonna talk to her?

CAMERON. Would you just leave me alone? I've got enough to deal with without some lamps talking to me.

MANDY. Who you callin' a lamp?

SANDRA. Next year Topshop will be all over these hats.

GEORGIA. Oh look, she's coming over.

SANDRA. We saved you something from earlier, just in case.

They shove a condom in his hand then go back to being lamps.

ETTA. Hi, Cameron.

CAMERON. Oh. Hey. I was just… looking for you.

ETTA. Were you?

CAMERON. It's good… good to see you… hey. (*Unsure what to do he awkwardly shakes her hand, inadvertently handing her the condom.*)

Shit. Sorry. That's not for you. It's… for… Riley. Sometimes he likes me to hold his thing… things… for emergencies you know?

ETTA.…right. So. I was wondering. Are you planning on going to the V-Day dance?

CAMERON. I… I dunno.

ETTA. Oh. Well.

Long pause.

CAMERON. Come here often?

ETTA. What?

CAMERON. I have no idea.

PIPPA. Cameron. I didn't know you were here.

CAMERON. Here I am.

Having a good night?

PIPPA. Yeah. Course course. We should definitely go out again the four of us. That was so fun. Wasn't that so fun?

CAMERON. Yeah… definitely.

PIPPA. What's up with Calum? He's been such a weirdo all night. Think he's on his period.

ZACH. Listen up listen up. Time. For. A gaaaaame!

PIPPA. I hate games. When I was a kid, my parents used to send me to like gymboree class and I'd just sit at the side throwing those plastic balls at other kids' heads. I just hate games, you know?

ZACH. In ode to our passing youth and days gone by, and in honour of the fact that it is Valentine's Day next week: It is time. For. Spin. The bottle!

People cheer.

PIPPA. That is so primary-school, don't you think?

ZACH. As it's my party, I shall decide who goes first… and I have chosennnn… Tanisha.

Catcalls.

TANISHA. Oh do I have to go first?

ZACH. You have to go first. It's in the constitution.

She goes in the middle and spins, then stands up.

Annnnnddd, ittttttttsssss… Falisha!

FALISHA. What? No. That's not fair. We're supposed to be sitting boy-girl.

ZACH. It's Falisha.

FALISHA. You organised the game wrong.

ZACH. A bottle spun…

RILEY. Is a bottle done.

ZACH. A bottle spun is a bottle done. Those are the rules.

FALISHA. I'm not kissing her.

RILEY. Go on, Tanisha. Kiss Falisha. It's just a game.

TANISHA. Yeah. It's just a game. Come on, Falisha. (*Pulls her into the middle.*)

RILEY. Listen to Tanisha.

(*Starts chanting*.) Kiss her. Kiss her. Kiss her.

Soon everyone has joined in the chant.

It's clear FALISHA *doesn't want to do it. But feels overwhelmed by the chanting. She caves, and quickly kisses her.*

Everyone reacts with ooohhhs, and claps.

MAX. That was hot.

RILEY. Totally going in the wank bank.

FALISHA. I kissed first so I choose who goes next, and I choose you, Zach.

ZACH. Alright. Alright.

He goes in middle and spins. It lands on MAX.

RILEY. Gotta spin again, mate.

FALISHA. No. He spun it. And it's Max.

ZACH. No way.

FALISHA. A bottle spun is a bottle done.

ZACH. I ain't kissing him.

MAX. No way.

RILEY. Spin again.

FALISHA. No. I had to kiss Tanisha.

ZACH. That's different, man.

FALISHA. How is that different?

ZACH. I'm not kissing a guy.

FALISHA. I kissed a girl.

ZACH. It's not the same thing. It's different.

FALISHA. How is it different?

ZACH. A girl kissing a girl is hot. Two guys is just fucking disgusting.

RILEY. Vile, man.

CALUM. Two guys kissing is just… (*Looks at* CAMERON.) wrong.

FALISHA. Too bad. Those are the rules, right?

ZACH. You know what? I'm bored of this game, we're gonna play a different game.

FALISHA. You can't do that.

ZACH. It's my party.

FALISHA. You're a dick.

ZACH. That's what your mum said last night when she was talking to my cock.

FALISHA. That makes no sense.

ZACH. If you don't like it, you can leave.

We're going to playyyyy… seven minutes in heaven!

Claps, cheers.

I choose two couples. And each go into a cupboard and they have seven minutes to do what they like in there – but when the seven minutes are up, you gotta come out of there.

In cupboard A, we'll have… Tanisha and Riley. And in cupboard B…

RILEY. I'll choose. Etta… and Cameron.

The four obediently go into their two cupboards/closets.

ZACH. Starting in five…

ALL. Four… three… two… one!

Scene Ten (b)

TANISHA *and* RILEY *in one closet.* ETTA *and* CAMERON *in another. Both are very cramped.*

First closet.

Silence.

ETTA. This is such a stupid game.

CAMERON. Yeah.

   Silence.

ETTA. Where are we anyway? I can barely see. What is this?…
   I think I feel… I'm touching a hoover.

CAMERON. That's not a hoover.

ETTA. What?

CAMERON. It was… bad joke.

ETTA. Oh. (*Laughs.*)

   Silence.

   SANDRA's *head appears in the cramped space.*

SANDRA. So how we getting on in here?

CAMERON. Oh God, no.

SANDRA. Any lovvvvve yet?

CAMERON. It's cramped enough as it is. Would you get out
   of here?

SANDRA. Just trying to help.

CAMERON. Well would you stop?

   GEORGIA *and* MANDY *appear.*

BANANA GIRLS (*sings The Supremes' song*). Stop! In the
   name of love…

CAMERON. Oh please God no. Just stop the music.

BANANA GIRLS (*sings The Shirelles' song*). Stop the music,
   stop the music, stop the music.

CAMERON. Seriously, I will run away from her again.

BANANA GIRLS (*sings The Crystals' song*). Da do run run run, da do run run.

CAMERON. Would you just shut up?!

They keep singing.

ETTA. I didn't say anything.

CAMERON. No. Not you. Sorry. I hear... I'm allergic... So I... hoover. I'm allergic to hoovers I think. The... carpets. Stuff in carpets. I just need some air. I'll be back.

He leaves.

Scene Ten (c)

Other closet.

RILEY. You seem nervous.

TANISHA. I'm... not.

RILEY. I don't bite. (*Suddenly bites the air.*)

She giggles.

He puts his hands on the back of her neck.

You're tense. (*Starts massaging.*) No need to be nervous.

TANISHA. I'm not. It's not like we have to do anything. No one ever does.

RILEY. Course. No. No.

So just relax. Unwind. Just concentrate on my fingers.

TANISHA. It's just... I've been anxious all day. Not about this. About. You know how I'm on the council. For the dance.

RILEY. Dance. Yeah. You can do all the dancing you like.

TANISHA. Well I was in charge of the finance. Keeping the money. And I... I just borrowed twenty quid. Just borrowed. But then my parents got all mad at me and didn't give me my allowance this week. And then Alisha's taken all the money back and she's done this like audit or something and says there's twenty missing, and Mr Lamb wants receipts for all the expenses by Monday to make sure it all adds up, and it's only twenty quid but I won't have it for Monday and if they find out they could suspend me. Seriously. And I can't tell Alisha cos she'll kill me.

RILEY. Relax. Relax. I'll give you the twenty quid.

TANISHA. Really?

RILEY. No probs.

TANISHA. I'll give it back next week when I –

He puts a finger to her lips.

RILEY. What are friends for, right? Here, you can have it right now.

Takes it out.

TANISHA. That's so – thank you, you have no idea –

RILEY. But you gotta lift up your top.

TANISHA (*giggles*). What?

RILEY. You've got a hot bod. I want something to remember for my twenty.

TANISHA. But I'm not… I'm not wearing –

RILEY. I know. I love that. I love feminist girls, all that burning-bra stuff. That's what makes you so special. That's why I asked Zach to put me in here with you. I've been too shy to talk to you before.

Sorry. I'm… I'm embarrassing myself. I'm an idiot.

TANISHA. No you're not.

RILEY. Just here take it. I can't believe I asked you to…

Here take it. (*Gives her the twenty quid.*)

I'm so embarrassed. I can't even look at you.

TANISHA. No. Look. Look.

She goes to lift up her top.

Scene Ten (d)

Outside the house.

CAMERON *stands near a bench and bush, smoking. The house party can be heard faintly from outside. He hears a rustling in the bushes, and, thinking it a fox or something, goes to have a look.*

CAMERON. Fucking hell.

> BEN *laughs.*

> What are you doing?

BEN. Pretending to be a bush.

CAMERON. Why are you always hiding?

BEN. Keep your head down, get through, right?

CAMERON. Doesn't mean you MI5 it in a bush. What are you doing?

BEN. Debating whether or not to go in.

CAMERON. You've probably made a wise decision.

BEN. I didn't know you smoked.

CAMERON. So you *don't* know everything.

BEN. You don't. Can tell by the way you hold it. Like they do in the movies.

CAMERON. Is there a right way to hold a cigarette?

BEN. You're not really inhaling.

> BEN *puts his hand out,* CAMERON *gives him the cigarette.* BEN *takes a puff, hands it back.*

> You look good. Not in your school uniform.

> *Beat.*

> So what's happening in there? Everyone pissed and making out in cupboards which they'll regret Monday at school?

CAMERON. Pretty much.

BEN. Such a cliché.

CAMERON. Secondary school is a cliché. Teenagers are a cliché.

BEN. And do you regret it? What happened earlier in the changing room?

Beat.

CAMERON. Aren't you cold?

BEN. I'm wearing a hat.

CAMERON. You're wearing a T-shirt.

BEN. You gonna offer me your jacket?

CAMERON. Already gave it away on my last date. Sorry.

BEN. Is this a date?

CAMERON. No… I just meant…

BEN. Did you mean what you said? In the card? About being my Valentine and that?

CAMERON. I don't know what a Valentine does.

BEN. Be my date to the Valentine's dance.

CAMERON. Are you mad?

BEN. No. Why?

CAMERON. You know why.

BEN. Don't you want to?

CAMERON. It doesn't matter what I want.

BEN. Doesn't it?

CAMERON. There's lots of things I want.

BEN. Like what?

CAMERON. I want to play football for the rest of my life. I want my dodgy leg to never act up again. I want to get all As in A levels. I want that spot on my forehead that comes and goes just to go. I want to speak French. I want to learn to like olives. I want to fly to New York. I want to go to Berlin. I want to go to Africa and ride an elephant, build an orphanage. I want to go to Thailand, get fucked off my face, wake up on the beach and not know where I am. I want to be a father. I want to look in the mirror and like what I see. I want to get my driver's licence. I want to drive to a festival and spend days not showering. I want to go to law school just so I can walk into a court, shout 'objection your honour' and then quit. I want to save someone. I want to find the cure to Aids. I want to win an Oscar. I want to try E. I want to have sex.

Pause.

BEN. Right.

CAMERON. But you can't do everything you want to. You have to choose.

BEN. So choose to go to the dance with me. Or will you be too busy riding an elephant in Africa that night?

CAMERON. It's not that simple.

BEN. Do you want… me?

CAMERON. When I kissed you… you tasted like… hot. Like summer. Like grass. Like the dew on grass in the morning. Do all boys taste like that? Is that what I taste like?

BEN. No.

CAMERON. Oh.

BEN. You taste like air. Like suede.

CAMERON. How many boys have you kissed?

BEN *shrugs.*

Have you had sex?

Beat.

Who with? Was it someone from school?

BEN. Maybe.

CAMERON. Who?

BEN. It wasn't someone from school.

CAMERON. Who?

BEN. Why are you angry?

CAMERON. I'm not.

BEN. I was only kidding. About the school part. Just wanted to see what you'd do.

CAMERON. Who is he?

BEN. I dunno. Just some guy.

CAMERON. Where did you meet him? Ben?

BEN. Does it matter?

CAMERON. You asked me what I want. I want to know about what it's like. Who was he?

BEN. I met him online.

CAMERON. Oh. So. What school does he go to? Ben?

BEN. He doesn't.

CAMERON. So…

BEN. So…

CAMERON. So he's like an adult? I mean we're adults I guess. But like a real one?

BEN. You're funny sometimes.

CAMERON. I wasn't trying to be. It was a serious question.

BEN. I know.

CAMERON. Sorry I asked.

BEN. He was thirty. An accountant at Ernst & Young.

CAMERON. Thirty? Oh. Okay. (*Beat*.) Thirty? Really?

Was it good?

BEN. Yeah. I guess.

CAMERON. Did you like… practise beforehand?

BEN. For fuck's sake.

CAMERON. I just… sorry… okay. Yeah. Sorry.

BEN. It was okay. He was a bit. I dunno. Just might have been nicer with someone my own age.

CAMERON. Like me?

Do you want to… with me?

BEN. We're in the freaking street.

CAMERON. I don't mean now. I just mean. Am I the sort of guy you want to – am I the sort of guy boys want to have sex with?

Keep thinking about it. The changing room earlier. How your face looks. Up close. How the little mole below your lip makes a perfect right-angle triangle. If you were to connect it by drawing lines. Like with your make-up. How wet your tongue was. I've added bits too.

I look at porn sometimes.

BEN. So do I.

CAMERON. And sometimes when I'd think of you, I'd imagine… and it would be all gentle. There'd be love. And other times… it would be like in the scenes I've seen. Rough. And I'd want to hurt you. There'd still be love. But I'd want to hurt you. Does that scare you? Is there something wrong with me?

BEN. I dunno. There's something wrong with everyone.

CAMERON. They'll wonder where I am.

BEN. You should go.

CAMERON. I don't want to.

BEN. Then don't.

CAMERON. There's so many things I want. I don't want to hurt you.

CAMERON *starts to make his way back toward the house*.

BEN. Valentine's Day dance. Wear a suit. I'll bring you a boutonnière.

CAMERON. What's that?

BEN. A flower. For your lapel. I'll even pin it on for you.

CAMERON. I'd like that. I'd want that. I would.

CAMERON *goes back in*.

Scene Ten (e)

Inside party.

Everyone is far drunker than before.

MAX. There you are.

Everyone, Cameron's back!

ZACH. You, my friend, did not finish your seven minutes.

So that means… what does that mean?

RILEY. It means you need to finish them now. Licky lucky.

Those are the rules.

CAMERON *goes toward the closet.*

No no no. You've got to finish them right here.

CAMERON. What?

RILEY. Those are the rules. Come on, Etta.

ETTA. Just leave it, Riley.

RILEY. Don't you want to kiss our man Cameron? Look at this face.

CALUM. I think it's Cameron who doesn't want to kiss her. Do you, Cameron?

Do you. Cameron.

And why is that, Cameron? Why is it you don't want to kiss Etta?

PIPPA. Calum.

CALUM. No no, I think everyone wants to know. Don't they?

Don't you think Etta's pretty?

PIPPA. Calum.

CALUM. Isn't Etta pretty, Cameron?

CAMERON. Yes. She's pretty.

CALUM. And she clearly likes you. So what's the problem?

PIPPA. Calum, stop. It's not funny.

CALUM. What? I'm just asking a question. I can ask a friend a question, can't I?

PIPPA. Well you're embarrassing your friends.

CALUM. I'm embarrassing them. Okay. Okay. You don't have to kiss her. Sorry. Sorry. I don't want to embarrass anyone. Certainly not my friend. My best friend.

But. I think, in the honour of friendship, there's something I should share, since we're all among friends here, about our friend in question, Cameron.

Cameron – our friend, my so-called best fucking friend is a big, fucking –

CAMERON *grabs* ETTA *and kisses her aggressively.*

Cheers, claps.

CALUM *pulls them apart.*

Get off her.

MAX. What are you doing, Calum?

CALUM. He's a fake. You're a fake, man.

RILEY. What you on about?

CALUM. You think you know someone, that they're your friend.

CAMERON. I am your friend.

CALUM. A liar. A dirty fucking liar is what you are.

PIPPA. Calum, I think it's time to go home.

CALUM. I'm not going anywhere while this filthy disgusting… him is here.

PIPPA. You've had too much to drink.

CALUM. This has nothing to do with me. It's him! I can't believe I was your friend. I can't believe I shared my brolly with you! A sneaky little fuck, you are. A traitor.

PIPPA. Come on, Calum. Enough.

CAMERON. She's right. You've had too much to drink.

CALUM. Don't tell me anything about me. Me. It's you. Mr captain-of-the-football-team. You're a joke!

CAMERON. Why don't we go outside, Calum.

CALUM. I'm not going anywhere with you. Fake! You're a fake!

CAMERON. Calum.

CALUM. Stop saying my name.

CAMERON. We'll go outside. Come on. (*Grabs* CALUM*'s arm to usher him outside*.)

CALUM. Don't touch me! Faggot!

CALUM *punches* CAMERON *in the face, then legs it out of the party in anger.*

ETTA. You okay?

FALISHA. Crap, your eye.

ALISHA. Get some ice.

CAMERON *runs out.*

ETTA. Cameron. Cameron!

Pause.

RILEY. Poppin' party, man.

THE BANANA GIRLS *begin to sing 'It's My Party and I'll Cry if I Want To' by Lesley Gore.*

Scene Eleven

CAMERON*'s bedroom/*CALUM *and* JORDAN*'s bedroom –*
two days later (*Sunday*).

CAMERON *puts on some loud sulky teenager music. Suddenly*
the music cuts out and turns into 'Why Do Fools Fall in Love?'
What we think are THE BANANA GIRLS *appear. They dance*
with their backs to us singing the doo-dah intro. When they turn
around we see the are in fact MAX, ZACH *and* RILEY *in drag.*

THREE BOYS (*sing*). Why do birds sing so gay?

MAX. Gay?

ZACH. Gay?

RILEY. Gay.

They all point at CAMERON.

THREE BOYS. Gay!

CAMERON. Get out! Get out! Just get out!

They disappear.

There's a knock at the door.

Get out!

BEN *pops his head in.*

I said – oh…

BEN. I heard there was a fight.

CAMERON. Why are you wearing make-up in my house? Shit.
Did my family see?

BEN. By the looks of it I'm not the only one that needs it.

Have you put ice on it?

CAMERON. It's fine.

BEN. Let me see.

CAMERON *pulls away.*

CAMERON. Sorry. I'm just a bit…

Why are you here?

BEN. I just wanted to check you were okay.

CAMERON. No. But I'm used to it.

BEN. I kind of like it. The eye. It's pretty sexy. It suits you.

CAMERON. Shut up.

BEN. It does. A bit Russell Crowe.

CAMERON. Russell Crowe?

BEN. Could be worse.

(*Of his eye*.) Calum?

CAMERON. Yeah.

BEN. I told you he was a wanker.

CAMERON. Don't say that.

BEN. He gave you a black eye.

CAMERON. He's still my best friend.

Beat.

What's in the bag?

BEN *pulls out a tie with hearts on it*.

BEN. What do you think?

CAMERON. It's a bit…

BEN. Gay?

It's for the Valentine's Day dance.

What are you going to wear?

CAMERON. I'm… I'm not…

BEN. Sure?

CAMERON. Going. I'm not going.

BEN. Oh.

CAMERON. It's not that I don't want to. It's that I –

BEN. Can't.

CAMERON. Exactly. You understand.

BEN. No. I don't understand. You can. You're choosing not to.

CAMERON. It's more complicated than that.

BEN. No it's not. It's a choice. You choose to go. You choose not to go.

CAMERON. It's not that I don't want to go with you.

BEN. Do you know what I want? The other night. You never asked me what it was I wanted. I want to walk into that dance, the two of us wearing, well whatever we're wearing, but holding your hand –

CAMERON (*sarcastic*). And everyone just smiles. Good for them. Being honest with themselves. With all of us. And the crowd parts as we walk down the stairs – I'm not sure why there's stairs, but there always is in those kinds of things – and the crowd looks up and applauds and we slow dance in the middle with everyone looking on, like some romantic movie and –

BEN. No. Nothing. That's what I want. For them all to do nothing. We walk in holding hands, and yes maybe we dance, but no one looks. No one smiles. No one looks on. No one even takes any fucking notice. They just keep dancing. Like it's nothing. That's what I want.

Is that too much to ask for? Nothing?

I hope you'll come.

BEN *exits*.

JORDAN. You wanna come?

CALUM. Nah.

JORDAN. What's up? Girl problems? Cos I can ident-i-fy. You get me?

CALUM. Nat?

JORDAN. She's all: I want this, you never do that, started talking about marriage and shit, you know. I'm only eighteen and she's talking 'bout marriage.

CALUM. So –

JORDAN. So I ended it. Got more seed to spread, you get me?

CALUM. I thought you loved her.

JORDAN. I did. I did. But there's lots of girls that I love. My love is long, man. Like something else, you know?

CALUM. Yeah.

JORDAN. You can love. But can't have it tying you down, you know. Love can lift you up, but it can also tie you down. Like a tie in a tie shop. Like a shoelace tied to a park bench. You get me?

CALUM. Yeah. Like a shoelace.

JORDAN. Exactly. Yeah. Don't you worry about me. I already be lovin' someone else.

You goin' out with Cameron today?

CALUM. No. We ain't friends.

JORDAN. I get ya. I get ya. See it's the same, right. Can't have your friends tie you down. They say bros before hos but let me tell you something. Bros and hos they're like one. They come and go. In the end you just got you. That's it, man. Everyone else is just in and out.

CAMERON *falls on his bed, exasperated, feels a bump, pulls back covers.* THE BANANA GIRLS *are in his bed smiling.*

SANDRA. Morning, honey!

CAMERON (*swatting them with pillows*). Get out get out get out!

SANDRA. Man, watch my beehive. You know how long it took me to put this up?

MANDY. He just sad because everybody's in love with him, and he ain't showin' no one any love.

CAMERON. What do you know about love? Huh? What do you actually know? This is all your fault. With your honesty and love and all that crap.

GEORGIA. We know there's a girl that really likes you. Who's quite upset.

CAMERON. You're the ones who told me to go out with her.

SANDRA. How were we supposed to know you were gonna choose to be one of them fruits, and we're not talking bananas.

CAMERON. I didn't choose anything.

MANDY. What about that boy with the make-up?

GEORGIA. It's really quite nice make-up. Is he available? I need a touch-up.

MANDY. You chose to kiss him.

CAMERON. But I didn't choose to l– to like him. I didn't choose to be… okay?

SANDRA. Life is a choice.

CAMERON. Did you choose to be black?

SANDRA. Who's talkin' 'bout black?

CAMERON. Did you?

GEORGIA. This boy's talkin' like a crazy.

CAMERON. Black and… [gay]. It's the same.

MANDY. This boy saying we're gay?

SANDRA. We sing with the ladies but we do not swing with the ladies.

CAMERON. You wake up in the morning, you look in the mirror. You're black. It's not all you are but it's part of you. You can't change that.

GEORGIA. Who wants to change it?

CAMERON. And I wake up in the morning and look in the mirror. And I'm…

Maybe I can hide it better than you can hide your skin. But it's the same. It's just… what's there. I wish it weren't. I wake up every morning and look in the mirror hoping it won't still be there. But it is. It's there. Some days I convince myself it's not. But it's there.

PIPPA (*entering* CALUM/JORDAN*'s room*). I'm here. Oh. Hey. I thought – like – you were going out with Cameron today.

CALUM. No. So why'd you come by?

PIPPA. I wanted to... see how you were after Friday. What was that all about?

CALUM. Doesn't matter.

PIPPA. You guys like... made up yet?

CALUM. No. And we ain't going to. Besides, I don't need him – I got you. (*Goes to give her a kiss*.)

She turns away, throwing a look at JORDAN, *which* CALUM *takes to mean is she's uncomfortable with his brother in the room.*

JORDAN. I'm out. (*Exits*.)

PIPPA. Since we're alone, we should probably... talk. Tomorrow's... Valentine's Day... and it's been about like two years... and it's come to a point... where... I'm... I'm trying to find the words, to explain... my feelings... when you've been with someone for two years, you start to ask yourself, well girls do, is this guy... is he *the* one, and I know that sounds scary, but you ask: am I gonna like settle down with this person...

What am I trying to say?

CALUM *thinks he knows.*

CALUM. I love you. I love you, Pippa.

Pause.

PIPPA. Right.

Ditto.

CAMERON. Love. Be honest with yourself. Be honest with each other. They were your rules. So why's it all gone so complicated?

SANDRA. You ain't followed the rules.

CAMERON. I have.

GEORGIA/MANDY. Nah-ah.

CAMERON. I've been honest with you.

SANDRA. And.

CAMERON. And I've loved, haven't I? I've tried.

SANDRA. And

CAMERON. And that's it.

SANDRA. The first rule.

CAMERON. Honest with myself. How have I not been honest with myself?

SANDRA. Look in the mirror.

CAMERON. I see me.

SANDRA. Do you?

CAMERON. Yes. I've told you. I see it.

SANDRA. Well say it then.

CAMERON. Why?

GEORGIA. Come on, honey. We're due in someone else's bedroom in a minute.

CAMERON. It's just a word.

MANDY. Just a word.

SANDRA. So say it.

CAMERON. I don't want to.

GEORGIA. Should we sing?

CAMERON. Please don't sing.

SANDRA. Just say the word.

Silence.

They start the intro of a song. To stop them:

CAMERON. Gay. Gay. Gay!

I'm…

THE BANANA GIRLS *are gone.*

Scene Twelve (a)

Boys' changing room/girls' changing room.

ZACH *and* MAX *getting changed.* CALUM *enters.*

CALUM. How many people d'you tell?

ZACH. Not many. I won't tell anyone else.

MAX. Ditto.

They laugh.

CALUM. I called you cos I was hoping for some advice, and you go tell the whole school.

ZACH. I was trying to help. Couldn't think of any advice on the matter. Wanted to get a wider opinion.

CALUM. And?

MAX. Ditto shitto.

ZACH. Can't believe you told her you love her – you are such a girl.

MAX. That girl has you whipped like a dog.

ZACH. A cocker spaniel.

MAX. A spaniel's cock.

CALUM. What you talking 'bout?

ZACH. Max is right. Girls like that. Make you think you love them. Like witchcraft.

MAX. My sister has this book *The Rules*. How to get a guy to do whatever you want. Ten quid Pippa's memorised the whole thing.

CALUM. She didn't *make* me do or think anything. I do. Love her.

They laugh.

What the fuck's so funny?

ZACH. You don't know shit about love.

CALUM. And you do?

ZACH. I don't put myself in a position to be rejected by
    some bird.

CALUM. She didn't reject me.

ZACH. 'Ditto'?

CALUM. Didn't you ever see the movie *Ghost*?

MAX/ZACH. No.

CALUM. Well that's how the guy, Patrick Swayze, shows he
    loves her. She knows he's there – as a ghost – knows he's
    there cos he tells her – Demi Moore –

MAX. Calum's hot for a pensioner.

CALUM. Tells her through the medium – that's Whoopi
    Goldberg – Demi's about to walk away, don't believe he's
    there, and he says – tell her ditto, tell her ditto!

    Beat.

ZACH. Sounds gay.

CALUM. I told you because I wanted some advice on what
    to do.

ZACH. Get rid.

MAX. Dump the humps.

ZACH. Ditto that.

    They both laugh.

CALUM. Glad you find this funny.

ZACH. It is. What guy tells a girl he loves her before they've
    even done it?

MAX. No giving flowers till you've deflowered. (*High-fives*
    ZACH.)

CALUM. Why you talking like that? You sound like Riley.

MAX. Well he ain't here.

ZACH. Yeah.

    Where is he?

MAX *shrugs*.

CALUM. So what do you think she meant? What should I do now?

ZACH. Seriously, man, we got more important things to worry about than your personal *EastEnders* drama. We got a game practice to think about.

MAX. Gotta get slickin' on our kickin'.

ZACH. You wanna take Riley's midfield?

CALUM. No. Why would I give up striker to do his midfield?

ZACH. Cos you ain't a forward striker.

CALUM. What you talkin' about?

ZACH. You're on the bench, but if you would like Riley's –

CALUM. Says who?

ZACH. Me.

CALUM. You can't decide that. Only the captain –

ZACH. Well Captain Cam hasn't shown up at school today, or answered his phone since your little rumble, so as deputy captain, I choose formations.

CALUM. This is bullshit. You're supposed to be my friend.

ZACH. Course I am, mate. But it's also about winning games. Cameron was too soft, putting you as striker, when you ain't.

CALUM. Oh let me guess, you've moved up to the front line.

ZACH. As a matter of fact.

CALUM. Cameron wouldn't stand for this crap.

ZACH. Well he ain't here.

MAX. Ditto that.

They laugh.

CALUM. This is bullshit.

MAX. Well why don't you go hang out with your girlfriend instead?

ZACH. Ditto.

MAX. Ditto.

ZACH. Ditto.

Keeps laughing as him and MAX *exit.*

See you out there, mate.

CALUM *throws his bag/things angrily across the changing room. Sits on a bench.*

BEN *enters, gets/puts something in his locker.*

CALUM *collects the things he's thrown. Can't find something.* BEN *sees it under the bench by his feet. Picks it up. Holds it out.* CALUM *takes it.*

BEN *exits.*

Scene Twelve (b)

RILEY *stands guard outside the girls' changing-room door.*

ALISHA. Excuse me.

RILEY. That's two quid, ladies.

FALISHA. What you on about?

RILEY. Two shiny ones to go in there.

FALISHA. Piss off.

They push past him into the changing room.

RILEY. Don't make me get the bouncer.

They enter the changing room. TANISHA *is standing there, with her eyes closed, about to lift up her top.*

FALISHA. What are you doing?

TANISHA. Oh. It's you.

ALISHA. We've been looking everywhere for you. You are supposed to help put up decorations.

FALISHA. She filed a report on you. Missing duties.

ALISHA. What are you doing?

TANISHA. Nothing.

ALISHA. And why is poo-brain acting as box-office manager? Tanisha?

TANISHA. It's just some fun.

FALISHA. What?

TANISHA. He's just… collecting the money.

ALISHA. For what? Are you scalping V-Day tickets because that is so not allowed.

TANISHA. No. He collects the money and I. And I…

ALISHA. You…?

TANISHA. Give them a little show.

FALISHA. Give who a show?

TANISHA. Some Year 9s. One at a time.

ALISHA. I thought you quit ballet.

FALISHA. Not dance, stupid. (*Mimes stripping/or having sex*.) That kind of show.

TANISHA. Ew. No. I only flash them.

ALISHA. You only what?

FALISHA. You mad?

ALISHA. You could get expelled.

TANISHA. No one's gonna know. Made ten quid already.

ALISHA. You're a prostitute! This is political scandal for the V-Day council.

TANISHA. I am not a –

FALISHA. This shit-mouth's idea?

TANISHA. He likes me.

FALISHA. He doesn't like you.

ALISHA. He doesn't like you.

TANISHA. He likes me.

FALISHA. In a pimping way.

ALISHA. We need to pay him. To shut him up. The school paper'll be all over this.

TANISHA. He's already taking fifty per cent.

ALISHA. Fifty? He is so ripping you off.

FALISHA. Come on. You are not staying here.

TANISHA. I think maybe he loves me. Wants to show me off. *He* likes that I don't wear a bra.

FALISHA. This is not how you show love, Tanisha. Didn't you pay attention to any of those romcoms we watched. You don't see Meg Ryan in the toilets flashing her tits for Tom Hanks.

TANISHA. Well that was the nineties.

And anyway, you don't even believe in love.

FALISHA. Come on.

RILEY *enters*.

RILEY. What's up in here?

ALISHA. You can't come in here. It's the girls' changing room.

RILEY. Nothing I haven't seen hundreds of times before.

FALISHA. Yeah. On your computer.

TANISHA. I gotta go, Riley.

RILEY. Alright. I respect that shaz.

TANISHA. You going to the dance tonight? I know it's dumb and all. But thought maybe we could go together.

RILEY. Aw, sweet, but I can't go with you.

TANISHA. I know it's not your thing but –

RILEY. Nah. I'm going. It's just…

TANISHA. Just?

RILEY. Well how would it look? I mean, you girls understand, right?

TANISHA. Understand what?

RILEY. Everyone's seen your goods now. I can't be showing up to the dance with a girl like that. I got a rep, you know?

TANISHA. But. It's Valentine's Day. Meant to take your GF aren't you?

RILEY. Girlfriend? Who said anything about girlfriend?

TANISHA. I thought…

RILEY. You hot. But you ain't GF material. Don't worry. With those you'll make lots of boys happy. Look I'm outty. But I'll see you there tonight, yeah? Who knows. Let's have a dance together or something.

Oh. Right. Your share. (*Goes to give it.*)

Give me one last show of 'em.

FALISHA. I'll show your face the underside of my boots in a second!

RILEY. Alright, alright. Don't need to get all jealous about it. (*Hands* TANISHA *the money, winks, and exits.*)

TANISHA *doesn't move. Then she turns to the mirror. Is about to cry.*

ALISHA. No way.

FALISHA. Don't even think of shedding a tear for that sorry-ass mumbo-jumbo-talking monkey.

TANISHA. I feel…

ALISHA. You've got a dance to get ready for.

TANISHA. I don't even have a date.

Looks at herself in the mirror.

FALISHA. Sure you do.

They put their arms around her.

You've got two.

The song 'You Can't Hurry Love' by The Supremes begins to play.

Scene Thirteen

As the song continues to play, there is a montage of characters getting ready for the dance, one at a time, in a separate spotlight or two, as follows:

FALISHA *and* ALISHA *doing* TANISHA's *hair, still in the school changing-room mirror.*

MAX *putting gel in his hair.*

ETTA *putting on make-up.*

RILEY *shaving his face.*

PIPPA *shaving her legs.*

ALISHA *adjusting an old-fashioned ball gown.*

ZACH *spraying Lynx all over himself. Pause. Sprays Lynx into his crotch.*

FALISHA *popping a zit.*

TANISHA *doing her hair.*

CALUM *adjusting his tie.*

CAMERON *doing the same.*

Scene Fourteen

CAMERON*'s room*/CALUM *and* JORDAN*'s room.*

CAMERON *is adjusting his tie in the mirror.*

RACHEL. You look nice.

CAMERON. I look stupid.

RACHEL. Nice-stupid.

Here. (*Fixes his tie.*)

CAMERON. When did you get to be so old?

RACHEL. When you were moping in your bedroom.

You and Calum made up yet?

CAMERON. No. And I don't think we're going to.

RACHEL. Course you will.

CAMERON. You know those monologues at the end of
movies? The voice-over that goes over that photograph or
final image of the friends running around together, and says
how after that they didn't see much of each other, grew
apart. Grew up. *Stand by Me*, *Mad Love*, *Now & Then*, *The
Wonder Years*. I think I've reached that monologue. Think
Cal and I have reached the final credits maybe, you know?

Beat.

RACHEL. That boy who was here yesterday. Ben.

CAMERON. I know – he's a bit weird. With the make-up.

RACHEL. That wasn't what I was going to say. I thought it
looked nice. The make-up.

Ben. Is he your boyfriend?

CAMERON. What? No.

RACHEL. Too bad. He's cute.

CAMERON. I guess. If you like that kind of thing.

RACHEL. It's not about what I like. It's about if you like that
kind of thing.

CAMERON. Why are you always the older sibling? It's supposed to be my job to dish out semi-sound advice.

Beat.

Am I a shit older brother?

RACHEL. A bit. I love you anyway though.

This is a bit too *Woman's Hour* for me.

CAMERON. Give me a hug anyway, will you?

They hug.

RACHEL. Here. (*Takes two boutonnières from her purse.*) These are –

CAMERON. Boutonnières.

RACHEL. Yeah. (*Puts one on him.*)

CAMERON. So who's this one for?

RACHEL. You figure it out.

Have fun.

I'm off to the cinema with Ryan.

She exits.

JORDAN *and* PIPPA *are fooling around.*

CALUM (*entering*). Jord – have you seen my? Oh sorry.

Pippa?

PIPPA. Awkward.

Yanks JORDAN *off her.*

CALUM. What the fuck, Jord?! Are you high?

PIPPA. Calum.

CALUM. What is wrong with you?

PIPPA. Calum.

CALUM. You okay? (*To* JORDAN.) What the hell, Jordan?

PIPPA. Calum!

CALUM. Did he hurt you?

PIPPA. Calum. Will you listen? He didn't hurt me. He didn't...
we're...

CALUM. You're...

JORDAN. Share the love, right?

CALUM. What you on about?

PIPPA. Calum. Listen. We're... you and I. You and I are... it's
been two years, right? Since we were fourteen. And well...
I wanna see the world, you know?

CALUM. No I don't. What are you saying?

PIPPA. That I'm seeing... Jordan.

CALUM. Seeing the world is seeing him?!

JORDAN. Chill out, man.

CALUM. Chill out?? I walk in on you with my girl and you
want me to chill out. I will not fucking chill! You said...
you – well you said '*ditto*'!

PIPPA. Calum. Don't be like that.

CALUM. Were you just talking trash?

PIPPA. Calum. I'm sixteen.

CALUM. So am I.

PIPPA. We've got our lives ahead of us.

CALUM. How long?

PIPPA. Sixty years. Maybe seventy. Ninety if we're lucky.

CALUM. No, how long you been with him? All along while
we've been –

PIPPA. Just this week, Cal.

CALUM. Were you gonna tell me? Or you two just gonna keep
laughing behind my back?

PIPPA. I was gonna tell you tonight.

CALUM. On Valentine's Day?

JORDAN. He has a point, Pippa.

CALUM. Shut up, Jordan.

PIPPA. Love just happens. You even said, right? When you
  know you know. Didn't you always say that?

CALUM. And you love him?

PIPPA. He sent me a Valentine.

CALUM. And that's love?!

PIPPA. Calum.

CALUM. Have you… have you two?

PIPPA. Can't we act like rational adults about this?

CALUM. I am sixteen! I will not be a rational adult for at least
  another two years! Have you…?!

  Silence.

  Fucking hell.

JORDAN. The girl couldn't wait for ever, Cal.

  CALUM *punches him in the nose*.

  Fuck. I'm bleeding. I'm bleeding.

PIPPA. I'm having déjà vu.

  I'm still your friend, right?

JORDAN. We're all friends.

CALUM. My brother. Maybe. But you know shit about being
  a friend.

PIPPA. Do you still want to go to the dance together?

  CALUM *storms out*.

Scene Fifteen (a)

The Valentine's Day dance.

There's a set of stairs leading down into the hall.

DJ. 'Sup, Camden Comp gals and guys. It's time to dance until
the sun doth rise. This is your American-style Valentine's
Day dance. So take a chance. That's right. Tonight's the
night. The matchmaking is done, the arrows have been
launched, I've got your music, whether hardcore, slow or
raunch. Time to grab the one you fancy, that beauty queen or
king, because love is a beautiful thing. So whether it's that
guy from science with fogged-up specs, or that math-whizz
bird making your heart a wreck. Tonight's the night, so take
a chance, spin the bottle for old romance. For we're bringing
you the purity of fifties and sixties when love was all tender,
flowers and love letters, and no return to sender. To get your
hearts a-throbbing and your bodies a-spinnin', here's our live
girls, The Watermelon Women!

THE WATERMELON WOMEN *enter. They are played by*
THE BANANA GIRLS. *But while they're still sixties-chic,
there's something that clearly says they're contemporary,
just dressed up in sixties attire for a tribute band.*

*They begin to sing 'Love Train' by The Supremes. As the
various dialogue and moments below happen, they continue
to sing, though we obviously need to be able to hear the
dialogue.*

Some couples dance.

BEN *enters down the stairs. He wears a suit, with cupid
wings and a bag of arrows.*

Everyone stares as he makes his way slowly down the stairs.

ZACH. Hey, Ben? You the faggot fairy?

BEN *pulls out an arrow. Aims it at him.*

Whoa, man. Just joking. Show some love. It's Valentine's Day.

ETTA. Do you have a date?

BEN. Uh… I'm not sure. You?

ETTA. Hasn't shown yet.

BEN. Mine either.

ETTA. You look… handsome.

BEN. Thanks. You look… pretty.

ETTA. We should dance. Do you want to dance?

He holds out his hand. They go onto the dance floor.

RILEY *and* MAX *approach* ALISHA.

RILEY. Hey, Alisha. Who knew you cleaned up so good?

ALISHA (*handing card to* RILEY). I'm supposed to give this to you.

RILEY *takes card and wanders away.*

MAX. Looking good.

ALISHA. Oh. Thanks. I just put my hair up.

MAX. I meant the dance. The dance is looking good.

ALISHA. Oh.

MAX. But you are too. Look… sophisticated.

ALISHA. Yeah. Thanks.

Beat.

MAX. Thanks for organising all this. Looking good.

ALISHA. You said that.

MAX. Yeah. I did.

ALISHA. Would you like to ask me to dance or something?

MAX. Are you asking me to dance with you?

ALISHA. No. I'm asking if you want to ask me to dance.

MAX. What's the difference?

ALISHA. The difference is you'd be the one asking to dance… the boy asks the girl. Don't you know anything?

MAX. Thought you were a feminist. Power to women.

ALISHA. Yeah, the power to say yes or no when you ask. You gonna ask me or what?

MAX. You wanna dance?

ALISHA (*hand out*). I'd be delighted.

He takes her hand, is about to lead her to dance floor.

Kiss it.

MAX. What?

ALISHA. My hand.

MAX. What?

ALISHA. You a gentleman or not?

He looks around. Kisses her hand.

You put your hands anywhere near my breasts I will bite your fingers off one by one.

Under the stairs.

RILEY (*reading*). To my secret Valentine.
You've always been the man for my eyes.
Meet me under the stairs
For some Valentine surprise.

FALISHA (*appearing from behind him*). You got my message.

RILEY. I knew it! Always the ones pretending to hate you, innit!

FALISHA. Stop talking.

RILEY. No worries. I find all that angry-bird stuff hot.

FALISHA. Stop talking. Undo your tie.

RILEY. Yes, ma'am. Love a girl who takes control. Got that Lara Croft thing going on.

FALISHA. Tie it over your eyes.

RILEY. What?

FALISHA. You wanna do this or not?

RILEY (*ties tie as blindfold*). Love that kinky shit. Happy Valentine's Day to me.

FALISHA. Undo your trousers.

His back to us, but facing FALISHA, *he unzips his trousers.*

RILEY. All the guys always saying how tight you are. But I knew. Just waitin' for a real man, right?

FALISHA. You gonna get it out or what?

Still with his back to us, he 'gets it out'.

FALISHA *kneels down.*

RILEY. The guys'll never believe this.

FALISHA. They will.

FALISHA *takes out a phone, snaps a photo of* RILEY's *package.*

Sorry, Riley. Don't think it's gonna work out after all. I've got a rep, you know. And everyone's seen your goods.

RILEY *takes the blindfold off.*

Send. All.

RILEY. No way. (*Goes to chase her, but is held up by having to do up his trousers.*)

Dance floor.

ETTA. What is it?

BEN. Huh?

ETTA. You keep looking around at everyone.

Everyone is involved in their dancing, no one's looking at them.

BEN. It's nothing. It's… nothing. Nothing.

RILEY *re-enters looking for* FALISHA. *Just then everyone's phones (except for* TANISHA's*) beep – text message. The music temporarily stops.*

Everyone pulls out their phones, look up at RILEY, *start laughing.*

RILEY. Well play the stupid music.

Music resumes. RILEY *tries to keep his cool, strutting/ dancing casually over to* TANISHA.

Hey, Tanisha.

'Sup?

TANISHA. What?

RILEY. How's it goin'?

TANISHA. What do you want?

RILEY. Don't be like that. Come on. You're lookin' great. Just wanted to know if you wanted to dance?

TANISHA. Course I wanna dance.

He holds out his hand.

But not with you.

She joins the dance floor, dancing confidently by herself. Eventually FALISHA *joins her.*

ZACH (*hands on* BEN*'s shoulders*). Hey, mate! There you are. You don't mind if cut in, do you?

BEN. Uh.

ETTA. I mind.

ZACH. Just for a minute?

ETTA. I guess.

BEN. You sure?

ETTA. I'm sure. Just keep the arrows handy in case.

ETTA *dances with* ZACH.

ZACH. Why the face of a cherry that's just been picked? A touch too sour.

ETTA. Why you talking like that?

ZACH. Like what, my peach?

ETTA. That. Peaches and cherries. You some kind of smoothie?

ZACH. I am just a man.
A man who wants to understand.

How it is a girl so sweet
Has me off my feet?

ETTA. Cos you're shorter than me.

ZACH. Etta Etta
What could be betta
Than a girl like you
Who makes grey skies blue

You make me sweat-a
You're the olive to my feta.
Oh what could be betta
Than Etta Etta Etta.

ETTA. Did you just make that up?

ZACH. I wrote it weeks ago.

Etta oh Etta.
You're so special to me.
Don't you see.
Me looking at yo
But too shy to say hello.

Could love be true?
I'll dream of that dance
In case I've the chance
To dance with you.

ETTA. Oh God. That was you.

ZACH. You sound surprised.

ETTA. But you're so... horrible. Crude.

ZACH. To cover my inner Romeo.

ETTA. Well sorry to ruin your poem but my name's not really
Etta. It's Ethel. Still interested?

ZACH. A rose by any other name would smell as sweet.

ETTA. That's beautiful.

ZACH. I wrote it.

ETTA. Did you?

ZACH. For you.

ETTA. It's lovely. No one's ever done anything romantic like that for me.

ZACH. So does that mean…

ETTA. Mean?

ZACH. I'll at least get to cop a feel later?

At this point BEN *is seated on the stairs, watching the dance.*

CAMERON *enters at the top of the stairs, unnoticed to the other characters.*

CAMERON. Cameron enters the room.

The music stops.

Everyone slowly looks up.

(*Alluding to* BEN.) Except for *him* of course. Because it's always the love interest that notices last.

CALUM (*entering*). And Calum arrives behind him.

CAMERON. The camera zooms in. Cal and Cam.

CALUM. Cam and Cal.

Because despite everything, he's still gonna go to the dance.

CAMERON. Show everyone how strong he is.

CALUM. How life goes on.

CAMERON. He'll love again.

CALUM. And Cameron makes his way down the stairs.

CAMERON. Slowly.

CALUM. Like a footballer getting ready for the winning penalty shot.

CAMERON. Like a ballet dancer making his entrance.

CALUM. And then he notices.

CAMERON. Ben.

CALUM. And Cameron puts out his hand.

And he says.

CAMERON. He says… what does he say?

CALUM. Be mine.

CAMERON. Or something like that. And they go down the stairs hand in hand.

CALUM. And no one says anything.

CAMERON. And they

CALUM. They

CAMERON. They dance.

CALUM. Like it's nothing.

CAMERON. Like it's something they do every day.

CALUM. Two blokes slow-dancing.

CAMERON. Like Zac Efron and Corbin Bleu slow-dancing together in the *High School Musical* director's cut Disney'd never let you see.

CALUM. Two blokes dancing.

CAMERON. Like it was nothing.

But was everything in the world.

Beat.

'Cept that's not what happened. Because shit like that only happens in movies.

Scene Fifteen (b)

The lights change and we realise CALUM *and* CAMERON *are actually standing in their spot at the Heath overlooking water.*

Though BEN *is still at the dance, he should still be faintly visible below on the stairs.*

CALUM. Shouldn't you be at the dance?

CAMERON. Shouldn't you?

> *Beat.*

> So who gets this spot?

CALUM. What?

CAMERON. This. I guess you can have it.

CALUM. You make it sound like we're getting divorced.

> *Beat.*

> D'you drop the team?

> CAMERON *shrugs*.

> Why?

CAMERON. What's it to you?

CALUM. Cos of me?

CAMERON. Cos of me.

CALUM. Cameron. How long?

> How long have you...

> Why'd you lie to me?

CAMERON. I didn't.

CALUM. No?

CAMERON. It wasn't like that.

CALUM. Well what was it like? What about all that stuff with Etta?

CAMERON. I don't [know]... it wasn't like that, alright? I can't [explain] – it just wasn't. It's not about you, Calum.

CALUM. You should've told me.

CAMERON. Right. And everything would've been fine, yeah?

Beat.

You know Valentine was some priest who got murdered or something. For marrying people. Messed up that's what we celebrate.

It's all… messed up.

CALUM. Maybe you can have that half. And I can have this half.

Beat.

Put a little fence between, some landscaping, so we don't have to see each other.

CAMERON (*smiles*). Sounds fair.

Beat.

So tonight's the big night, right? Or have you already…?

CALUM. She's screwing my brother.

CAMERON. Oh. That's a bit… shit.

CALUM. A proper big diarrhoea shit.

CAMERON. Yeah.

CALUM. You think you know people. Your friends. But no one knows anyone. Not really. We don't even know ourselves.

CAMERON. I know you.

CALUM. I guess.

CAMERON. You know me.

CALUM. Do I?

CAMERON. Cam and Cal.

CALUM. Everything's different now.

CAMERON. No.

CALUM. No?

CAMERON. I don't know.

Cam and Cal.

CALUM. Cal and Cam.

We're not eight any more.

CAMERON. When we were eight we couldn't wait to be sixteen. All the stuff we could do then. The whole world. Now… sometimes I wish I was eight again.

CALUM. Yeah. Yeah.

Fuck.

CAMERON. I'm sorry. About Pippa.

CALUM. I'm sorry too.

CAMERON. Not your fault. Couldn't have known she was… you know.

CALUM. I meant about your eye.

CAMERON. Oh.

CALUM. Looks pretty bad.

CAMERON. Nah. You shoulda seen the other guy.

CALUM *laughs. Then* CAMERON *does too.*

You should go to the dance. Do you good.

CALUM. Nah. I don't even have… the flower thing.

CAMERON. Boutonnière.

CALUM. Bet she didn't even get me one.

CAMERON (*takes out second one*). Here.

CALUM. Did you buy that for me?

CAMERON. Yes.

No.

But you should have it.

Is about to put it on him, quickly changes his mind, goes to hand it over instead.

Here.

CALUM. You put it on.

CAMERON. I'll have to cross the line.

CALUM. I'll grant you a day pass.

CAMERON puts it on him.

Does it hurt?

CAMERON. What?

CALUM. Bum sex.

CAMERON. Cal! Hell.

CALUM. What?

CAMERON. We've only... kissed.

CALUM. Alright, alright. Just make sure to use a condom. Just cos you can't get pregnant, doesn't mean –

CAMERON (*playfully*). Would you fuck off?

CALUM. So is he like... your boyfriend... or you're supposed to say 'partner' right?

CAMERON. No. I don't know. He's just... I don't know.

CALUM. You should go to the dance. Before your boutonnière withers.

CAMERON. Yeah. Maybe.

Beat.

CALUM *suddenly starts crying.*

Okay, I'll go [to the dance].

CALUM. I loved her so much you know.

CAMERON. I know.

CAMERON hesitates. Puts a hand on CALUM's shoulder.

CALUM *grabs his hand, holds it.*

Crying subsides. CALUM takes his own hand down from his shoulder, but he's still holding CAMERON's hand so they're standing side by side holding hands like at the start of the play.

CALUM. Don't tell anyone I cried. I don't want her to know.

CAMERON. Course.

Beat.

You can let go [of my hand] now.

CALUM. No. I can't.

Long pause. The two boys looking out, holding hands.

So what the hell do we do now?

Beat.

CAMERON. We jump.

End.

HOLLOWAY JONES

*For the tens of thousands of
'looked-after' children in the UK*

A single edition of *Holloway Jones* can be printed on demand if
you wish to read, study or perform the play separately.
Please contact info@nickhernbooks.co.uk

Acknowledgements

Neil Grutchfield for pulling the play out of me.

Esther Baker, Paula Hamilton, and Jennie McClure at Synergy.

The men and women who'd been parents while in prison, and the young people in prison, who told me their stories – thank you for bringing a richness and humanity to the play.

The young people in schools and youth groups who workshopped draft scenes from the play, and gave me their feedback – your insights were invaluable and made me work harder.

E.P.

Holloway Jones was commissioned and produced by Synergy Theatre Project, and was first performed at the Unicorn Theatre, London, on 2 November 2011, following a tour to schools and pupil referral units. The cast was as follows:

HOLLOWAY JONES	Danielle Vitalis
MUM/CHORUS	Doreene Blackstock
GEM/CHORUS	Mandeep Dhillon and Holli Dempsey
AVERY/CHORUS	Femi Wilhelm
COACH/CHORUS	Frank Prosper
POLICEMAN/CHORUS	Karl Smith

Director	Esther Baker
Dramaturg	Neil Grutchfield
Set Designer	Katy McPhee
Video Designer	Peter H. Oliver
Video Editor	Chris Beston
Costume Designer	Emmett de Monterey
Voice Coach	Kate Godfrey
Company Manager	Kirsty Henderson
Assistant Stage Managers	Ronnie Actil and Lloyd O'Neill

Characters

HOLLOWAY JONES, *female, teenager*
MUM, *female*
AVERY, *male, teenager*
GEM, *female, teenager*
COACH, *male*
POLICEMAN, *male*
CHORUS, *played by the cast* (*except for Holloway*)

Author's Note

The lines the Chorus speak have not been assigned to individual characters – the division is up to the director. It may be that they speak them in unison, or different people take on different lines. Or a bit of both.

In any case the effect is that they are a sort of modern-day Greek chorus who take on different forms throughout the play (cyclists, nosy neighbours, security guards, teachers…).

It's imagined that they are always on stage. Even when they're not in a scene, or 'exit' a scene, they are still present, watching the action as bystanders.

Setting

Primarily: London. 2008–2012.

Scenes should flow easily and quickly from one to the next, so settings should be suggested rather than fully realised in the set. Integrated into the set design should be a large screen.

A Note on Punctuation

A dash (–) is a cut-off, sometimes of one's own thought with a different thought (not a pause or beat).

An ellipsis (…) is a loss or search for words.

Words in square brackets [ ] are not spoken, but there to clarify a line's meaning.

A lack of punctuation at the end of a line means the next line comes right in.

The sound of a heart beating fast. Heavy breathing.

HOLLOWAY *cycles onto the stage.*

HOLLOWAY. Heart race
keep pace
got only one decision, which is about more than the
precision of the land, avoiding collisions with other bikes,
like, need to understand there's no team
so win or lose you need to choose what you gonna do.
Choice is: Them. Or You.

The CHORUS *enters as* TEENAGE BMX RIDERS *on
bikes. They stop and watch* HOLLOWAY.

CHORUS. They say she always ride alone
a hooded silhouette 'gainst the sky
no lie?
No family, no friends, loner at the start and at the ends
freak barely speak about it, just ride around town with that
frown pedalling like the Grim Reaper, digging her past, her
future, deeper and deeper.

The RIDERS *take their place alongside* HOLLOWAY *at the
start of a race. The screen reads: '2008 BMX SOUTH-WEST
REGIONALS, JUNIOR DIVISION'.*

*The beep of the race starting – a timer on the screen begins
to roll forward. While the* CHORUS *are in the race, they act
to carry* HOLLOWAY *– a piece of choreography focusing
on* HOLLOWAY *on her bike. While the choreography will
be interpretive of her on her bike – the screen behind comes
alive with the race. Throughout, the race freezes,*
HOLLOWAY *mid-flight, allowing the* CHORUS *to speak.*

They say her blood is cold
like the metal bed where she was born

Say beneath her skin is poisonous bones

So the story goes for Holloway Jones.

Race continues. Two of the RIDERS *fall off their bikes…
Race pauses again.*

Say she came out kickin'

Say she came out with fury in her eyes

Perhaps one of the fallen RIDERS *removes her helmet and
becomes* MUM *giving birth.*

Say she came out screamin', chanting death cries.

What you expect from prison baby.

Born to Mama like she
behind bars
so even we see
she can only go so far

Perhaps another becomes the NURSE.

Even nurse say, she say this out aloud:
'Baby born in prison, die in prison
Might go out, but eventually they all come back around.'

Holloway Prison spit you onto the ground, into this world,
but then it get hungry and swallow you back down.

Race continues… then pauses again.

Keep pace
her mama, warm and smitten, holdin' kickin' baby close to
her face,
but too drugged-up, junked-up, to make a sound choice
her sounding voice goes:

Prison baby. Holloway baby. Holloway Jones.

HOLLOWAY. Gate down, bike up down forward
forward, forward
bunny-hop, avoid the berm
no looking back, behind, what's past,
no apologies, no second guessing, no second chances.
Forward, a jump, a bump, a push, a corner, the lot, make a
choice, ride the whoop
forward. That's all you got.

CHORUS. Her mama don't need to be missin'
her for long, cos soon Holloway Jones be joining in the
Holloway Prison song.

ANNOUNCER (*off*). And in first it's: Holloway Jones!

*She crosses the finish line. Takes off her helmet. Pants, out of
breath. She has a medal round her neck. The mild sound of a
crowd fades.*

HOLLOWAY. Better luck next time, yeah?

RIDER. How old are you anyway?

HOLLOWAY. Old enough to be your mama.

RIDER. What?

HOLLOWAY. Dunno, always wanted to say that.

RIDER. It true your mum banged up?

HOLLOWAY. Who told you that?

RIDER. What they say.

HOLLOWAY. What who say?

RIDER. Makes sense.

HOLLOWAY. I won fair.

RIDER. I meant your kit. And you being here. You one of them
charity cases? You know 'keep 'em out of trouble, donate a
bike' schemes or something.

RIDERS *laugh*.

Holloway baby look like she gonna cry.

ANOTHER RIDER. I would too with that kit. Who's your
sponsor? Tesco?

RIDER. Run home, little girl. Run home to Mummy. Oh that's
right. She havin' some orange-suit love.

HOLLOWAY *gives her a death stare*.

Wot?

HOLLOWAY *jumps on the* RIDER*'s back, trying to wrestle
her down.*

COACH *enters, pulls* HOLLOWAY *off, kicking*.

COACH. What you doing?

HOLLOWAY. She said, she said…

COACH. No one likes a telltale, Holloway.

RIDER. You need to control your Girl Scout.

RIDERS *clear off*.

COACH. Holloway.

HOLLOWAY. Don't 'Holloway' me, coach. I just won you a regional medal.

COACH. Think you won *you* a medal.

HOLLOWAY. Yeah, you see me out there. I was flying.

COACH. I saw you. Jeremy Lake saw you out there too. Said keep this up, he'll come see you again in a year or two, have a shot at the Olympic Development Programme.

HOLLOWAY. You just saying that.

COACH. Why would I make that up?

HOLLOWAY. An adult thing to say. Dangle over me so you can do your adult voodoo stuff, get me to do what you want.

COACH. Well it's not working, going by what I just walked in on.

HOLLOWAY. She just…

COACH. How is it even in the middle of Surrey, after you win, you still find your way into trouble?

HOLLOWAY. I don't find trouble. Trouble find me.

COACH. A twelve-year-old shouldn't be picking on fourteen-year-olds.

HOLLOWAY. That girl fourteen? Puberty hit late for some, huh.

COACH. You got anger, you put it into that bike. You got sadness you put it into that bike. That's where you channel it, Holloway.

HOLLOWAY. I know, I know. But I did good, right? I did good, right?

COACH *laughs*.

Come on, say it.

COACH. This ain't a film, and I'm trying to talk serious here about your temper.

HOLLOWAY. Go on say it. Like in those old films. I did good, right?

COACH. You did good, kid. You did real good.

HOLLOWAY *laughs*.

HOLLOWAY. Never gets old.

COACH. Come on. Grab your bike. Gotta get you back to London.

HOLLOWAY *looks up – the screen starts to show the race we've just seen in reverse.* HOLLOWAY*'s lifted up by the* CHORUS*, riding again.*

CHORUS (RIDERS). Start rewinding, reminding yourself of the moment, the broken flow, where you failed, where your shoddy body impaled itself on the dirt below, where you went wrong.

HOLLOWAY. Where you went right. Cos there's no looking back. Only forward. To my future self: You're not rewinding but fast-forwarding to future you.

And the timer starts fast-forwarding through years… 2011, 2012, 2013, 2014, 2015, 2016.

Crowd roars up, sea of faces, the people who ignored you in secondary school, on the street… who's laughing now? Yeah? Who's…
Who's cheering now?
Sound of their claps, their voices
sound of metal, of pedals,
but the clanging clearer, nearer
no pedals, but metal bars
as your future legs start reversing, traversing the road,
sending bike wheels spinning back to reality. To now.

The timer starts reversing on itself, going backwards to where we started – while the CHORUS *lift* HOLLOWAY, *pedalling backwards, until she lands in a chair just as the timer ends firmly on 2008, and the video turns into CCTV of prison.*

And we're in: Holloway Prison visiting room. Across the table from HOLLOWAY *sits* MUM. *An individually wrapped vending-machine fairy cake sits between them. The* CHORUS *as* GUARDS *stand by.* HOLLOWAY *opens a card.*

MUM. Happy birthday, baby. Twelve years old. Remember my twelfth. Let me tell you a story. My mum bought me these rollerblades. Never been rollerblading in my life but all I wanted was these blades. Morning of my birthday go out on my own with the blades.

So I'm going forward, fast, and suddenly going down this hill and I realise I don't know how to stop! I'm going down down like a speed-skater in th' Olympics, and bam! go sailing right through Ms Jensen's white fence – break the thing into pieces! She says to me, Ms Jensen says: You shouldn't have been speeding down the lane like that! And I say, I say:

BOTH. You shouldn't have built a fence there!

MUM (*laughing*). Yeah… yeah. That's what I said. Yeah.

HOLLOWAY. It was a skateboard.

MUM. What?

HOLLOWAY. It was a skateboard. Not rollerblades. And it was your sister's birthday. You took the skateboard cos you were jealous.

MUM. How do you know? You weren't there.

HOLLOWAY. You've told me the story before.

MUM. So? Good to repeat stuff. Stops the memory going.

HOLLOWAY. Last time you told it it wasn't –

MUM. Well last time I was mistaken.

Don't be sucking teeth at me. Suddenly you're twelve you think you're some know-it-all. What?

HOLLOWAY. I'm thirteen.

MUM. What you mean?

HOLLOWAY. What you think I mean? I'm thirteen years old.

MUM. Nah.

HOLLOWAY. Think I know how old I am.

MUM. What does that say?

HOLLOWAY. I know what it says.

MUM. Well read it out. You can read can't you? Not done
    something stupid 'n' left school?

HOLLOWAY. No.

MUM. Well what's it say?

HOLLOWAY. 'Happy Twelfth Birthday.'

MUM. Well then.

    Know how I know. Cos last year you come for your eleventh
    birthday. Went to the play area, didn't we? Swimming pool.
    What? You don't remember? Got Alzheimer's or something?

HOLLOWAY. That was two years ago.

MUM. What'd we do last year then, you so clever?

HOLLOWAY. Wasn't here last year on my birthday.

MUM. Where else would you be?

HOLLOWAY. Lost your privileges. No visitors that month.
    Didn't tell me though. So I sat in the car park. In the taxi.
    Ali. That was the taxi driver's name. Gave me some salt-
    and-vinegar crisps. Then we listened to Radio One. They did
    a listener vote. Ali and I called in. Our song lost. Then some
    lady cried walking back to her car. Then a bird shat on the
    windscreen. Then it got dark and Ali drove me home. That's
    what I did for my birthday last year.

MUM. You go on remembering things as you do, gonna get you
    into trouble. Get through this world faster if you start
    forgettin'. Not gonna eat your birthday cake?

    Don't you like chocolate no more?

HOLLOWAY. Got loads of calories innit?

MUM. You some Naomi Campbell now? Gonna be hitting people with your mobile soon. Eat your cake.

HOLLOWAY *does*.

That's my baby. Give you strength. Make you strong. What?

HOLLOWAY. Meant to eat healthy. For my cycling and that.

MUM. What's that got to do with nothing?

HOLLOWAY. Say I got a chance at Junior European. Say I'm real good.

MUM. Say lots of things get a girl's hopes up, say lots of things take advantage of a girl.

HOLLOWAY. Coach ain't like that.

MUM. How you know?

HOLLOWAY. I *am* good. I won South-West Regional.

MUM. What you win?

HOLLOWAY. Just said, the South-West.

MUM. But *what* you win, what they give you? Money?

HOLLOWAY *pulls out her medal from under her shirt, still around her neck*.

What you gonna do with that?

That gonna buy a girl clothes, that gonna pay the rent? *That* gonna get a girl a ride?

HOLLOWAY. I got a bike.

MUM. That what flash now? People riding round on two wheels? That what your friends do?

HOLLOWAY *shrugs*.

Ain't you still got no friends?

HOLLOWAY. Got Gem.

MUM. Gem. Need be careful round girls like that, can't trust 'em. Don't roll your eyes at me, Holloway Jones, or soon I roll them back in your head for you. Just listen, alright. Get yourself a man, with prospects. Support you, protect you. What?

HOLLOWAY. Nothing. I dunno. Suzanne don't like boys coming round.

MUM. That Suzanne [who] went to get the tea?

HOLLOWAY *nods*.

Why you bring her here? To make me feel bad?

HOLLOWAY. No. The rules, innit. Have to be supervised till I'm sixteen. You know the rules.

MUM. I been abidin' the rules my whole life. Don't let Suzanne tell you different. How come you not with Margarite no more?

HOLLOWAY *shrugs*.

You misbehavin'?

HOLLOWAY *shrugs*.

Soon you find yourself in here with me.

HOLLOWAY. So?

MUM. What you mean so?

HOLLOWAY. You look alright.

MUM *grabs her hand fiercely*.

MUM. Listen to me, Holloway Jones, don't say things like that to me.

HOLLOWAY. I was just saying

MUM. Well don't be.

HOLLOWAY. Okay. Sorry, Mum.

MUM. Cos you not careful, don't control that temper, no foster gonna take you. Then where will you be?

HOLLOWAY. Better off.

Beat. MUM *starts laughing hysterically*.

MUM. Better off! You got your mum's sense of humour.

Continues to laugh, then turns to tears.

HOLLOWAY. Mum? You okay?

MUM. Give me a tissue.

HOLLOWAY. What?

MUM. You brought the tissue, didn't you? Before Suzanne gets back.

Holloway. D'you bring the tissue?

Long pause.

HOLLOWAY. Course I did.

HOLLOWAY *hands tissue to her.* MUM *pretends to dab eyes, blows nose. Takes a pill from the tissue, puts it in her mouth. Hands back the tissue.*

MUM. That's my girl. That's my Holloway baby. Happy Birthday, Holloway baby.

CHORUS (GUARDS). Can't change your history, no mystery that you can't change the destiny you're given, that you got, say what you like, but any fool can ride a bike.

AVERY, *picking a bike lock.*

HOLLOWAY. What you doing? Hey, I'm talking to you.

AVERY. What's it to you?

HOLLOWAY. You trying to steal that bike?

AVERY. What's it to you?

HOLLOWAY. It's my bike.

Beat.

AVERY. That's awkward.

Beat.

HOLLOWAY. You Avery.

AVERY. Who wants to know?

HOLLOWAY. Wasn't a question. You got a rep.

AVERY. How would you know?

HOLLOWAY. We gone to the same school since primary. You just ain't never seen me – not through that fog of Lynx you always covered in.

AVERY. You gonna rat me out?

HOLLOWAY. [I'm] no snitch.
Can I have my bike now?

AVERY. What's your name?

HOLLOWAY. Who wants to know?

Beat.

AVERY. Holloway.

HOLLOWAY. How you know that?

AVERY (*smiles*). Gone to the same school since primary.
See you got a pretty face, Holloway. But a crap lock.

He holds up lock, she goes to take it. He pulls it away.

See dilemma: now that I got your lock, what kind of message would it send if I didn't go and take it?

Goes to leave.

HOLLOWAY *grabs him, flips him to the floor (self-defence class put to use) ending with her having him pinned to the ground – her foot or knee resting threateningly on his crotch.*

HOLLOWAY. Got a pretty face, but a crap attitude. See dilemma is: now that I got your balls, what kind of message would it send if I didn't go and break them?

AVERY. Girl talks dirty.

HOLLOWAY *tightens grip.*

Right. Man gives in.

She lets him go.

Used to think my ex-girlfriend had me by the balls, but damn…

Goes to leave.

HOLLOWAY. Hey. My lock.

AVERY. Right.

Gives lock. Keeps hold of other end.

Say. You wanna go for a bike ride some time?

AVERY *disappears.*

HOLLOWAY *races. Speaks to us as she does.*

HOLLOWAY. People say your kit makes all the difference.

COACH. Where are your gloves, Holloway?

HOLLOWAY. That a mistake in the kit, the way you look, can cost you it all. Hair catching the wind the wrong way, shoe catching the pedal the wrong way

COACH. And I don't remember Shanaze Reade wearing hoops as she cycled to gold.

HOLLOWAY. Like a second skin, not just something that's protecting you. It is you.

COACH. Focus, Holloway. Focus on what's in front of you. Don't fall –

HOLLOWAY. Focus on my lungs, the breath coming up through my throat, out my lips.

Lots of peeps don't got relationships. Not serious ones. You know why? Not just the time it takes away from training, not what you'd think. But oxygen. They lone riders.

COACH. You're not breathing, Holloway.

HOLLOWAY. Don't want someone taking your oxygen. True. Specially not before a race. Don't want some guy in your room stealing, hogging the oxygen while you sleep. Can never be too careful.

COACH. What you smiling like that for?

HOLLOWAY. My time, innit.

COACH. No, girls don't smile like that 'less there's a boy involved. Good time but at the cost of recklessness on those jumps. You be careful.

She continues to cycle, but COACH *goes and* AVERY*'s now trailing behind her.*

CHORUS (SECURITY). But careful never lead to good
Never by doing what you should.
Discovery of the world, of its treasures, its many pleasures
come from going off-track.
Cos there's always time to go back to where you're meant, yeah?
But now there's romance. The chance to be young and free
without conscience or care, or dare I say, gents: love?

They arrive outside the partially built Olympic Stadium.

AVERY. Wait up. Can't keep up with you.

HOLLOWAY. Your idea to come so far.

Worried? A girl faster than you.

AVERY. I'm alright with that. [I] Like a fast girl.

HOLLOWAY. Woman.

AVERY. Where'd you learn to ride like that?

HOLLOWAY. Was eleven years old, cycling between some cars
when this guy goes –

COACH *appears on the other side of her.*

COACH. Where'd you learn to ride like that?

HOLLOWAY. When you got places to get away from, you learn
quick.

COACH (*laughs*). Makes sense. Though at that speed, I reckon
you got quite a few places to get away from.

HOLLOWAY. What's it to you?

COACH. My car bonnet you just used as your bump. Shouldn't
ride on other people's cars.

HOLLOWAY. Shouldn't park your car there.

COACH (*smiles*). Impressive jump anyhow.

HOLLOWAY. Yeah? You some kind of expert?

COACH. Yeah. I am.

Beat. He hands her a business card.

Come by. We'll try you out.

HOLLOWAY. You're not some kind of paedo are you?

COACH. No. How old are you?

HOLLOWAY. I knew it.

COACH. If you're under sixteen, need to bring a parent with you.

HOLLOWAY. Might be difficult.

COACH. Those are the rules.

HOLLOWAY. Never met my dad. And Mum's in Holloway Prison.

COACH....oh.

She goes to give him back his card.

HOLLOWAY. Guess you want your card back. Where'd you get these made anyhow – Poundsavers?

COACH. Keep it. Put the same energy into your performance as you do your lip and we might make a right athlete out of you.

COACH *disappears.*

AVERY. Same coach you with now? Same coach tell you you can't do twenty-twelve?

HOLLOWAY. Don't work like that. I only just made Olympic *Talent Team*, and that's the lowest one. Takes years – move up different teams. I mean I only been training properly two years.

AVERY. Ask me, get a new coach – one that get you in twenty-twelve.

HOLLOWAY. Coach a bit tight, rules and that, but he's alright. He sticks by, y'know?

AVERY. Loyalty. I respect that. So he the one first got you hooked on bikes?

HOLLOWAY. No. Doreen Finley.

AVERY. Who's she?

HOLLOWAY. Foster mum when I was eight. Old lady. But she was – gave me this bike. Used to be her little girl's, cheap old thing, but a gift. You know. For me.

AVERY. This old lady taught you to ride?

HOLLOWAY. No taught myself. Bike sat in corner for weeks, kept asking when I was gonna ride it, didn't I like it? I loved it. Only I couldn't ride it. No one'd ever taught me. Didn't want to disappoint her I guess. So I'd sneak out at night, unlock the garage, and practise. Got good. Thought I'd impress her.

AVERY. And you blew her away?

HOLLOWAY. No. Forgot to lock the garage one time. Some lads cleared out all her stuff. She found out I was sneaking out at night. Placed me somewhere else after that. (*Laughs*.) Cleared everything from the garage, but left the bike, rubbish old thing. Houses always changed for me, but the bike stayed the same.

Beat.

AVERY. Come on.

HOLLOWAY. What we doing at Olympic Stadium anyhow? Still a building site.

AVERY. Shh… through here.

HOLLOWAY. How you know about this entrance?

AVERY. I know a guy, a cleaner.

HOLLOWAY. Get arrested, breaking and entering.

AVERY. Didn't break anything, did we?

CHORUS (SECURITY). It's no crime, sneak into a stadium for a short time. No victim you've seen so we avert our eyes from the CCTV screen.

AVERY. Said coach can't get you to race twenty-twelve. So I did. All yours. Well for eight minutes then nightwatch back on this side.

Wait hold on. Got you something.

AVERY *gets down on one knee.*

HOLLOWAY. You best not be proposing.

He puts a box at her feet. Bowing like a prince as he does. She looks at the box hesitantly.

AVERY. Not gonna blow up.

She opens the box. Gleaming white trainers.

HOLLOWAY. What… how'd you get these?

AVERY. Ones you wanted, innit? All the cyclists have 'em.

HOLLOWAY. But how'd you get 'em? Avery?

CHORUS (SECURITY). Don't ask questions to which you won't like the reply, or where there's always a tightly wrapped, freshly boxed lie.

HOLLOWAY. These are like… the best shoes.

AVERY. And don't you deserve the best?

HOLLOWAY. Deserve's a funny word. Where'd you get 'em?

He helps her into them, does her laces, and then onto her bike, as the following is said:

CHORUS (SECURITY). Is that a real question? Or just something you say to be polite, because it's the right thing to ask? The danger is that question leads to other questions that your smile masks. *Where'd* you get 'em leads to *how'd* you get 'em. And somewhere in your liver you know the answer – and a shiver of doubt slithers a route through your spine, a cancer at its tiny start, but in your heart you convince yourself it's fine, not thinking of the contract you've signed. You don't pursue, after all what harm can a shoe do?

AVERY. I'll take care of you.

They kiss.

HOLLOWAY *begins to ride, and* AVERY *laughs with delight.*

(*Laughing.*) Holloway Jones is off! The nation watches. Can she do it?

Sound of roaring crowd comes in.

Holloway! Holloway! Watch her go!

HOLLOWAY. Choose a path. Follow it.

The sound of a crowd roars.

And then HOLLOWAY *is standing at a corner with* GEM, *en route home from school.* (*The bike and sound go.*) GEM *applies make-up. A* POLICEMAN *eyes them up nearby.*

Staring. You see that, Gem? That Fed keep looking over here, staring, so I'm staring right back. (*Calls out.*) Staring contest, innit?

HOLLOWAY *goes into* GEM*'s make-up bag to borrow some herself, and pulls out a fifty-pound note.*

Where you get this fifty?

GEM. Mum.

HOLLOWAY. Your mum gave you that.

GEM. No, she's tight. Just borrowed it from the till at her shop.

HOLLOWAY. You mean you stole it.

GEM. Nah, when you take from family it's not stealing. Just cashing in on estimate of your future inheritance. Kinda like a hedge fund, innit?

HOLLOWAY. Theft-fund maybe, and your mum got them CCTV cameras.

GEM. They just for show – none of them actually work. Hey, d'you remember in Year 4, Miss Smith?

HOLLOWAY. Heard she went and had a mental breakdown. Proper.

GEM. Heard she sang some YouTube video and now she's proper famous.

HOLLOWAY. Is it?

GEM. Anyway, remember we had to do that project: 'To My Future Self. When I Grow Up.'

HOLLOWAY. So?

GEM. Just been thinking about it is all. I was gonna be a veterinarian.

HOLLOWAY. Need biology for that, innit?

GEM. And we had to write letters and stuff to our future self. Who we were gonna be when we grew up.

HOLLOWAY. I dunno how you remember stuff from Year 4.

GEM. And. And we had to come dressed up. Like our future self. Miss took our picture. Put 'em on the wall. Our future selves staring down at us.

HOLLOWAY. You were wearing a white coat.

GEM. But we weren't allowed to keep them. The pictures.

HOLLOWAY. Good thing, the haircut you had.

GEM. Just had to remember the picture in our head, Miss said. That's what she said.

HOLLOWAY. Yeah. So? (*Pulls out her iPhone, takes a photo of the staring* POLICEMAN.)

POLICEMAN. Excuse me, what do you think you're doing?

HOLLOWAY. Keeping a record of guys perving on us.

POLICEMAN. Can't just take pictures of people. Privacy laws.

HOLLOWAY. There's cameras everywhere here, taking pics of *me*.

GEM. Where'd you get that phone?

AVERY *appears*. (*A scene within a scene, as it were – though* GEM *is watching the scene, and* HOLLOWAY *can speak between both*.)

AVERY. Where you been? Said you'd ring after training.

HOLLOWAY. Out of credit.

AVERY. You always say that.

HOLLOWAY. Well 's always true.

AVERY. Lemme see your phone.

HOLLOWAY. Why?

AVERY. You don't trust me.

Beat. Hands it over.

AVERY *throws it in the river.*

Should be able to reach you.

HOLLOWAY. I hope you're a good swimmer.

AVERY. I'm Tom Daley I am. Should be able to reach my girl, right?

Pulls out iPhone.

Saw you approaching on your bike. Looked beautiful. Come here, ain't gonna bite.

(*Presses play on video on phone.*) Look how good you look.

Beat. She's flattered.

HOLLOWAY. Don't think sweet-talking gonna get you out of diving in for my phone. And don't be filming me on your phone. It's sweet, but creepy sweet.

AVERY. It's not my phone.

HOLLOWAY. Whose is it?

AVERY. Yours. Only best for my girl, right?

Beat. She kisses him. He goes to kiss again, but she stops.

GEM. Where he get that?

HOLLOWAY (*to* AVERY). Where you get that?

AVERY. What's it matter?

HOLLOWAY (*to* GEM). What's it matter?

(*To* AVERY.) Already got someone else's numbers in here.

AVERY. Thas why there a delete button, right?

CHORUS. Harmless names – friends of whoever's phone it was before. Easy enough to ignore. Easier to accept the gift, the toy, than cause a rift with the boy.

AVERY. Don't my girl deserve the best.

He films her, starts kissing her, filming them kissing.

GEM. Like that is it. Hello? Holloway?

POLICEMAN. 'Scuse me. I'm talking to you.

She breaks from kissing. AVERY *disappears.*

What you girls doing here?

GEM. What it look like we're doing? Planning bank robberies. (*To* HOLLOWAY.) Ask me –

POLICEMAN. Think it's time you girls moved on.

GEM. We ain't botherin' no one.

POLICEMAN. No loitering.

HOLLOWAY. We ain't dropped no rubbish.

POLICEMAN. Not littering, loitering. Best make your way home. Don't want Mum worrying you getting into trouble.

HOLLOWAY. My mum's dead.

GEM. Ask me, man buys you phone, man expect to reach you. Man expect to control you.

HOLLOWAY. Lucky no one asking you.

GEM. Avery Lewis used to steal people's lunches, don't you remember?

HOLLOWAY. What you talking about?

GEM. In Year 3, got suspended for stealing kids' lunches and selling them to other kids.

HOLLOWAY. Not healthy how you remember things from Year 3.

POLICEMAN. Excuse me, girls, I'm saying –

GEM. Just saying. Man buy you something he want something in return.

HOLLOWAY *passes a matching phone to* GEM.

What's this?

HOLLOWAY. From Shawn, Avery's mate. Said give it you. You gonna take it or worried where it came from.

GEM. No use it going to waste.

Just best not ditch me now you got a man. Don't forget your roots.

HOLLOWAY. What roots? Mine soiled up in cell, dropping leaves in care homes up and down London.

GEM. You know what I mean.

HOLLOWAY. You.

GEM. Yeah.

HOLLOWAY. You hang out with us too.

We going to Club Destiny tonight.

GEM. How you gonna get in there?

HOLLOWAY. Avery gonna get us in.

POLICEMAN. Girls.

HOLLOWAY. Can't you see we trying to have an important conversation here?

POLICEMAN. What's your name?

HOLLOWAY. Ain't telling you my name. One thing my mum taught me: don't tell no pig nothing.

POLICEMAN. Thought your mum was dead.

GEM. She can talk to the dead. She's a clairvoyant.

HOLLOWAY *starts shaking*.

HOLLOWAY. Mama saying be nice to this man for he's a… banker?… anchor?… oh. A wanker. I ain't giving you my name or anything else. I know my rights.

GEM (*leaving*). Come on, Holloway.

POLICEMAN. Holloway.

HOLLOWAY. Gem!

GEM. Sorry.

POLICEMAN. Till we meet again, Holloway.

CHORUS (POLICEMEN). A promise made
    Or a warning laid, of things to come?

Club music comes blasting in. HOLLOWAY *and the cast
dance as though in a club – young, free, without
responsibility. In the dance, her scruffy jacket is removed,
and the* CHORUS (CLUBBERS) *put her in a swish new one.*

COACH *interrupts the club scene. The club turns into
training scene.*

COACH. Where you been, Holloway? Hurry up, need to
    catch up.

The CLASS *dance/train to music.*

HOLLOWAY*'s phone rings.*

Holloway!

HOLLOWAY. Sorry. I gotta take this.

Takes phone which merges her back into club scene.

Her phone rings.

AVERY. Leave it.

HOLLOWAY. It's coach.

AVERY. Leave it.

She does. The CHORUS (CLUBBERS) *again redress her –
again a not-cool item is replaced with something much more
cool. The screen timer turns forward, reading 2009.*

AVERY *films her dancing – the screen comes alive with their
image (or perhaps a montage) of them out having fun…
think early-days-romance stuff they're filming on their
iPhones. Then we're on a bus and the images turn darker –
some sort of harassment/mugging/robbery is taking place.*
HOLLOWAY *stands with her back to us watching the film*

during the following while holding up her phone as though it's filming it – she's part of what's going on but at the same time separate.

The CHORUS (*as various everyday people*) *sit in chairs as though they're on a bus.*

CHORUS. Look down
    book up
    avoid detection
    stare at your own reflection
    unfazed, avert your gaze, look anywhere but at
    anywhere but
    anywhere but
    at that you don't see
    thankful it's not me
    Cos I fear…
    hear nothing
    see nothing
    say nothing
    just stay in your seat
    glued in your seat
    subdued in your seat

    dead meat – you do the same
    stay out of the frame, right?
    Out of sight, what could be a fight
    my right to stay in my chair, my fair due.
    And what do you do?
    What do you do?
    Same as us, as me, as we
    don't make a fuss
    just sit and the bus and
    ignore, the problem's not yours
    what problem?
    I didn't see nothing
    I didn't hear nothing
    didn't interfere with nothing
    cos nothing to interfere with
    you better off when you hear nothing
    see nothing
    know nothing
    so the bus go, on its way

carry on your day
and the event –
what, what event?
Memory came and went
I forgot like I ought to
Like you, like we do
like she do.

Beat.

AVERY *puts his arm around her and the video returns us to happy/fun images and we're immersed back into some sort of club scene. And the timer tumbles forward again landing on 2010. Another aspect of her appearance is upgraded by the* CHORUS.

And we break out into two scenes that happen at the same time – HOLLOWAY *in both at once. The scene happens as a training class – exercise-weight balls being thrown back and forth (by* AVERY *when she's in that scene, by* COACH *in the other) and other training exercises… eventually* COACH *and* AVERY *spin a skipping rope for her which she jumps in.*

AVERY. Someone has. Someone has not. The natural order. Survival of the fittest, right?

Someone always on top, someone always on the bottom.

HOLLOWAY. What about equal rights?

COACH. Everyone starts at the same place, and then you drive 'em out.

AVERY. Equal rights? It's the equal right for everyone to take what they deserve. We have the same right to that bloke on the bus's stuff as he does.

COACH. It's anyone's race.

AVERY. So if you don't take it, that top, if you don't fight for it –

COACH. Do what you can –

AVERY. Someone else gonna get there first. Circle of life, right?

HOLLOWAY. I guess.

AVERY. Like your cycling. Only one person can cross the finish line first.

COACH. Someone falls down in front of you, you fall over. You're done, right?

HOLLOWAY. Yeah.

AVERY. Don't you deserve to win?

HOLLOWAY. Yeah. Course.

COACH. You gonna let someone else force you to lose?

HOLLOWAY. No. Course not.

AVERY. Everybody on the bus stood by cos they knew their place now in the natural order.

COACH. Can't just stand by, cycle idly by.

AVERY. They knew he didn't deserve this stuff any more than we did.

COACH. Need to be aggressive.

AVERY. What he do to get it that's better than us?

COACH. What you gonna do?

HOLLOWAY. Take the lead. Fight for what's mine.

COACH. Only one person wins. Only one person's on top.

COACH/AVERY. You gotta choose: it's either them. Or you.

HOLLOWAY. I choose me.

She's immersed back into club scene – final change to appearance – the effect being when she exits it she looks like a different woman than when she started the club sequence – older yes, but also more confident and in expensive gear. The CHORUS *turn into* TEAMMATES *on bikes circling her. The timer on the screen comes to life, tumbles forward, so much so that it lands on 2011.*

COACH. Where've you been, Holloway?

HOLLOWAY. I'm here ain't I?

COACH. You're late. And you been late the last three practices.

HOLLOWAY. Don't dwell on the past, man, alright?

COACH. You can't just come when you like. This isn't Butlins holiday camp.

HOLLOWAY. Got that right.

COACH. You need to watch your lip too.

HOLLOWAY. Did I not just win you the Junior British Series? Do you get that?

COACH. I got Jeremy Lake coming down. Just for you, Holloway. He doesn't come to London for just anyone. You show up late for that, it reflects on me. And you come waltzing in when you like, I promise you right now he won't put you on the Olympic Development Team, no matter how good you are. Do you get *that*?

HOLLOWAY. Do you want me to warm up or not? I'm not bothered.

Beat.

COACH. Hurry up. We're timing today.

She mounts bike, joins others. Starting sound and timer starts – HOLLOWAY *begins the race landing beside* GEM *and* AVERY.

AVERY. Where you been? I been ringing you.

HOLLOWAY. Got the Europeans coming up.

AVERY. No point paying your contract, you don't even answer the phone.

GEM. Just said didn't she, was on a bike – you ever answered the phone while jumping berms?

AVERY. You ever keep your snout outta other dog's food?

HOLLOWAY. Alright, we're all friends here right. Right?

AVERY. We cool. I was just worried 'bout where my girl was.

HOLLOWAY. I'm here.

AVERY. Need you girls to come along tomorrow night.

GEM. We going to that new club, Fate?

AVERY. Maybe. First we gotta swing by Simon Street.

GEM. What's happening at Simon Street? What business we have being there?

AVERY. Not for you to worry about, Gem.

HOLLOWAY. Then what we gotta be doing there?

AVERY. Don't gotta do nothing. Cos it ain't nothing. You'll just be the pretty dressing, you get me. Looks more casual if there's some pretty girls around.

HOLLOWAY. I got practice. Coach said Jeremy Lake's coming.

AVERY. What's that mean?

GEM. Don't you listen? Means moving from Talent Team where she's been for two years to Olympic Development Programme.

AVERY. So what that mean?

GEM. Means she's for real. After that it's the Olympic *Academy* Programme, which is the hardcore seven days a week, on your way to Olympic glory. I hear Athlete's Village is sick, all these fitties around, pent-up energy out of control.

AVERY. So this *Development* Programme which you *might* move to if this Jeremy Lake sees you, *if* – ain't even the full thing?

GEM. It's one step closer. An *important* step closer.

AVERY. Sounds shady to me so many steps, so many years. Anyway, this won't take long. You can go there right after.

GEM. She got practice.

AVERY. There go your snout again.

GEM. Cos my snout smell trouble.

AVERY. It getting confused with that pound of perfume you wearing.

HOLLOWAY. Alright, you two.

AVERY. It's cool. I get you sore Shawn dumped your ass, but don't need to put it on us.

GEM. Dumped me? That what he said?

AVERY. This between me and my girl. Don't get involved.

GEM. But that's exactly what you asking. For us to be
involved. 'None of your business' but we *involved*. And that
business that's none of ours gonna be the business that get us
in trouble.

AVERY. You don't know what you're talking about. Just asking
a *favour*.

GEM. Same favour Shawn start asking me which is why I
dumped *his* ass. Same reason you should...

AVERY. What? She should what?

GEM *kisses her teeth*.

Just keep out, man.

GEM. Why you getting messed up in his dirty work?

AVERY. Ain't so dirty paying for that leash round your neck,
those studs on your claws.

GEM *takes off her necklace and rings – throws them at
his feet*.

HOLLOWAY. Gem.

AVERY. Now you just disrespecting, man.

GEM. Used to be fun, all of you, the group – just a laugh. When
did it all turn so serious? Suddenly comes like we always
reporting in to you all or something. Like you own us. Now
it's all serious and boring. I don't want to be here no more.

HOLLOWAY. She don't mean that.

GEM. How do you know what I mean?

AVERY. All for one and one for all, huh? If there's one thing
worse than those who take without giving anything back, it's
a lack of loyalty. You leave us, this, it don't show much
loyalty. And a lack of loyalty is a lack of respect. And
without that, you got nothing. And you disrespect us, this, no
saying what could happen. You get me?

GEM. I get that you talk so much come so you don't even know what you saying half the time. You boys all the same with your talk – you, Shawn, all of you. Think you're some Obama, some Martin Luther with your words of wisdom, your view on society. You all just scared little boys.

Call it what you want. But I'm done. It's not fun no more.

She exits.

AVERY. That girl looking for a slap.

HOLLOWAY. She'll be back. She just in a bit of a mood since Shawn find a new girl.

AVERY. You feel like she do? Like you gotta report in and stuff?

HOLLOWAY. No.

AVERY. Cos you can leave any time if you –

HOLLOWAY. Avery. She's my friend but she don't talk for me, alright.

AVERY. So you'll come tomorrow?

Beat.

You trust me, right?

HOLLOWAY. Course.

AVERY. Without trust, there's nothing.

HOLLOWAY. I trust you. I'll be there.

COACH *appears.*

COACH. You'll be there right on time, right? He's coming down special, just to meet you.

HOLLOWAY. Said I'll be there.

COACH. Trust me. Show him your stuff and the Development Team will be yours next year.

HOLLOWAY. I trust you. I'll be there.

During the following, HOLLOWAY'*s passed from one* CHORUS *member to another, or perhaps she does a more erratic version of her training and dancing from earlier. Whatever it is, she's starting to lose control.*

CHORUS (NEIGHBOURHOOD PEOPLE). Say there's been a
stitch-up on Simon Street
A hiccup on Simon Street
I heard

She heard

A little bird told me

I see

She see it with her own two eyes – bunch of guys in hoods,
no good, on Simon Street, taking off, breaking off like in a
race, alarm going, leaving no trace but a girl

Always a stupid girl left behind

The kind who doesn't know what she's doing there. No fair.

Boohoo

Imagine it was you

Well it's not, not some stupid femme

Anyway she was carted off by them.

No, wait, the attempt was *aborted*, reported no crime took
place. So cop car raced to Simon Street like he knew,
stopping before anything broke.

Like that bloke in *Minority Report*

Exactly.

As someone with seniority, can say I'm glad authorities get
the bad off our street *before* they do harm. Lock 'em up! Put
'em on a farm for all I care. I swear, when I was young, in
my day –

Say it was that Holloway, you know –

I know the one, lock her up and be done with it.

Poor girl, if you ask me, got nought to do with she, she just
stand there cos her man is there.

Teach her a lesson. You start messin' with boys of that kind,
you find their charm, their shiny cars don't stop you being
put behind bars. And all that branded stuff suddenly look
cheap as rubble, as you suddenly waist-deep in trouble.

Stupid bird.

Not so absurd, you'd do the same for your man without hesitation. A shame it's landed her at the station.

HOLLOWAY. Told you I don't know nothing, just standing there – alone.

CHORUS. Baby born in prison, die in prison. Might go out, but eventually they all come back around.

HOLLOWAY. Can I go now? I got somewhere to be.

POLICEMAN. Someone to pick you up? Parent? Foster-mum?

HOLLOWAY. Only been with this one a week. She permanent screw-face. She ain't gonna come.

POLICEMAN. Then I guess you're staying here overnight.

HOLLOWAY. No way.

POLICEMAN. Those are the rules.

The CHORUS/COPS *lift her into a cell. Then they begin cycling around her as a* GANG.

HOLLOWAY. I didn't do nothing!

CHORUS (GANG). And you think maybe you're getting deeper, that you're on the brink,
a narrow path that's only getting steeper.
And for a split second – you think of your career
for a split second you think of saying what they want to hear
for a split second, yeah, you think of telling them who was there…

HOLLOWAY. I didn't do nothing! No one listening! Didn't do nothing!

CHORUS (GANG). But you won't. Don't. You swear.
You care about your self-respect.
Him you gonna protect.
So a split second later the thought disappears cos you ain't a SNITCH.
Not about fear, it's just what you know
something you've always known
You don't snitch.

A scratch you never itch, you know it in your blood, in your
veins, in your brain, it's written on your skin as well.
No matter what, you never ever tell.

HOLLOWAY. Hey, can't I get another phone call? I know my
rights!

CHORUS (TEACHER). After spending a night in a cell,
doesn't tell, comes to school like it's all okay, just another
day, but as a teacher, you see through, you do, to what she's
thinkin'. I'm no preacher, just a teacher, but still I shake her,
make her see the light, see what's right, tell her it's a warning
heeded, Avery's not what she needed and stay away and
just... focus on my class.

Except none of this do I actually do or say... I mean I'm not
a social worker, to get involved, try to solve, would be...
see... I've got a hundred and eighty students, need to show
some prudence when deciding to – all you can do is hope
they can cope when the bell rings. Thing is I hope she sticks
with her plan and stays away from the man. But... the pull,
right? Try as she might, she'll be pulled back to his arms, to
his charms. So... I mean where else has she got to go?

She approaches AVERY (*and* CHORUS).

AVERY. Where you been, Holloway?

HOLLOWAY. Where've I been? Where were you? You know
where I was. Cos I left you a message. Sitting in with police
overnight. Why didn't you come?

AVERY. Devon's party, innit?

HOLLOWAY (*sarcastic*). Oh, well. How was Devon's party?

AVERY. Good, yeah.

Look, you know we couldn't come by there. But you're
alright now. Just like I knew you would be.

Goes to touch her, but she pulls away.

Don't be like that. So what'd you say?

HOLLOWAY. What did I say?

AVERY. To the police.

HOLLOWAY. Didn't have anything to say, cos I didn't know what I was doing, did I?

AVERY. Exactly. Told you I gonna protect you, right? You tell 'em about us?

HOLLOWAY. I'm not a snitch.

AVERY. Course you ain't.

HOLLOWAY. Just left me standing on Simon Street.

AVERY. We called to you to run, thought you heard.

Got you something.

HOLLOWAY. What for?

AVERY. Was worried about you. What I got without you? Thinking about you in there, got me all broken up, you know.

But you done alright. (*Gives her a gift.*) Yeah, you done alright.

HOLLOWAY (*American accent*). Easiest time I ever did.

All laugh.

CHORUS (GANG). And like that, a shared joke, a laugh, the night before up in smoke, forgot and gone, she worries no longer and their bond grows stronger.

AVERY. You know what been bothering me about that night though – how they know we gonna be there? Before we even done nothing.

HOLLOWAY. Lucky for me.

AVERY. But how they know we gonna be there?

HOLLOWAY. They didn't.

AVERY. How the police get there so quick then? Don't make sense.

CHORUS. You all thinking the unsaid, in your head a thought you all share but you all dare not speak – the bleak, cold possibility someone... told.

HOLLOWAY. Who knew you gonna be there?

AVERY. Only person who knew who wasn't there was Gem.

HOLLOWAY. Gem ain't a snitch.

AVERY. You heard her that day.

HOLLOWAY. She just angry. I known her since I was six. She's loyal, okay?

AVERY. Yeah. Okay.

Anyway, good to have you back.

COACH *appears. We're at the training ground.*

COACH. You're back.

HOLLOWAY. I ain't never gone.

COACH. No?

HOLLOWAY. Why you always gotta give me a hard time?

COACH. You make it hard for yourself.

You going to tell me about the other day? And I don't want no excuses.

HOLLOWAY. You don't want no excuses, then why you asking then?

Beat.

When Jeremy Lake gonna come again?

COACH. Whenever I ask him to.

HOLLOWAY. So when you gonna ask him to?

COACH. When you prove to me you're committed.

HOLLOWAY. I prove it right now.

COACH. Not your riding. It's more than that.

HOLLOWAY. Well tell me what. And I do it. Tell me what to do and I do it.

COACH. Just got to make a choice for yourself, Holloway.

HOLLOWAY. Well then I choose to get on my bike.

What?

COACH. You serious about this, then you come here, no more excuses, and in a year we'll reassess it, and then maybe I'll invite him down to see you.

HOLLOWAY. A year? You joking me?

COACH. No.

HOLLOWAY. What all the BS you tell me about *this* year?

COACH. I meant it. But then you start coming and going as you please and you didn't turn up.

HOLLOWAY. Said I was sorry didn't I.

COACH. No, actually. You didn't. But I'm not interested in apologies. I'm interested in you being loyal. In you being here every day. And then we'll see.

HOLLOWAY. I'm not waiting no year.

COACH *shrugs*.

You just like the rest of 'em, you know that?

COACH. Maybe. But at some point it's no longer about the rest of 'em. And it's about you.

HOLLOWAY. You a liar like the rest of 'em. I don't need you. I'm the one who can ride the bike! Me! I'm Holloway Jones!

COACH *disappears*.

AVERY. Thought you had practice.

HOLLOWAY. Who needs practice when you're already perfect? Seriously coach keeps having me do all these practice runs while everyone else doing the real competitions.

CHORUS (GANG). Should be you doing the real deal.
Sealing the win
Not just peddling some spin class.

HOLLOWAY. That's what I said.

CHORUS. He don't respect you
don't detect the speed of your shoe
Coach forgettin' he need you.

HOLLOWAY. That's what I said.

CHORUS. Show 'em.

HOLLOWAY. I'll show 'em. Show 'em all.

CHORUS. Show 'em who's boss.

And we're in prison waiting room.

MUM. Cycling never got no one no job. Cycling never got no one no money. 'Less you sell the bike. Done right thing stopping with that. How much you pay for them clothes?

HOLLOWAY. Free.

MUM. Ain't nothing free.

HOLLOWAY. Avery.

MUM. He good to you?

HOLLOWAY. He good to me.

MUM. Look like it.

HOLLOWAY. He better than anyone ever was to me. Better than you was to me.

MUM. You like one of them wind-up toys, always on repeat, never a visit you don't bring that up. You want my advice, that kinda thinking about the past make a girl angry, that kinda thinking get a girl worked up, and next thing she know she wind up on same side as me. And don't think you'd like that too much.

HOLLOWAY. Liked it fine enough when I was in a cell last week.

That's right. But unlike you, I got out. So your threats bounce off me. Prison? That's a joke.

MUM. Alright. You turning into a fine young woman, Holloway Jones. Strong young woman. I always believed you would. I...

MUM *starts to cry.*

Holloway.

HOLLOWAY *takes out tissue. Stops short.*

What you doing?

HOLLOWAY. Money.

MUM. What?

HOLLOWAY. Pay up.

MUM. Holloway.

HOLLOWAY. Said so yourself. Ain't nothing free. You want your treat, you pay fifty quid.

MUM. Fifty quid?

HOLLOWAY. Includes transport and delivery.

MUM. You lost your mind.

> HOLLOWAY *puts it away.*

> What kinda girl treats her mum like that?

> HOLLOWAY *goes to leave.*

> Alright. Alright. I don't got money with me now. Give it now, pay later.

HOLLOWAY. Do I like like an Argos catalogue?

MUM. This ain't like you, Holloway.

HOLLOWAY. And how would you know?

MUM. You becoming. You becoming…

HOLLOWAY. Like you?

> Scary, innit?

> AVERY *stands with a bright-red sports bag. We're outside* HOLLOWAY*'s foster home.*

> What you doin' out here?

AVERY. I been calling and calling you, you don't answer the phone.

HOLLOWAY. Sorry I was –

AVERY. You don't answer it what's the point me paying for it?

HOLLOWAY. Sorry I – That blood on your shirt?

AVERY. Can I come in?

HOLLOWAY. You know Ms Thomas don't like visitors. You look shook. Something happened?

AVERY. Nah, nah, you do something for me?

HOLLOWAY. That blood?

AVERY. It's not blood.

HOLLOWAY. You bleeding?

AVERY (*shows he's not*). Just mud is all. Now you do something for me?

HOLLOWAY. What it involve me doing?

AVERY. Doing nothing. Just gotta keep something for me. You keep this bag for me?

HOLLOWAY. What is it?

AVERY. Nothing for you to worry about.

HOLLOWAY. Thas what worries me.

AVERY. I just need you to hold on to it. It ain't gonna blow up or nothing.

HOLLOWAY. I wanna know what I'm holding on to. Is it drugs?

AVERY. You know I don't do that crap. Don't you trust me?

HOLLOWAY. Don't you trust *me*?

AVERY. You right. Okay. Look if you want. Go on. Just... trying to protect you. After what happened to you at Simon Street, thought the less you knew the better, to protect you. But I trust you...

Beat. She goes to open the bag. Unzips it – looks to AVERY. *Beat. She zips it back up, having not looked in bag.*

HOLLOWAY. I trust you.

AVERY. Blind trust. I love you, you know that.

CHORUS (NEIGHBOUR). Blind trust. Love blind. Just mean you can't rewind.

HOLLOWAY. What?

AVERY. You heard me. I love you.

HOLLOWAY. Don't say that.

AVERY. Why?

HOLLOWAY. They just words.

AVERY. If they just words, why you acting so bothered? Ain't no one told you they loved you before?

I love you, Holloway Jones.

She takes the bag. AVERY *disappears and we're in* HOLLOWAY*'s bedroom. She slips the red bag under her bed.*

She puts on a different backpack and then we're in the street.

GEM. Holloway Jones.

HOLLOWAY. Where you been?

GEM. Where I been?

HOLLOWAY. Last couple days. Look I ain't sore 'bout what you said to Avery 'n' that.

GEM. Oh well. I sleep easier then, Holloway Jones ain't sore with me.

HOLLOWAY. Who's on the reds today?

GEM. You not heard?

HOLLOWAY. Heard what?

GEM. When you last seen Avery?

HOLLOWAY. Yesterday, why?

GEM. He talk about me?

HOLLOWAY. What he be talking bout you for?

GEM. Say nothing about me or Mum's shop? On Rawley Road?

HOLLOWAY. I know where your mum's shop is. What business he got with your mum's shop?

GEM. That's what I'm trying to find out. He ain't said nothing about me then?

HOLLOWAY. No. 'Cept…

GEM. 'Cept what?

HOLLOWAY. 'Cept nothing.

GEM. It's like that now is it?

HOLLOWAY. Just asked – not even asked – maybe you snitched us up in Simon Street.

GEM. I'm no snitch.

HOLLOWAY. I told him.

GEM. Though if I'd known you'd end up banged up for a night, then I woulda done. Good warning for you.

HOLLOWAY. What warning? Dead easy. Everyone do a night in the cells.

GEM. I never did.

HOLLOWAY. That make you Miss Special, now? What's the story with your mum's shop?

GEM. Burgled, innit.

HOLLOWAY. No.

GEM. Armed burglary. Done shanked my cousin Tye in the neck.

HOLLOWAY. What? He dead?

POLICEMAN. Well if it isn't Holloway Jones.

HOLLOWAY. You like my stalker – why you always everywhere?

POLICEMAN. Off your perch, stop and search.

HOLLOWAY. You just done searched us last week.

POLICEMAN. Quotas.

HOLLOWAY. Since when young girls like us become quotas?

POLICEMAN. Since you started hanging out with who you do.

HOLLOWAY. That's discrimination.

GEM. I don't hang out with them no more anyway. (*Off HOLLOWAY's look.*) Well I don't.

HOLLOWAY. Point is it's discrimination. 'Sides you boys not allowed to search girls. Need a female officer. I know my rights.

(*To* GEM.) Your cousin – he?

GEM. No he gonna live. Missed the artery. You know it was meant to be me working that night, but Tye covered so I could study for biology GCSE.

HOLLOWAY. Sorry. I...

They get the guys? On camera?

GEM. Those cameras haven't worked for years.

HOLLOWAY. Your cousin seen the guys?

POLICEMAN. Bag.

GEM. D'you not hear what she just said?

POLICEMAN. Allowed to check your bags.

HOLLOWAY. Can't you see we're in the middle of something?

(*To* GEM.) Your cousin seen the guys?

GEM. No. Wearing hoods and masks.

HOLLOWAY. Masks?

GEM. You know them dumb neutral ones, like Miss make us wear in drama?

HOLLOWAY. Maybe was Miss done it, you know teachers be on benefits these days.

Sorry. I...

What's all this got to do with Avery?

GEM. Said so yourself. Avery got beef with me.

HOLLOWAY. No, Avery done lots of things none of my business, but he ain't no shanker and he ain't in my friend's shop.

GEM. You know everything he do?

HOLLOWAY. You be careful 'fore you go round making accusations like that.

GEM. As a friend, I'm telling you, that boy gonna be your fall.

HOLLOWAY. That the only boy who got my back.

GEM. That why you end up with the police?

HOLLOWAY. That boy's my family.

GEM. He ain't your family.

HOLLOWAY. Who then? Who my family? Lady I'm with now? Different lady I'm with last week, different lady I'm with last month, last year? Different name, different bed, different smell. Who?

He's all I have. With Avery, I'm somebody.

Beat.

He loves me.

Beat.

GEM. Holloway.

HOLLOWAY. And you go round making up rumours about him, then it's like you disrespecting me.

POLICEMAN. Look, you girls don't hand over your bags, gonna have to take you both in.

In sync, they both suck their teeth at him.

GEM. You remember when we were kids

HOLLOWAY. Well we're not kids no more

GEM. Used to say that one thing you wouldn't do when you're older is spend your life in a cell like your – don't you see that's where this boy's leading you. I don't trust him.

HOLLOWAY. You want to talk about when we were kids. When we were kids you always had all the toys and the clothes. And did I ever say nothing – no I kept my mouth shut. Just happy to be your friend. Now I got something. So it's your turn to stand by and keep your mouth shut. Now that I got credit, I got currency. Now that it's me who's somebody.

GEM. Yeah? Who are you, Holloway Jones? What, cos you decked out in Prada you a somebody now. Cos you're wearing some white shoes, so white they blinding you to what's real. Maybe you ought to look at them and see your reflection, what you've become.

POLICEMAN. Ladies.

GEM. For Christ's sake.

They both throw their bags to him.

HOLLOWAY. You keep talking lies about Avery you gonna find yourself hurt.

GEM. You couldn't hurt a fly, Holloway Jones.

HOLLOWAY. You leave me alone. You leave Avery alone.

GEM. You're right you know. Avery has made you somebody. You know who you've become? Your mum.

HOLLOWAY *slaps her across the face.*

GEM *takes her bag from* POLICEMAN *and exits. He hands* HOLLOWAY *hers.*

HOLLOWAY. What?

HOLLOWAY *gets on her bike.*

Being an athlete's all about focus, doing what you're told. Discipline. Don't gotta think. Simpler that way. So when he say:

AVERY. All you gotta do is stand there. On Arden Avenue. Like last time on Simon Street.

HOLLOWAY. Last time land me at the station.

AVERY. Only cos they knew. Not this time. Just stand there. All you gotta do. Simple. (*Goes.*)

HOLLOWAY. Simple. All I gotta do. So there's *some* choice, but when you make it, you *choose* it, you gotta keep it. When to jump, when to ride the wave, or choose a different path to the finish line altogether. You make a choice, act on it, and stick to it. Only way to stop yourself falling.

AVERY *runs out.*

AVERY. Go, go, go!

HOLLOWAY. What?

AVERY. Gotta get out of here.

HOLLOWAY. Told me I just had to stand here.

AVERY. And now I'm telling you you can't stand here.

Sound of cops/sirens.

Go!

She cycles fast, jumps, etc. as the following is said:

CHORUS (SPORTS ANNOUNCERS). It's Holloway Jones in
the lead,
like she's been freed
the way she navigates those trees,
avoids that cop
can't be stopped.
It's a breeze
siren wailing
tyres flailing behind her
flashing red to remind her she's being tracked
they're on her back,
scrape that wall
but she's sailing
over that railing
that bump
she jumps!
She jumps!
She jumps! And...

She falls.
Falls.
Falls.

I'm afraid to say today there's no first place – for Holloway
Jones, it's the end of the race.

HOLLOWAY *being questioned by police.*

CHORUS (POLICE OFFICER). This isn't a joke, some TV
show, where we offer you a smoke. You know that? Yes. So
it's best I'd suggest that we skip this little prelude and get
right to the point. *Joint. Enterprise.* Don't give me surprised,

or some puppydog eyes like you didn't know or didn't mean it, I've seen it all before, so the score is this: Armed Robbery.

Now shut up and think a second, we don't wanna hear your 'didn't know no one had a weapon'.

So before you open your trap and reel off crap that you were just there, leaning on bricks, for Joint Enterprise, that's enough to convict. Prison four to seven – if you're lucky a year less. But bottom line, we've got you stuck right in the middle of this mess.

So take ten and then when I get back I want details about this attack.

OFFICER *leaves*.

OTHER OFFICER. I'd suggest you listen to him.

HOLLOWAY. My fate already decided then what the point?

OTHER OFFICER. There's room to manoeuvre. Make you a deal. Tell us who was with you.

HOLLOWAY. I ain't a snitch.

OTHER OFFICER. They're going to take you to trial. They're going to find you guilty.

You're going to grow up in prison. That the plan?

CHORUS. Prison baby. Holloway baby. Holloway Jones.

HOLLOWAY. Maybe. Maybe it is the plan.

Can I go?

OTHER OFFICER. You can go. When someone posts bail for you.

HOLLOWAY. Who gonna do that for me?

OTHER OFFICER. Friend. Family. Not for me to worry about.

CHORUS. Mama don't need to be missin' her for long. Soon Holloway Jones be joining in the Holloway Prison song.

COACH *appears*.

HOLLOWAY. Didn't know who else to call.

They sit in silence (perhaps in the car).

COACH. What they going to give you?

HOLLOWAY. Four to seven probably.

COACH. Bail's on my house. You leave town, they'll take my house, you know that.

HOLLOWAY. I'm not going nowhere. I was never going nowhere.

COACH *goes.* HOLLOWAY *watches the video screen – a young girl on a BMX bike.*

AVERY. What they say?

HOLLOWAY. Say it was Joint Enterprise. Say I'm going to jail.

AVERY. You ain't done nothing but stand there.

HOLLOWAY. Standing there enough.

Say you was armed.

AVERY. They know me?

HOLLOWAY. No I meant –

AVERY. You tell them 'bout me?

HOLLOWAY. I ain't a snitch. Not you you, you whoever done it, they say – man at shop on Arden Avenue say, you was armed.

AVERY. I didn't know Shawn had no shank.

HOLLOWAY. You didn't know.

AVERY. Swear down. You know I don't do that stuff. Man's got to have rules.

So how long they gonna give you?

HOLLOWAY. Four to seven… unless…

AVERY. Less what?

HOLLOWAY. Nothing. Four to seven.

AVERY. Everyone do time. Good behaviour you out in half that, won't even know you been gone. We gonna get through this.

HOLLOWAY. We?

AVERY. You brave, you strong. Why I love you. I'm sorry
I never woulda asked you to come if I knew put you into
trouble. You trust me, right?

AVERY *goes.*

The sound of HOLLOWAY*'s heart beating, breathing…*

HOLLOWAY. You make a decision, you stick to it. There are no
second chances.

You make a decision, you stick to it. There are no second
chances.

She continues to repeat her biking mantra while:

HOLLOWAY *retrieves the red bag* AVERY *had given her
previously.*

She opens it.

Inside are knives.

*And neutral masks. She puts down the bag. Deflated.
Defeated.*

HOLLOWAY *opens the bag again, takes out one of the
knives, boards her bike determined.*

HOLLOWAY *cycles, at the same moment, the video comes
to life:*

The happy images of HOLLOWAY *and* AVERY *as we saw
earlier which turns into the attack on the bus we also saw
before which turns into security monitoring of* HOLLOWAY
and her MUM *in the visiting room which turns into images
of* HOLLOWAY *and* GEM *as eight-year-olds.*

As she cycles, the CHORUS *appear (possibly cycling also)
closing in on her – each of them in hoods and neutral masks.*

HOLLOWAY *finally screams. Raises the knife and brings it
into the metal of her bike – a futile attempt to destroy it. The
images on the screen repeat themselves faster and faster. To
stop them, she smashes her iPhone repeatedly. The screen
flickers, broken, the repeated CCTV image of* HOLLOWAY
on the screen. Staring up at us, and herself.

HOLLOWAY *watches herself on the screen.*

Then MUM *appears and the image turns into the CCTV of the prison visiting room.* HOLLOWAY *reads a card.*

'Happy Sixtieth Birthday.'

MUM. All I could get on short notice.

HOLLOWAY. Not even my birthday.

MUM. Needed the card to get you money.

HOLLOWAY. I don't want it.

MUM. You said.

HOLLOWAY. I don't want it.

I… I have done some things. I have allowed some bad things to happen. I have stood by and done nothing. I have been an active participant. People have been hurt by my actions, my inactions, and they have been too scared to report it. Or too respectful to report it. Or too stubborn to ask for help. And so I'm… I'm asking for help. Are you listening to me? (*Calls out to prison, and to the CCTV screen.*) Are you catching this on CCTV?! This is my confession! My cry for help! My… my…

Starts to cry. MUM *goes to comfort her. And for a brief moment, she is making* HOLLOWAY *feel better.*

MUM. Oh Holloway baby… But did you bring…?

HOLLOWAY *throws tissue at her.*

HOLLOWAY. That's all I got to give you. Ain't nothing else in here. Holloway Jones just hollow bones.

MUM. You're just like me, Holloway.

HOLLOWAY. No. I'm not like you. Not like anyone. I'm nobody. Not even me.

She takes off her earrings, her jacket, all the things she was dressed in in the club scene earlier.

MUM. What you doing, Holloway? Holloway?

Finally she takes off her white shoes. Hands everything to MUM.

HOLLOWAY. You won't be seeing me for a while.

MUM. How come? Holloway? Holloway?

HOLLOWAY *begins to run*. MUM *disappears*.

CHORUS. This girl running through the street, like shackles lifted
like a rift mended, her honour defended, no signs of defeat.

Running from somewhere? Maybe. Who knows? But it's somewhere she's running to, forward the motion goes.

AVERY. Hey.

HOLLOWAY. Hey. (*Starts to cry*.)

AVERY. Don't be like that, Holloway Jones. You're tougher than that. You'll survive better [if you] don't show people that side. Girls in there is tough – you just stay the Holloway I know.

HOLLOWAY. Not about that.

AVERY. Then what?

HOLLOWAY. Us. You.

AVERY. Aw. Ain't nothing to cry for. Nothing gonna change for us.

HOLLOWAY. Avery. I… I love you.

AVERY. That's what I'm saying. No prison wall gonna break what we have. I'll still be here. Okay?

Two POLICEMEN *appear. One on each side of them*.

HOLLOWAY (*to audience*). Say you don't get second chances. You hit that bump, mis-measure the landing – you're done.

But you gotta get off that track eventually, get on the bike, or walk but get to the finish line, even though you know you lost.

Maybe that's your second chance.

If you're a road-racer cyclist, there's these lead-out riders right – their job to slow down the race of others, help their leader to win, by them losing; take one for the team.

But in BMX, there ain't no team to take one for. So you gotta choose. It's them. Or you.

HOLLOWAY *hands the* POLICEMEN *the red bag of knives and masks.*

(*To audience.*) I choose me.

The POLICEMAN *handcuffs* AVERY.

(*Crying.*) I choose me, Avery. I choose me.

POLICEMAN *takes* AVERY *away.*

AVERY. Holloway! Holloway!

HOLLOWAY *rides.*

CHORUS (NEIGHBOURS). They say her blood is cold
like the metal bed where she was born
So we're told
Now explain why sixteen years old, the girl just cycle round and round,
empty or mourning for some other life, a knife that dealt a
blow or the life the way it was supposed to go.

CHORUS *become* GANG, *blocking her path, forcing her to demount.*

Stay.
Away.
From here.
You hear me? I'd be fearin' me if I were you.
You chose your own ends, so don't look to us for friends.
Snitches get stitches
so eyes on your back, never know when an attack will strike
Looking for your bike?

Her bike is strung up in the air to a post or a tree.

Don't wanna see your face anywhere round this place
Avery been stung, and next time not your bike that gonna be
hung.
So get, Sket!
Snitch!
Bitch!

HOLLOWAY *walks around the stage in a circle, slowly.
Defeated, scared. She repeats this three times – each time
she passes where the bike is hung is a new season which can*

be demonstrated through a change in clothes (i.e. winter hat)
and/or the aid of the CHORUS *(throwing leaves or snow)*
and/or video. Each rotation also coincides with the
character change of the CHORUS *and their lines below. It's*
also possible that the club music and atmosphere from
earlier returns, a return of this sequence – but this time
HOLLOWAY *outside it – and each* CHORUS *and season*
breaks out of that dancing group.

No friends, no ends, she goes toward no destination
the sensation of a ghost living in flesh, empty skin – for
what sin?

Last I heard they say she's a snitch,
a traitor
so berate her, she deserves it unreservedly,
or brand a scarlet letter on her forehead.
Better all should know: 'There the snitch go!'

And how they do know indeed – from her they keep a
distance wide, lest it be conceived by others they're on
her side.

And good thing they leave her well alone, that Holloway
Jones.

Leaves changing green to brown, still that bike not
taken down
She pass it, we pass it every day, as if to say:
This what happens to a rat, don't forget that.

CHORUS (TEACHER). Now I'm trying to remember, it was
probably December, when I knew something was really
wrong. Like amongst the throng of faces I could spot the
traces of regret in her eyes. I mean what was her prize – for
being honest? What they promised: fear all year, a hanging
bike, which was like a constant reminder, always looking
behind her, leaving class early, so she surely wouldn't run
into anyone, with good reason. Change of season, it's
freezin' and I slow to see the cycle covered in snow, in a tree,
and were it me, giving her advice… well I'd tell her to do the
same… but is it too big a price?

The timer goes forward, reads 2012.

CHORUS (RIDERS). I think we saw her in April or March
Not that I care, but to be fair it was pretty harsh – what
they'd done. Sun's out, been about eight months and still no
stunts, no bike to ride

No friends, yeah I'd have cried.

But she wasn't –

No. But she doesn't look up, averts her gaze, just stays with
her eyes to the floor, to ignore her bike up there.

But I swear, for me, been there so long that it starts to get…
that you forget. And it's not like before. It's almost like…
like it's not there any more.

*The screen comes to life with a BMX race in the 2012
Olympics. The* CHORUS *party – drinking, throwing
streamers, while watching the screen cheering.*
HOLLOWAY *watches them from a distance. The party goes.*

HOLLOWAY *knocks on a door. She holds papers.* GEM
answers.

HOLLOWAY. I uh… I found these at home. Not sure why I
have them… Well I do. Think we said. Think we said I'd
hold on to them. So one day. So. In ten years we could dig
'em up. Compare.

GEM. It hasn't been ten years.

HOLLOWAY. No…

Hear you're going to uni next week.

GEM. Yeah.

HOLLOWAY. Veterinary college.

GEM. Yeah.

HOLLOWAY. I guess yours came true.

GEM. Guess so.

HOLLOWAY. Well in part. Think you were gonna have a pet
horse by now too…

GEM. Well hasn't been ten years yet. Give me time. (*Smiles.*)

HOLLOWAY. I wanted to say... uh... have a good time and that.

GEM. Yeah. Thanks.

Hands her the letters. Lingers...

HOLLOWAY. Maybe we should read them.

GEM. What for?

HOLLOWAY *shrugs*.

Hasn't been ten years.

HOLLOWAY. Let's read 'em anyway.

Read it out loud.

GEM. 'When I grow up...' This is stupid.

HOLLOWAY. No it isn't. And I know you don't think so.

GEM (*reads*). 'When I grow up I'm going to be a veterinarian.
I will have to go away to veterinary school for a long time –
five or six years. I will work very hard. I will come home all
the time to see my... my best friend, Holloway. We will be
friends forever. We will go on holidays together with our
children – I'm going to have two boys, Holloway is going to
have two girls. Maybe our kids will marry each other and
then we'll be almost related – we're pretty much sisters.
I can't wait to grow up, because then we can do what we
want...' (*Beat*.) I gotta go, more stuff to pack and that.

HOLLOWAY. Right. Well. Whenever you're back, give me a
nudge or something. We can do something.

CHORUS (STREET CLEANERS). The words practised,
rehearsed, relayed over and over, but delayed now that she's
here – cos it's clear, that which words can't ever fix. The scar
that will always remind and remain. The hurt that will
always sustain. And sometimes a lie, a white lie, is better
than acknowledging the goodbye.

GEM. Sure. See you, Holloway.

GEM *exits*.

Left standing there, HOLLOWAY *begins to read her paper
aloud:*

HOLLOWAY. 'My name is Holloway Jones and when I grow up I want to be – '

GEM *re-enters.*

GEM. Oh Holloway. Happy birthday.

She exits again.

HOLLOWAY *turns to find the* STREET CLEANERS *have stopped sweeping and are taking down her bike.*

HOLLOWAY. Hey, what are you doing?

CLEANER. What's it look like? Olympics over. Clean up begins.

HOLLOWAY. Oh. That's… that's my bike…

CLEANER. Not a very sensible place for it, is it? (*Gives it to her.*) Bloody kids. (*Exits.*)

HOLLOWAY *holds her bike, almost afraid to mount it. Looks around. Deserted. Gets on the bike, then she turns to face* COACH. *We're at the training ground.*

Long pause.

HOLLOWAY. Saw one of your girls on TV. (*Complimenting.*) They done alright.

COACH. Yeah. They done alright.

Beat.

He throws her some gloves/shoes…

Good to have you back.

She puts on the gloves.

Then begins to get dressed into full cycling gear as she speaks.

HOLLOWAY. People say the uniform makes all the difference. That one mistake can cost you all. I have a ritual I do before every race. How I get ready. It helps me clear my head. Stay calm. But I don't actually think the uniform makes all the difference. That one mistake can cost you all. I don't believe that.

Not any more.

She turns. MUM *is standing there.*

Pause.

MUM. Was gonna wait till after, but someone said this is where
the athletes all get ready. Apparently don't normally let
people back here. But family are allowed. So...

Here I got you this.

Holds out card.

You can open it.

She does.

HOLLOWAY. It's not my birthday.

MUM. I know. But for the last five.

HOLLOWAY. Thanks.

You flew all the way here?

MUM. Thought I deserved a holiday.

HOLLOWAY. You look good.

MUM. Clean three years.

HOLLOWAY. That's good...

MUM. Cos of you. When you stopped coming, I kind of – well
I thought was time to change, that maybe if I... that you'd
come back.

HOLLOWAY. I couldn't.

MUM. I know. I know. I don't blame you, baby.

Pause.

Well I'll let you get ready. Get to my seat – you know charge
an absolute fortune to see you race.

HOLLOWAY. I know, it's a rip-off.

MUM. Well. Make it worth every penny will you?

See you after maybe.

She goes to leave.

HOLLOWAY. Mum?

CHORUS. The words practised, rehearsed, relayed...

HOLLOWAY goes and hugs her. Holds her.

The sounds of crowd cheers.

CHORUS (ANNOUNCERS). We're at the Women's BMX here at the 2016 Olympics in sunny Rio de Janeiro.

The timer reads 00:00.

HOLLOWAY mounts her bike in front of the screen, alongside the CHORUS who have become RIDERS beside her.

CHORUS (RIDERS). They say her blood is cold
like the metal bed where she was born
Say beneath her skin is poisonous bones
So the story goes for Holloway Jones.
Holloway born in prison, die in prison, so they say
they say
but guess... it don't mean it actually end that way.
Cos what do we know –
of that what an eight-year-old once said
When an eight-year-old in white trainers read:

HOLLOWAY, still poised on her bike, now holds her letter in front of her.

HOLLOWAY. My name is Holloway Jones and when I grow up...

ANNOUNCER (*off*). Look at that focus. The drive. Anticipation.

HOLLOWAY. I want to be... somebody.

The sound of a race beginning. The numbers start to tumble forward and continue to do so...

End.

GIRLS LIKE THAT

For Zoey, and the woman she grows up to be

A single edition of *Girls Like That* is also available
from Nick Hern Books, www.nickhernbooks.co.uk

Acknowledgements

This play was a team effort, involving the dedication and support of many people. Thank you to:

Everyone at Birmingham Rep, West Yorkshire Playhouse, and Theatre Royal Plymouth, and especially: Gemma Woffinden, Beth Shouler, Daniel Tyler, Alex Chisholm, Jessica Farmer, Victoria Allen, Jane Pawson, David Prescott, Tessa Walker, and Caroline Jester.

Everyone at the Unicorn Theatre and Synergy Theatre, especially Esther Baker, for bringing renewed life and creativity to the play.

The many young people – too many to name here – who shared with me their insights and ideas; thank you all for your honesty.

Tanya Tillett, for talking sense into me every once in a while.

Mom, Dad, Lindsay and Jay, for your constant support.

Daniel, for believing in me and loving me even when I act like a teenager.

E.P.

Girls Like That was commissioned by Birmingham Repertory Theatre, Theatre Royal Plymouth and West Yorkshire Playhouse.

The play was first performed by The Young REP as part of The Young Rep Festival at The Old Rep Theatre, Birmingham, on 12 July 2013; the West Yorkshire Playhouse Youth Theatre at the Courtyard Theatre, West Yorkshire Playhouse, Leeds, on 18 July 2013; and by the Theatre Royal Plymouth Young Company at the Theatre Royal Plymouth, on 14 August 2013.

The three companies were as follows:

BIRMINGHAM REPERTORY THEATRE

Kimberley Atkiss
Dayna Batman
Victoria Bowes
Anushka Chakravarti
Heather Fantham
Rebekka Ford
Sophie Lines
Anna Piper
Jordan Perkins
Nathan Queeley-Dennis
Roisin Richardson
Kesia Schofield
Aurora Tanda
Melissa Uppal

Director	Daniel Tyler
Festival Designer	Oliver Shapley
Festival Stage Manager	Amber Curtis
Festival Production Manager	Tomas Wright
Festival Costumes by	Birmingham Repertory Theatre
Festival Lighting by	The Old Rep Theatre
Festival Technician	Anthony Aston
Young REP Company Support	Emma Ledsam

172

Daisy Addison
Emily Anderson-Wallace
Lydia Crosland
Megan Dawson
Jessica Finlay
Mabel Goulden
Zoe Hamilton
Catherine Hawthorn
Edward House
Bethan Johnson
Hannah Kilcoyne
Hal Lockwood
Laura Marsden
Alistair McKenzie
Holly Pennington
Harri Pitches
Uma Ramachadran
Alice Rayner
Natasha Brotherdale Smith
Lizzie Turner

Director	Gemma Woffinden
Set Designer	Chris Cully
YP Design	Dylon Rawnsley
& Construction Assistants	& Abena Weston
Costume Designer	Victoria Marzetti
YP Costume Design Assistants	Samantha Metcalfe
	& Ella Robbins
Lighting Designer	Paul Lovett
YP Lighting Design Assistants	Sam Gosling & Ben Lander
Sound Designer	Ian Robert Trollope
YP Sound Design Assistant	Joe Bellwood
Movement Director	Sophie Hudson
Fight Director	Gavin Harding
Assistant to the Director	Amy Oddy
Production Manager	Suzi Cubbage
YP Production Manager	Loren Rayner
Stage Manager	Julie Issott
YP Stage Manager	Rachel Robertson

Special thanks to: Andrew Potterton for original music, Air Transport Auxiliary Museum, Maidenhead Carphone Warehouse

THEATRE ROYAL PLYMOUTH YOUNG COMPANY

Alice Cadmore
Senga Clarke-Côté
Elizabeth Edwards
Alisha Lee
Libby Long
Sinead Millar
Lorrine Penwarden
Rosie Stevenson
Abigail Summers
Amy Wallace
Zoe Walton
Talia Winn
Simon Hill
Danny Laine
William Lewis
JJ McColl
Lewis Peek

Director	Beth Shouler
Assistant Director	Liam Salmon
Designer	Fiona Evans
Assistant Designer	Nina Raines
Producer	Jane Pawson
Production Manager	Nick Soper
Lighting Designer	John Perkis
Sound Designer	Holly Harbottle
Theatre Technician	Matt Hoyle
Stage Manager	Brooke Tippett
Deputy Stage Manager	Natasha Whitley
Assistant Stage Manager	Thomas Michaels

Characters

GIRLS, *up to nineteen of them, division of lines up to the company*
GIRL IN FLAPPER DRESS
GIRL WITH AVIATOR HELMET AND GOGGLES
GIRL WITH FLOWERS IN HER HAIR
GIRL WITH SHOULDER PADS
SCARLETT

A Note on Stage Directions and Punctuation

Change is a change in time. It should be quite quick. It might be indicated by a change in light, or a sound, or in the actors changing position on stage or all of these or none of these.

An ellipsis (…) is a trailing off/loss of words/search for words. It is not a cut-off.

A dash (–) is a cut-off. Sometimes by one's own thought being intercepted by another thought. These are not pauses or beats.

A lack of punctuation means the next line comes right in.

The GIRLS *stand at the front of the stage facing the audience.*

GIRLS   Slut

Skank

Sket

Ho

Prossie

Whore

Slag

Tart

Tramp

Hussy

Floozie

Ho-bag

Slapper

You deserve everything coming to you

Skanky Scarlett

Slutty Scarlett

Scarlett the Harlot

Slut

Slut

Slut

Slut

Slut

Slut

Slut

Slut.

Beat.

*Music. 'Run the World (Girls)' by Beyoncé. The
GIRLS put on headphones. The GIRLS sing along and
dance – a routine they've clearly practised before. The
music suddenly stops. The GIRLS take off their
headphones. Five years old.*

When Scarlett arrives her hair is in these two messy
pigtail braids, and she has Ribena stained around her
mouth.

We are five years old. I am by the sandbox making a
princess castle that more accurately resembles a large
horse's shit.

I am by the water tub – I like the way the water feels
when it runs through the little blonde hairs on my wrist.

I'm on the carpet picking my nose still unsure why this
lady who looks like Nanny McPhee is to replace my
mother when another girl makes a beeline straight for
me. She sits right next to me, our knees touching. And
I know I am special. I have been chosen.

My mother told me not to pick my nose in public.

My mother told me not to bite my nails.

My mother told me not to be so loud.

What my mother told me means nothing on the first
day of reception at St Helen's School for Girls.

Clearly my mother is an idiot. I have been duped.
Because the girl picking her nose with the chewed-
down pinky is now sitting next to the most popular girl
in class. I will never listen to my mother again.

St Helen's is a special school. I know this because my
mother told me so.

St Helen's is a special school because it only accepts
twenty five-year-olds each year, selected for our gifted

academic ability and creative potential to think outside the box, demonstrated through a test with questions like 'Sophie has a car with only one working door. She has five friends who each take forty-five seconds to enter through the door and get in their seat. How many of them will be seated ninety seconds after Sophie unlocks the door?'

All of them. The car is a convertible.

St Helen's is special because me and these twenty girls

These twenty girls and I will progress through the next seven years of primary together, always the same classmates, the same twenty girls, forging long-lasting friendships, and bonds of camaraderie and sisterhood. My mother would call this special. I would call this hell.

Twenty girls from different parts of the city, different backgrounds, who might not otherwise have ever crossed paths.

If only.

But here at St Helen's, in this grey classroom we will become a family. A Benetton ad. In prison.

I live on a farm. We have chickens. And every time we get some new hens, it starts again – it lasts no more than five minutes, but they battle it out, to determine the pecking order. They jump on each other's backs, push the other with their chests, rip feathers out of each other with their beaks. They go until it's clear who goes where in the hierarchy. My brother, he's older, he's seven, he cries whenever this happens, tries to pull them apart, the referee. But I am a five-year-old girl. I stand back and watch. I understand.

At St Helen's we are civilised little girls. We humans are much more clever than hens. We do not need to fight. We know it, the pecking order.

Who's at the top

Who's in the middle

Who's at the bottom

Just as every girl at every other school in the city
knows it

Is sitting in their own classroom, eyeing up the others

Smelling the others

Positioning themselves in the order that will determine
the rest of their lives.

I am in the middle. A comfortable place to be. I'd
recommend to any five-year-old that this is the wisest
place to be.

Definitely.

Scarlett is at the bottom. Full stop.

Beat.

I join the others on the carpet for circle time. I don't
know if it's for a game or maybe we just do it –
instinctively just reach out to our neighbours, interlock
fingers – but we're all holding hands.

An unspoken pact sealed.

These girls are my friends. My mother told me these
girls are my friends for life.

And she's got chocolate on her fingers from breakfast.

And she's got bits of Play-Doh under her fingernails.

And her hands are wet from the water tub.

But we let it pass. It's the first day. And we're happy to
be here. Twenty special girls.

Twenty little girls holding hands.

Change. Present.

We're in history when it comes.

Miss is droning on, highlighting keywords on the board, and every time she raises her arm to write you can like see her bingo wings through the opening of her sleeve. Like someone should really tell her it's illegal for fifty-year-olds to wear short sleeves. Maybe I'll like write her a note. Anonymously of course. But as a courtesy like.

I am texting a boy. There are no boys in history.

Secondary school is mixed, so we can see the male species in the corridors and stuff, make sure we don't all turn out to be lesbians, but otherwise it's still just the girls. But other girls too. Three schools feed into St Margaret's. And so it's nice, like really honestly nice to still have all my primary-school friends with me. The St Helen's girls.

The St Helen's girls. Or the Satan Hell girls as some of the others call us. As a joke y'know.

It's nice to have girls that really know me, that remember in Year 3 when I won the singing competition with my rendition of 'Since U Been Gone'.

It's nice to have girls that remember our school trip in Year 5 when the bus broke down and we had a slumber party on the bus.

Girls who remember the swimming relay when I came first

Girls who remember the music teacher's meltdown

Girls who remember the time I laughed so hard I pee'd a bit

Girls who remember when my period went on the cafeteria bench and I refused to get up

Girls who remember that my mum had an affair with the maths teacher

Girls who remember that I was the only one in the year not invited to the end-of-year pool party

Girls who remember when I was in the toilet and missed my entrance in the school play

Girls who remember when I put my tampon in cord-end first and had to go to hospital

Girls who remember when I asked Nurse Nancy if a clitoris was a kind of dinosaur

Girls who never forget.

Beat.

Us girls are sitting in history not listening to Miss's McMuffin-breath ramble on about voting or suffering jets or something when it comes.

Buzz

Click

Pop

Flash

A text

An email

A message

A tweet

And the classroom is brighter as phones come alight

It's not like I was the only one checking

Everyone got it, not just me so it's not like

Which is why, when I, like it wouldn't have changed anything

A photo of Scarlett. Naked.

Beat.

Buzz

Click

Pop

Flash

O-M-G

What a little slut

What a little skank

When the chickens start attacking each other, like really going for it, they can draw blood, and that's when, that's when you need to be really careful. Because if they see blood, the other chickens, they can turn into murderers. They'll keep pecking until there's more blood and more. So you have to get this antiseptic spray that sprays purple, so the chickens don't notice the red blood. Or else they'll peck the chicken to death. I don't know why. But I think it's maybe cos a vulnerable chicken is putting the whole flock at risk. Or something.

And it's funny

And it's kind of sexy

And it's ugly

And so I

And so I

And so I

DELETE.

Beat.

And it's over.

Beat.

Except I don't.

Because someone else will

Someone else will definitely anyway

So I

Forward

Tweet

Poke

Send

Forward

Tweet

Poke

Send

Buzz

Click

Pop

Flash.

And it's not like…

I didn't send the photo out in the first place

If a photo's taken and no one's there to see it, was it really taken? I mean didn't Plato or someone say that?

And there's a rumour that the school internet crashes from all the activity.

There's a rumour that makes no sense whatsoever since obviously no one's allowed to use the school internet on their phones and they're using 3G

What is definitely true is that within three minutes of receiving the photo in the middle of Miss saying something about a woman who got tied up to Parliament – some crazy *Fifty Shades* shit or something – everyone in the school has acquired the photo.

Or maybe it's not to do with protecting the flock at all. Maybe it's just that chickens are horrible murderous bitches. You'd have to ask a chicken farmer really.

Music. 'Wings' by Little Mix. GIRLS put their headphones on. Again they sing along and do a dance to it – this time leading it though is a GIRL IN FLAPPER DRESS. Her appearance and manner are

*at odds with the contemporary song, but she knows all
the words and the dance.*

The song suddenly stops. The GIRLS *keep their
headphones on, face the back/away.*

GIRL IN FLAPPER DRESS
The invitation reads: 'Mrs Plunkett Greene, Miss
Ponsonby, Mr Edward Gathorne-Hardy and Mr Brian
Howard request the pleasure of my company at St
George's Swimming Baths, Buckingham Palace Road,
11 o'clock p.m. on Friday, 12th of July, 1928. Please
wear a bathing suit and bring a bath towel and a bottle.
Each guest is required to show his invitation on arrival.'

The colours of the other girls' suits are dazzling. Some
of them change suits two or three times throughout the
evening. I've only brought the one. But I don't mind.

I flirt with the trumpet player from the Negro band. I
flirt with one of the cocktail mixers, who's also wearing
a bathing costume. I even flirt with the rubber horses
that float above the water. This is the single-most
greatest night in my life thus far. I shall never forget it.

And then I see him. Out of place in his full suit
amongst the semi-naked bodies. Eyes darting
nervously. Until he spots what he's looking for: me.

'I'm taking you home right now.'

And one of the other girls wanders over. 'I didn't know
you had a fella.'

'I don't. He's my brother.'

'Cute. I hope he's brought a bathing costume.'

'I haven't,' he interjects. He doesn't like being spoken
about in the third person.

'Well then I guess you'll have to go nude. You won't
be the first.' And she laughs.

My clothes are somewhere inside. So my brother
drapes his jacket around my bare arms. 'We can get
them tomorrow.'

'She's only just got here. She hasn't even swum yet.'

And then he turns on her. 'I'm not talking to you.'

But the girl's not listening, or doesn't care. 'Do you have a light,' she wants to know. A cigarette dangling from her lips.

I want to avoid this. But a Negro saxophonist is riffing and some girls are splashing in the water and some girls are spilling their Martini glasses and he can't contain himself.

'No. And I don't think it's very ladylike to be smoking in public.'

And this time she hears him loud and clear. She smiles. She can't tell if he's flirting or challenging her. She doesn't care either way. 'Oh. And why is that?'

And now I'm suddenly ready to go. I don't want to swim. I just want to leave. And why doesn't the band play louder? Why have they gone quiet just at the moment my brother says:

'Because people will mistake you for an ordinary whore.'

Play goddamit, why won't the band just play! And everyone is looking over. Everyone who a moment ago I was dancing with and drinking with are now looking over at my eighteen-year-old brother.

And then the music starts up again. Only it's not the band. It's the people. And they're not singing, they're laughing. My brother has underestimated his audience. Because if he'd looked around he'd have noticed girls all over the pool shamelessly smoking.

And the girl, she says: 'Shall I take that as a no then? You don't have a light?'

And the girls laugh even harder. And even I, I can't help it, and I start laughing too. I'm laughing so hard that I don't even see it coming.

Slap.

'If you want to act like a slut I'll treat you like one.'

My cheek is throbbing but the effort to touch it feels too much. My face is wet and I don't know whether it's tears or if someone has splashed from the pool. So I stand there clutching the inside pockets of my brother's jacket. And I wish I'd never come out tonight. I wish I'd just stayed home like a girl should. I'm sorry, I'm sorry, I'm sorry.

'You think our mother fought for your rights so you could behave like this?'

And as I'm leaving, my bare feet on the concrete – I feel something in my hand. In the pocket. Matches.

And I don't think about what I'm doing. My body takes on a life of its own and I've turned back. Everyone still watching. I strike a match.

Fizz. Pop.

And I light her cigarette.

And it feels like the best thing I've ever done in my life.

And my brother just looks at me. A look that says I won't forget this. A look that says just wait until we get home. And I know that I don't have a choice.

I throw off his jacket. And dive into the pool.

She exits. The GIRLS *take off their headphones and turn around.*

GIRLS   Scarlett has a mole on the top of her left breast. Well my left, her right. And it, or actually maybe it's her left too, cos the camera does it in reverse, right? Does it? I'm confused.

She probably wants to get that checked out. Check it's not Aids or something.

Probably should get that mole removed. Cos you never know. And boys don't like markings. Unless they're one of those Goth types who likes girls with tattoos and piercings – boys like girls with smooth skin.

I saw a movie once where this girl had a piercing in her fanny.

On closer inspection, I decide it's actually a freckle. When I enlarge it on my screen, zoom in, you can see it's a freckle.

And her nipples are large, like really – like that's not normal is it?

And the way she's positioned, there's like this line on her stomach, this line of blubber on her belly. I didn't know she was fat until now. But she is. She's fat.

Fat slut

And she hasn't even bothered to, I mean it's a jungle, like if you're going to, at least wax beforehand, it's like a guinea pig died.

Looks pretty normal to me.

It's a dead guinea pig.

And I feel good because she's a hairy ape

And I feel good because my breasts are bigger than hers

And I feel good because my breasts are smaller than her abnormally large ones

And I feel good because her arms are short

And I feel good because her shoulders are bony

And I feel good because her belly button is an outie

And I feel good because her nail polish is chipped

And I feel good because she has a mole on her right or left breast

And I feel good because she's a slut and not even that pretty.

There are rumours that Scarlett gave Russell a BJ in the toilets after school last week. I didn't believe it at the time, but this proves it. This is like… rock-hard evidence.

I believed it all along. With girls like that you can just tell.

And the thing with rumours, yeah, is that they wouldn't be rumours if there weren't at least some truth in them. Like they wouldn't have come about in the first place if they weren't at least say seventy percent true. So like maybe it wasn't in the toilets, or maybe it wasn't after school – that's the thirty percent that might be wrong, but she definitely gave him a blowjob. That's what matters.

Miss is still talking about *feminism* and the word reminds me of *femidom* like Nurse Nancy told us about so I start laughing, and when she asks me why I'm laughing I tell her I have a disability.

I secretly take a photo of Miss, and while she's blubbering on about voting I have put her face on Scarlett's naked body. My mum once got detention for making a cartoon drawing of one of her teachers. But I'm not worried, my phone is password protected.

At lunch the corridor is buzzing, is popping, and boys are smirking. The first moments of lunch when classes spill out and the sexes come tumbling together in the corridor is a bit like when I used to volunteer at the dogs' home. The dogs are all anxious to come out of their cages, can't sit still, but as soon as you open the doors, most of 'em barely come out at first. Tentative. Backs against the cage, against the lockers, but pretty soon they get over that and everybody's humping and smelling each other's arses.

Girls flick immaculate hair, boys steal furtive glances while pretending to talk to their friends, holding tight to the straps of their rucksacks as if they're cords of a bomb and they might combust.

A boy says: 'Guess I know what I'm doing tonight.'

Another laughs and says: 'Wank bank.'

'Slut.'

'Whore.'

But that's not the boys. That's what's weirdest, while the girls are zooming, highlighting, cutting, pasting, analysing, comparing thoughts and insights into Scarlett, the boys are… well they're not doing much of anything. Just smirking. Like fucking buffoons. Like they don't get it. Like they… y'know?

And then one of them finally speaks.

'I'd tap it.' Tyler. That's what he says.

Like even though she's a, and she's just…

'I don't think you should be looking at that.' A boy says this. Jay.

Maybe he fancies Scarlett, or maybe he's drunk, or maybe he's looking for a fight.

But Jay's not the fighting type. He's not a boy like that. He's just a boy who happens to be at his locker.

'You what?' It's Tyler.

'You what? Do you got a little hard-on for her do you? Want the photo all to yourself?'

'No. That's not. I haven't seen it actually.'

Like he's above it or something. Though probably he's lying. Everyone's seen it.

And Tyler laughs. 'Well here mate. Share and share alike.' And Tyler passes the phone to him.

But Jay averts his gaze. 'No. Thanks.'

'You what?'

'It's none of my…' His resolve's fading. 'I just don't think…'

'You gay or something?' Some other boy has piped up.

'Bet you are. That's why your parents named you Jay. Cos it rhymes with gay.'

Logic doesn't really matter at this point.

It doesn't matter that Jay has a girlfriend which even douchebag Tyler knows.

It also doesn't matter that Jay plays football with them and scored a winning shot last week and that they put him on their shoulders.

What matters is Jay has temporarily set everything off-balance. He has told them there is no Santa Claus. He has questioned gravity. The cosmos need to be realigned.

'Maybe if it was a photo of you Tyler, then he'd look.'

'Oh, is that it gay Jay? Are you saving your eyes for my – '

And before he can finish with some awful metaphor for his genitals, Jay does it. He looks at the photo. And I'm a bit angry at how easily he gives in. How easily he sighs and looks.

'I knew it. You totally have a woody for her. You'd tap it right?'

And he: 'Yeah. I'd tap it.' And even from where I'm standing I can hear the monotone. He'd make a terrible actor. Jay goes. And I wait for the boys to talk about Jay, to talk about what's just happened. But they don't. It's like. It's like it didn't happen.

Snog marry kill. Harry, Niall, Zayn.

And then the corridor goes silent, like proper.

And it reminds me of the time I met Lady Gaga. Well not really met, but you know what I mean. And I had this CD cover of Gaga's face for her to sign, and she's there like two feet in front of me, and it's her, it's definitely her from the cover, but just less... I dunno. Like she was still as hot and as cool as the her on the cover, but just a bit... normal.
And there's Scarlett looking up at me from my phone screen, and there she is two feet away from me, and the two images, the two Scarletts... they're just

different is all. One's just a bit more... *human*. Though I'm not totally sure which one.

And another thing about boys is they don't have any social awareness. Like they are completely socially unaware. They do not have what my mother would call *tact*. Because us girls don't say anything. Like obviously we would never say anything to her face. Cos that would just be... outrageous.

That would be completely rude.

And so we say nothing.

And Scarlett says: 'Hey.'

And it's kind of to all of us and none of us.

'Hey.'

But we don't say anything. Cos we're not like the boys.

No.

Beat.

We just pretend she's not there.

Personally, I don't think she was actually talking to me.

Nor me.

Personally, I don't think she was talking to anyone. It was more of a 'hey'. More like a sound really.

The problem with girls like that is they ruin it for everyone.

The problem with girls like that is they give all girls a bad name.

The problem with girls like that is that their reputation is contagious. And if you hang around girls like that, it's not necessarily that you'll start behaving like she does – we are intelligent young women, we have minds of our own – but people will think you do. And that's worse really.

We did a history class on the Holocaust, and learned about bystanders, who watched, stood by and even

though they weren't performing the acts themselves,
but just like being there, doing nothing, it's like…
they're condoning it. And this is a bit like that. Like if I
hang out with her, I'm approving of her behaviour.

And it wasn't planned, but we all just turn away, like
turn our backs. Like a wave. All the St Helen's girls
just silently turning. And I feel… part of something,
y'know. I feel deeply connected to these girls I grew
up with. And that's really nice.

These girls will be my friends for life.

And I'm gutted I didn't film it. Because it looked
really beautiful. Balletic almost. It felt beautiful.

And my locker's open, so even though my back –
through the mirror I can see what's happening. And
Scarlett just stands there looking at us all. Willing our
backs to move with her eyes or something like a witch.

And then she turns and looks to Russell.

Muscle Russell.

Tussled-hair Russell.

Lusty Russy.

Snog marry kill. Bed-head Russell. Football Russell.
And dining-hall-eating Russell.

And that look, before he even says anything, confirms
for me the rumours.

And I can't for sure say what her look was – as I can
only see the back of her head. Pleading? Flirting?
Accusing?

But he says: 'Again? I'm a bit worn out Scarlett.'

The boys laugh, some of them high-five.

I've never really understood the high-five. When I was
twelve I tried it out, started high-fiving my best friend
every time I saw her or I made a joke. But it just never
really took off.

Boys can be such dicks.

Russell can do so much better. Hope he didn't catch an STI or something.

And as she slinks away, I feel really sorry for her. We all do I think. Maybe it's not all her fault. Maybe if her mother had just taught her better.

Change. Eight years old.

We are twenty girls squished into a teeny changing room at the local pool.

Arms touching arms. Legs touching legs.

I wish someone would move over.

I think they purposely make the changing rooms tiny and dirty and smelly so that people will not come to the local pool. I am fairly certain this is a conspiracy put in place by the moustache-lady who always yells at us for swimming in the wrong lane.

We are eight years old.

It is someone's birthday party and we are all there. That's the kind of close friends we are.

We are all there because the four mothers of the four girls who were not invited spoke to the mother of the girl who did the inviting. It wasn't me, I'm invited to everything on account of my mother being a local councillor.

About fifty percent of the girls wear one-pieces. Fifty percent wear bikinis.

Two-pieces, not bikinis.

And I change in the corner so no one can really see me.

I change in the middle, the other girls' bodies as a shield.

I change wherever cos comparatively I'm definitely one of the skinnier ones.

For a moment I'm worried I'll grow up to be fat.

For a moment I'm worried I'll grow up and become a lesbian.

For a moment I'm worried I'll grow up to be a cat lady who lives by herself.

For a moment I'm worried I'll never be pretty enough to get a boyfriend.

But then we're in the pre-showers and the water is freezing and we all scream and we forget.

Someone is not talking to Scarlett, and Scarlett is not talking to someone else, and someone else is not talking to someone else and I'm not sure what happened but I have to take someone's side so I take someone else's side, and we all reshuffle so someone else doesn't have to be near Scarlett. And someone, maybe me, has to act as messenger passing messages between the two.

And then we go swimming. Twenty squealing floral-printed bodies cannonballing into the water.

We count how long we can hold our breath.

We are mermaids.

Scarlett has brought Swimming Barbie who comes with waterproof make-up and we forgive Scarlett and the fight whatever it was about is forgotten.

And one of us pretends to be Ken asking Barbie out on a date, and we take turns to see who can think of the bestest line.

'Hey Barbie, wanna go for a ride in my convertible?'

'Hey Barbie, you've got to be the prettiest girl I ever did see. If you don't go out with me, I will kill myself.'

'Hey Barbie I want to kiss you with tongues.'

Ew.

Gross.

'Hey Barbie'

And Ken always has an American accent. We've never heard Ken speak before but decide he's such a hunk that he must be from California.

We do these somersault things over the rings that divide the lanes and moustache-lady yells at us. So we take turns secretly touching the rings, sitting on the rings when she's not looking, while the other girls distract her. Girls got to stick together right?

And she can't catch us, can't stop us. Because we are twenty and she is one. And we are only eight and she is more than that and still we are smarter.

Full up on pizza and cake and fizzy pop we run to the park next door and lie down damp in the grass.

We put our heads on each other's bellies so we're all connected. My head on her belly.

My head on hers.

Hers on hers.

And hers on hers.

And hers on hers.

Like a giant zigzagging water snake.

And we close our eyes to the flashing sun and listen to each girl's belly breath.

In. Out. In. Out.

And it is quiet.

Beat.

And then someone laughs, her belly vibrating into some other girl's wet hair.

So she in turn starts laughing

And then she in turn

And then she in turn

And soon there are twenty chuckling bellies, heads bouncing up and down, and still we keep our eyes closed.

And we laugh for what feels like hours.

We are in love with swimming, and summer, and each other, and Ken.

We are Barbie. We are mermaids. We are indestructible.

Change. Present.

After school Scarlett is nowhere to be seen.

Scarlett the Harlot.

Like no one has seen her since lunch.

If I were her I would totally kill myself. Talk about embarrassing. I just couldn't, y'know?

And I'm a bit worried.

We're all a bit worried. Because you hear stories and stuff. And it's just a stupid picture. She wouldn't do something stupid…

'We should call her,' someone says. Someone. Maybe me. Or one of the other – it doesn't really matter. What matters is we call her. All of us huddled around the phone on speaker.

…

'Hello?'

Scarlett?

'Hello?'

Yeah, Scarlett?

'Gotchya! You've reached Scarlett's VM. You know what to do. And if you don't I can't help you.'

She's not there, and we're worried, naturally, so we leave a message.

Scarlett, hi, this is a message for Scarlett Smith. This is *Playboy* magazine. We uh… (*Lowers voice.*) We uh loved your pics and would love for you to pose for us. So um… (*Laughs.*)

We hang up. We call again. We hang up. We call again. We hang up. We call again. We hang up. We call again. We call again. We call again. We call again. We call again.

This is um *Playboy* magazine

This is um *Penthouse* magazine

This is um *Nuts* magazine

This is um *Loaded* magazine

This is um *Zoo* magazine

This is um *FHM* magazine

This is um *New Statesman* magazine.

That's a political magazine you moron.

Sorry. Wrong number.
What? I saw my dad read it once.

We hang up. We call again. We hang up. We call again. We hang up. We call again. We call again. We call again. We call again. We go home.

En route I buy a *Closer* magazine.

En route I buy a *Heat* magazine.

En route I buy an *OK!* and a *Now* and a *HELLO!* because you get all three now in one package which is quite a good deal actually.

Kim Kardashian has gained a stone and has cellulite which is a shame because she was doing so well on her post-kid diet and now she looks disgusting.

And Cheryl Cole has lost a stone and her bingo wings and got a flat stomach and has the ideal body so Ashley Cole will be really jealous.

And Nicki Minaj is looking unhealthily skinny and an insider friend is worried about her.

And Drake is now single, and so is Taylor Lautner and so is Conor Maynard, they're all looking for a girl who knows how to have fun and doesn't take herself too seriously.

Kill marry snog. Drake, Lautner, Maynard.

Anyway you can't believe everything you read. Those magazines aren't always realistic. They probably all have girlfriends.

At home someone sends me the Scarlett photo. You're a bit behind the times my friend. As if I don't already have it. I look at it again anyway.

I look at it again.

I look at it again.

I read the comments people have posted on her Facebook page.

I look at it again.

My mother asks me what I'm looking at.

I tell her 'nothing'.

I tell her 'homework'.

I don't tell her anything.

She doesn't actually want to know the answer.

She's marking Year 11 essays.

She's making a PowerPoint.

She's on the phone whinging about the bitch from work who stole her promotion.

She's telling my father about the girl from work who's going on maternity at what is a most inconvenient time for the company.

She's telling Grandma about the girl from the office who has to leave at three o'clock every day to pick up her kids, talk about a lack of commitment.

She's telling me about the slutty girl whose skirt was so short you could almost see the brand of her knickers.

She's telling no one in particular about how she got ID'd at Sainsbury's buying wine thank you very much.

She never actually asks.

She isn't home.

Buzz

Click

Pop

Flash

And a new photo has come through.

Someone else who is behind the times.

Except this time it's not Scarlett.

It's a different photo.

Russell. Completely naked.

Music. 'California Gurls' by Katy Perry. Again the girls put on headphones, sing along and do a dance. This time the dance is led by a GIRL WITH AVIATOR HELMET AND GOGGLES.

The music suddenly stops. The GIRLS *face away with their headphones.*

GIRL WITH AVIATOR HELMET AND GOGGLES
Let me give you some advice. Don't drink tea before ya fly. I tell ya I couldn't *live* without me mornin' tea, but nothing worse than bein' seven thousand feet in the air, clouds everywhere, no navigation equipment or radio aids and thinkin' I don't know how much longer 'fore I go in me knickers.

I try to tell this to the man who I've been assigned for the day drinkin' a steamin' hot cup. It's February 1945. Just another mornin' like any other at the Airport Transport Auxillary – only today it's a Hudson I gotta deliver for maintenance, which means there's gotta be two of us. Me and this lad. And I'm tryin t' tell him, give 'em some advice so I don't gotta be worried about him needin' to wee up in the air, but he's havin' none of it. Don't want t' hear it. Don't want t' hear none of it.

Don't even want t' be flyin with me. He's not takin' orders from a lass.

Starts mumblin' 'bout what's the world coming to. World at war, Britain bein' bombed, and t' top it all off we got some lass flyin' planes. As though I'm the only one. As though of the six hundred 'n' fifty ATA pilots, a hundred 'n' sixty-four aren't women.

But he's insistin' he take charge. He's insistin' otherwise this plane's goin' nowhere. And I can see he's a stubborn so and so, so sometimes you gotta take the higher ground, sometimes you gotta sit back and say okay, you got a willy – you know best. Sometimes when he's inspectin' the plane you gotta slip a laxative into his tea.

It's about an hour later, I'm ready to go, but he's not feelin' so good, so they get some other pilot – and let's say he's much more amenable. As we're getting' into the plane I see the lad again, face ashen. So I tell him: 'Shoulda listened to my advice. Told you not to drink before ya fly.'

She exits. The GIRLS *take off their headphones, turn back to face us.*

GIRLS   Russell's body is what you would expect.

He goes to the gym.

He plays rugby.

It's as I imagined. That's not to say I spend my days picturing Russell naked, but if I did, that's what he would like look – like he does.

And the boys' nickname for him – Big Mac – well let's just say it's now clear it has nothing to do with his love of fast food.

And let's just say that when people said he was a bit ginger and I said no he's definitely blond – that I was right, thank God.

He should work in Hollister or something.

What is almost one hundred percent certain is that it was Scarlett who put the photo online. A likely hypothesis is that she did this as an act of revenge. What is less clear-cut is the motive for revenge which can be narrowed down to one of two possibilities: one – it was Russell who sent round the photo of her naked. Whether or not it actually was I can neither confirm nor deny, nor is it actually relevant, what's important is she believes it to be the case. Two – as revenge for embarrassing her in the corridor yesterday in front of everyone. What I can say for definite is that the photo of Russell has made its way round the entire school.

We should know this because girls are laughing. And boys are yelling 'man-whore' down the corridor. And Russell is standing alone by his locker with his head down.

Beat.

Except this is not what is happening. This is not how we know.

We know because one girl is heard stating she has changed her mind and she wants to marry Russell instead of snog him and is it too late to change?

We know this because a boy is heard saying: 'He's a legend, dude.'

We know this because Russell's friends are high-fiving him and acting like it is any other day.

The thing, yeah, and I'm sorry to have to be the one to say this, is that Scarlett, well she's obviously even dumber than she acts.

She obviously doesn't get it's fine for boys to be, you know.

They're supposed to be, right? Like it's part of their DNA, part of their puberty... blue balls or something. Wait. Is that right?

It is nature. It's not just chickens and cocks. I was watching the BBC and like even elephants, right, like there'll be like twelve female elephants, and one male for like all those women. The women will only have sex with the one male their whole life, but the male, well you do the math.

It's how it's meant to be. If you don't believe me ask David Attenborough.

Like my brother says: if a key can open lots of locks, it's a really good key. Like a master key. But if a lock can be opened by lots of keys then it's a really shit lock. Do you see?

And this is what Scarlett has failed to understand. Maybe her mother didn't teach her.

Boys will be boys.

Boys like Russell, a boy like that can't help himself.

A boy like that has to try before he buys.

One of the GIRLS *quotes the first four lines of 'A Boy Like That' from* West Side Story.

Actually, those are just the lyrics from *West Side Story*

Yeah, but. Well maybe. I was Anita on account of their being no Puerto Ricans at the school and my being a quarter Indian.

There's a group of boys looking at the photo, but it's weird. Cos like they're looking at it, but not. Like each of them keep flicking their eyes away from the screen, like if they look at it too long their eyes will burn.

Like they're afraid.

Like they're scared of being caught looking at it. By other boys.

And watching this group of boys not looking at the photo, you'd think that actually none of them really saw it. If we hadn't noticed one of them later, alone in the caff line, secretly looking again.

And if we hadn't noticed the subtle changes that day.

A boy stretching his arms down, trying to casually check his bicep.

A boy lifting his shirt to scratch his stomach but really checking his abs. Or lack thereof.

A boy buying a salad for lunch.

A boy swiping a ruler from maths so he could later try to calculate how he measured up.

A boy with no facial hair in Boots buying an electric razor to trim his pubes.

Miss is explaining this project we have to do next term. We've got to trace our own family history, and specifically our family's *female* history, whatever that means.

We're in period three and Slutty Scarlett actually has the nerve to come to class.

And two girls, neither of which are me I don't think, are doodling on the photo of Russell. One of them has a colour printer at home, so.

They're drawing a tattoo of their name on his appendage when Miss turns round and confiscates it. And I bet it's the first time she's ever seen one.

I bet it is. I bet she's still a virgin.

And before she even has time to ask it, one of the two girls, or someone else says:

'Scarlett sent it round.'

And Miss asks Scarlett if it's true. And one of the other girls starts to speak but Miss silences her – 'I'm asking Scarlett' – and I can't help but think of that scene from *The Crucible*, that's the school play this year, I'm

playing John Proctor on account of there not being
enough boys who auditioned, and there's that scene
where I say: 'Tell the truth!' to my wife just like Miss
is saying now and our not being condemned to death
hangs on what comes out of her mouth.

Except this is nothing like that. Because Scarlett
knows she's condemned no matter what she says. And
so when Miss asks again: 'Did you send it, tell the
truth,' she says:

'Sure.'

Sure. Not yes, not no, but…

And it's weird cos for a moment I think maybe she
didn't – like if she'd protested her innocence I'd have
thought for sure she's actually done it, liar, but her
just…

Maybe she thinks in taking the blame she'll win favour
with the girls.

Or maybe she knows the headteacher's office is safer
than the corridors.

Or maybe she knows that it doesn't matter what she
says or whether she did or not because it's already
been decided.

Or maybe she thinks that this will end it. And the past
two days will be a distant memory, forgotten.

And that's what I mean about Scarlett being dumber
than she acts, bless her. I actually feel really bad.
Because still, after all these years, she hasn't learned
that St Helen's girls never forget. She thinks this is the
end. But I know it's just the start. And there's nothing
not one of us can do to stop it.

Change. Eleven years old.

I get my period. Thank fuck I'm not the last. So Sir says I don't have to go swimming. And I realise this will be a convenient excuse in future PE lessons.

We are all getting changed, nervous in our new school that has a swimming pool.

We are eleven years old. And though we are quiet pretending to concentrate on the arduous task of putting on swimsuits, we are really concentrating on taking casual glances at the others.

See who else has hair down there.

Who else doesn't really have boobs yet

Who is wearing a sports bra

Who is wearing no bra

Who is wearing a real bra.

No one. Except Scarlett.

And in the change-room after swim, she starts like putting on this lotion. Because her skin is dry she says. This lotion that smells like strawberries.

And this cherry-smelling Vaseline on her lips, because her lips are dry she says.

And it's like waving a steak rump around when my dog's wandered off. She'll walk down the corridor and the boys will come running.

Which is just the strangest thing, because this is Scarlett. Scarlett who wasn't even invited to all the parties, Scarlett who was last to get the accessory that everyone else already had, last to be picked.

And she has this confidence, this quiet confidence even when she's getting changed for swim. And it's like where did that come from? And she's suddenly started making these jokes. Like she's a comedian. I can't think of any, but yeah she makes these jokes.

And the boys always flock. Like bees to honey

Bees don't actually flock, they swarm

Sweating through their tight shirts

Nervously running hands through their faux-messy gelled coiffed hair

Annoyingly fingering the branded bands of their pants, cos all the boys were suddenly wearing boxers. And like branded ones

Stupidly laughing at her jokes

They're not even funny, not really

She has to barely utter two words and the boys start panting, wagging their tails.

Beat.

Maneater.

Beat.

The boys are disgusting anyway.

But really we get it. We get that it's not really about the boys for Scarlett. It's about attention. It's about for once not being at the bottom. Which is a bit pathetic really.

We take turns showing Sir our dives.

And Scarlett makes a big ugly splash on account of her boobs adding weight, serves her right.

Sir gives us five minutes' free time at the end and plays classical music over the speaker so we play calmly.

Someone gets the idea that we should pretend we're synchronised swimmers, which is dumb, but we do it anyway.

We lie on our backs in the water, a circle

My hands on her shoulder and her shoulder

Hers on her shoulder and her shoulder

Hers on her shoulder and her shoulder

Hers on her shoulder and her shoulder

And then we kick our legs up into the air.

It only lasts a moment before we all go underwater, the weight of someone's hands on our shoulders, drowning us

But for a moment it's the prettiest thing you ever saw.

Change. Present.

Last night my sister asked me why? 'Why did she take the photo?' Like I know.

But I did wonder about it. For a minute like. When I got the photo.

Probably it was a boy. Russell. Or. And probably he made her feel that if she didn't he'd lose interest. Cos some other girl would.

Probably he told her he'd be her boyfriend if she did.

Probably he threatened to tell everyone they slept together if she didn't.

Or. No. No.

Probably he made her feel special.

Probably he said it was just a bit of fun.

Probably he said: 'Show me yours I'll show you mine.'

Probably he made her feel pretty. Probably he made her feel like the most beautiful girl in the world.

Beat.

Or maybe he didn't.

Probably he made her feel ugly.

Probably he made her feel she could never get a guy like him.

Probably he made her feel worthless.

Probably he rejected her.

Probably he said he regretted what they'd done.

Probably she thought, if I just – flash, click, buzz – then he'll... pay attention.

Beat.

Or maybe it wasn't a boy. Maybe she just took it. Just to... see.

Maybe she wanted to know what she'd look like if she were a page-three girl.

And maybe it was innocent and maybe she can't wait to get home to delete the photo from her desktop to make sure the same thing doesn't happen to her! I mean. I don't know what I'm saying. Never mind.

And thank God my ex-boyfriend is a decent loyal guy. That's all I'm saying.

My sister is asking again *why.* As though somehow this matters, as though this changes things. She does not understand that this question is miles away, is a question from another dimension. And when I ignore her, she asks: 'Why does a photo make someone a slut?' But it's too complicated to explain, so I don't.

I'm thinking *why.* We're all wondering *why* when we see Scarlett in the corridor after school. Why didn't she just go home, leave school, leave the country, move to Mozambique.

There she is in the corridor like always. As though she's been asleep these past two days.

And I can feel it. My grandma, who had arthritis, used to say she could feel when it was gonna rain. Feel it in her bones. Well I can feel it, a storm's coming. And so when Scarlett glances at me, I say – with my eyes, I say, 'Run, run as fast as you can, get away from here'. But she doesn't hear me, or chooses not to.

And I should probably leave. I should probably not be here.

But then I'll miss something and tomorrow when everyone's –

'There's the ho.'

It's this girl I've never seen before. She doesn't go to our school I don't think.

And we find out later, that she text Scarlett while she was in the headteacher's office all afternoon. 'Meet me after school.' And like a moron, she comes.

Didn't her mother teach her anything?

Maybe she thinks she can explain.

Maybe she thinks at least a crowded corridor will keep her protected. What with students and teachers.

But the teachers have reports to write, and though their doors be open, they got invisible earplugs. They teach 'em how to do that in teacher training. And the students... well we're just kids.

'I hear you got with my man Russ. That true?'

And she looks to Russ. But he doesn't say anything.

'I said is that true bitch?'

And I wonder why he doesn't say anything.

And I wonder why if it's true, this girl isn't angry at *him*. Why she's not confronting *him*.

And I wonder what school she goes to.

And I didn't know Russell had a girlfriend.

'You a retarded mute or something? I'm gonna ask you one last time – and stop looking at my man. Did. You. Get. With. Him?'

We watch. Frozen.

And she says. Scarlett says:

'Sure.'

She could've just said no. She could've run away. But Scarlett's not as dumb as she seems. Because at long last she gets it. As she takes in the girls she went to school with in a circle around her, these girls she grew up with, she understands that this was all decided in nursery when we sat in a circle holding hands. She understands that it doesn't matter what she says. Which is why she:

'Sure.'

Pause.

There's a silence for what feels like for ever.

And I know a teacher will come and ruin it. Not let us see the ending. (*Pause.*) But no one comes. And then some guy's voice yells:

'Hit the slut already.'

A slap doesn't sound how you think it will. Not like in the movies. It's… louder.

And a punch sounds like… gardening. Like a spade tapping soil.

And a kick sounds like windscreen wipers when it's not raining.

And I want to click to another video, close the tab. But I can't.

And it's different than YouTube. Cos in person you can smell it. And I understand now when people talk about 'smelling the fear', because it actually does. Smells like salt. It smells like piss.

And you can taste the blood. Like when you breathe it tastes sour.

But suddenly Scarlett raises her arm, scratches the girl's face.

Scarlett's a nail-biter, so it doesn't really… but still.

And Scarlett's kicking in all directions, and her body's writhing on the ground, and she manages to get herself on top somehow, and she comes away with a chunk of the girl's hair in her hands.

Because this girl, us, have all underestimated Scarlett.
Because Scarlett knows she has nothing to lose.

She slaps the girl back and then she like… pauses.
Looks at me.

At me I think.

I think at me.

As if to say…

To say…

The girl seizes the opportunity to get back on top, and
seeing her hair in Scarlett's hands, she goes… mental.
Like proper mental.

And even Scarlett knows she's no match now. So she
just covers her head with her hands.

And I worry this girl is gonna kill her. If she keeps on,
then Scarlett might…

And why doesn't someone do something? Why won't
someone do something?
Why won't Russell say something, stop this?!

Why doesn't he pull them apart?

Why doesn't he run and get a teacher?

Why does he just.
Stand there.

Pause.

The next week someone asks where Scarlett is?

Miss answers that she has transferred to another school.

Which means there's only nineteen St Helen's girls at
the school now. Which is a bit of an awkward number.
It's a prime number.

And it's only later that I realise Russell was the only
boy there. And the guy who called out, who said 'hit
the slut' was in fact a girl. It was one of us.

*Music. 'Better Than Revenge' by Taylor Swift. Again
the girls put on headphones, sing along and do a
dance. This time the dance is led by a* GIRL WITH
FLOWERS IN HER HAIR.

The music suddenly stops. The GIRLS *face away with
their headphones.*

GIRL WITH FLOWERS IN HER HAIR
'Were you going to tell me?' He's looking at me like
I've shot Martin Luther King or something. Like *I've*
shot Bobby Kennedy.

'I'm telling you now.'

We're sitting in a park, enjoying one of the few days of
sunshine. It's August 1968, one of the worst summers
on record.

'Besides there's nothing to tell.'

He stares at a group of people our age smoking in the
distance. A girl dances, moving her lips to a song we
can't hear. And as if she has whispered some answer to
him, he: 'We can live with my parents.'

And I laugh. I can't help it. And I remember why I
love him.

'Well do you have a better idea?'

When did we become so old? We're only sixteen but I
feel a century. And I wonder what the next century
will look like. I start thinking about the year 2000 and
what a strange number that seems and I picture us in
flying cars.

And he's still talking. I catch the end of his diatribe
when he: 'We don't have a choice.'

And just like that I know that while I love him, we will
not grow old together. We will not fly a car together
into the next millennium. Because like that, the free-
wheeling laissez-faire hippy eco-warrior I have fallen
in love with has dropped his costume and become just
another traditional boy.

'We have to accept the consequences.'

Last year when we met, at a rally, I fell in love with the way he'd have to fill silences. Could always talk. Now it's just annoying.

'Are you sure it's mine?'

I say nothing.

'It doesn't matter. I'll love it anyway. We'll live at my parents' and – '

'It doesn't matter.' Finally I speak. 'It doesn't matter because it doesn't exist.'

And he gives me this look. An ugly look. A look of disdain.

'Have you…?'

'Not yet.'

And he's relieved. His face loves me again.

And he starts talking again. But my mind is somewhere else. My mind is in some sci-fi future in the 2000s when my daughter and I fly our car to parliament where she is Prime Minister, a lady Prime Minister, when there is only love and not war. But even in the daydream I know that my daughter is not the same one, not this one inside me.

He's still talking about his parents' loft when I say: 'I'm sixteen.'

And before I can say more he's right in there as always – 'Sixteen's practically an adult. My parents were sixteen when they got married. We're capable of making mature decisions.'

And I agree. 'Which is why I can make this one. It's my body.'

And the look is back. He looks at me like I'm a…

And before he can say more, I'm up, I'm walking away from his voice in the park. And as I pass the other young people, the girl grabs my hand. She starts dancing with me. I don't hear any music – I'm fairly certain it's in her head, but I figure out the rhythm by copying her body. She leans in. For a second I think she's going to kiss me, but instead puts her mouth to my ear.

Whispers.

'Us girls need to stick together.'

She exits. The GIRLS *take off their headphones, turn back to face us.*

GIRLS   I stand in front of a full-length mirror.

My get-ready soundtrack.

She sings about how last Friday night we went skinny-dipping then had a *ménage à trois*.

She sings about how chains and whips excite me.

She sings about letting her see what you're hiding underneath, let her see your peacock, and it puts me in the mood.

I shave my pits

I wax my legs

I pluck my brows

I paint my nails

I colour my lips

I rose my cheeks

I darken my lashes

I straighten my hair

I lotion my stomach

I sparkle my arms

I dangle my ears

I spray my neck

I shave. Wax. Pluck. Paint. Colour. Rose. Darken. Straighten. Lotion. Sparkle. Dangle. Spray. Wax. Pluck. Paint. Colour. Rose. Darken. Straighten. Lotion.

Sparkle. Dangle. Spray. Wax. Pluck. Paint. Colour. Rose. Darken. Straighten. Lotion. Sparkle. Dangle. Spray. And take a photo.

Flash.

I hate the way I look

I hate how my ears stick out

I hate how small my lips are

I hate the little hairs above my lip

I hate the veins on my neck

I hate my stomach blubber

I hate my chunky arse

I hate my tiny breasts

I hate my wide hips

I hate my wrinkly knees

I hate my stubby hands

I hate my long feet

I take another photo. And it's time to go.

The party is at Tyler's house. He greets us in shorts, a fur coat and no shirt. It's a 'pimps 'n' hos' party.

Rihanna plays and we love her.

Even though I've boycotted Rihanna on account of her getting back together with Chris Brown, I make an exception.

But that just shows what a strong woman Rihanna is. That she sticks by him despite what he did. That shows loyalty.

And we have a good time. I know this because people's Facebook statuses are updated to 'having a bare good time at Tyler's party'.

I know this because there are photos on Facebook showing us having a good time so we must be.

I know this because even though one of the girls is crying in a corner with mascara running down her face, we are still dancing and drinking.

And I hear Tyler tell one of the boys she's a cock-tease

Prude

Tight

Cold

Ice queen

Lead him on

Vamp

Prick-tease

Which is true. If you're gonna dress like that and then not, y'know?

And if you get a guy excited and then don't... like they can have problems, have to go to hospital, right?

What a bitch.

And I want to say, it's all bullshit. I want to say it doesn't make any sense. I want to ask about the space in-between. Cos she's a prick-tease cos she didn't, and she'd be a slut if she did, so how does she get to the space between? I want to be in the space between! I want to say this, but Rihanna is swirling through my brain, and alcohol is swirling through my veins or the other way round and I can't get the words to come out. And anyway, somewhere deep down I know the answer. In-between doesn't exist. So I just dance. And take a photo.

It is two in the morning and I could totally kill a Big Mac right now. Like a real one. Not Russell's.

We all could.

There's a good chance we won't notice. She's making a big effort to keep her head down, to be invisible. And through vodka-eyes focused on dipping fries into BBQ sauce there's a good chance no one will notice her.

Except someone, I don't think it's me, someone says: 'Look'. And the skulk of foxes raise their ketchup-blushed faces in unison.

It's been a good two months since we've seen her. I almost don't recognise her.

She's had a haircut, she's dyed her hair. And except for the tiny scar by her eyebrow, you wouldn't even know.

What she's doing at McDonald's with some guy in the middle of the night, I can't say.

Some guy from her new school.

And even when we were little we understood the rules always still applied – even out of school. Unless you ran into someone with their mum, and then it was smiles and a wave or small talk while your stupid mothers chatted to each other. But otherwise, the rules still applied, which is why –

'Scarlett.'

Someone says it quietly. She doesn't hear. Or pretends not to.

'Scarlett.'

And still she focuses her eyes hard on the guy, not blinking. Like maybe if she focuses hard enough we'll just disappear. Or maybe she will.

'Scarlett.'

You know the penis game we used to play in Year 9? Like someone starts quietly then the next person says it a bit louder, then louder?

They get louder with each 'Scarlett'.

'Scarlett'

'Scarlett'

'Scarlett'

'Scarlett'

'Scarlett'

'Scarlett!'

Till even the fifty-year-old Ronald McDonald behind the counter is looking over at us. And more importantly the boy with Scarlett is looking over. And we're all barking:

'Scarlett! Scarlett! Scarlett!'

And it's funny. Cos I can't remember the last time I played a game.

And then someone goes over. Not me. I don't – I would never… I just watch.

'Scarlett, how are you?
Scarlett, don't you recognise me? Scarlett and I grew up together.'

Scarlett still just stares ahead. Like she's scared or something. Like she's mixed us up with the girl who came after school that day. Like in Scarlett's mind we're all the same person.

'Scarlett? Hello? Anyone in there?'

And I don't understand why she doesn't say something. Speak up! It is 2013! Women have earned the right to speak! She just keeps staring at the guy like she's a statue, still not blinking.

And I think maybe she's died. You hear about it.

But then some water starts to come out of one of her eyes so I know she's alive.

'Scarlett is an amazing photographer. Has she shown you any?'

But the girl can't find it on her phone. And Scarlett's eyes finally blink. A hint of relief. A different ending.

But then another girl, I, or whoever it is, says: 'I've got it.' And finds the boy's phone on her Bluetooth and presses send.

Buzz. Click.

And then we leave. Or else it'll be another thirty
minutes for the next night bus.

Change. Twelve years old.

'Gimme Whatchya Got' by Chris Brown plays.

We are sat in a circle.

An empty Coca-Cola bottle spins fast.

We are twelve years old. We are sat in the loft of a boy
called Tyler's house.

My mother has let me come because Tyler's parents
will be there. Though you wouldn't know it. I have yet
to see them. But when someone went to the loo
downstairs she said she heard a loud TV so they
probably are.

The bottle lands on one of us, and the girl who it lands
on is nervous.

She's petrified. Scarlett.

But she doesn't show it. She acts like it's every day
that she kisses Russell with the sweep-away hair. She
doesn't let on that this will be the first time she has
ever kissed a boy.

She doesn't let on that while she fancies Russell –
everyone does – this wasn't how she'd pictured it in
her head.

A room full of the girls she's grown up with and boys
she doesn't really know chanting:

'Kiss kiss kiss tongue tongue tongue.'

She doesn't let on that it was supposed to be on their
fifth date, it was supposed to be just the two of them, it

was supposed to be with a rose in her hand, it was supposed to be like in the movies, it was supposed to be like how her mother told her.

And his tongue tastes of Doritos and Orange Fanta.

And when we've finished counting back from ten Russell says: 'Want to do it again?'

And she doesn't. Not really. But we're watching. And she knows we'll never forget if she doesn't. So she says:

'Sure.'

Beat.

Later we're sitting on couches and it feels like we're kids again or something because all the boys are on one couch and all the girls are on the other. And of course we can't all fit, so we sit on each other's knees

We sit on the floor leaning our heads on other girls' legs

We lie with our feet in other girls' laps.

And then Tyler brings out a laptop, hooks it up the TV. And says: 'Wanna see something?'

There are two men and one woman on the screen. All of them naked.

And at first I don't quite understand what I'm watching.

And I don't like it.

And I want to close my eyes.

And I want to say turn it off please.

And I want to get up and leave.

But she's sitting on my knee

And she has her head on my legs

And she has her feet in my lap

And I can't move.

So we sit there all of us and watch. Eating Doritos.

Change. Present.

If anything happens it will be his fault.

Yes, I blame the boy from McDonald's.

Why couldn't he have just kept it for himself?

Why couldn't he have just deleted it?

Why is it he felt so compelled to send it to others from his school?

What was it about the photo that offended him so?

It makes me really angry, the senseless things people do. His mother should have taught him better.

And if anything, if she like – then like it will be his fault. I hope he realises that. I hope he can like live with the consequences.

Scarlett is missing. She has been missing for over twenty-four hours. We know this because the police officer who comes to talk to our class tells us so.

He wants to know if any of us have heard from her.

'She doesn't go to this school any more,' I, or one of the other girls volunteer helpfully.

He's aware but thought perhaps some of us were still in touch with her. She was a St Helen's girl after all.

After all St Helen's girls are friends for life.

He thinks she may try to kill herself or have already done so. He doesn't say this in so many words.

He doesn't say this at all.

But we know. We are intelligent girls.

He also doesn't tell us that on the Monday after we saw her at McDonald's everyone at her new school had seen the photo. But we know this too. We have Twitter.

He also doesn't tell us that she left behind a note. We can't remember how we know this.

There is a girl in Canada who made a video before she killed herself.

And it's one of the first times a suicide was widely reported. Normally they don't cos they don't want it influencing impressionable young people.

In case we get ideas.

I mean how dumb is that? We're not so stupid that we're gonna kill ourselves just cos some girl on the news did.

The girl in Canada made this whole video, you can YouTube it, with cards and stuff talking about her naked photo that was sent around and her tormentors. It's pretty grim. I thought Canadians were supposed to be nice. I'm not so sure any more.

At lunch, I decide to go for a walk

I decide to go home

I decide to eat by myself

I can't explain it, but I just. I don't want to see anyone. I don't want to see any of the girls.

And at night, the news is showing her school photo.

And I wish they'd stop showing it.

And the newsreaders keep asking – where did she go? Why did this happen? Who is responsible? When what they should really be asking is why isn't she smiling in the photo?

Why are her eyes in the school photo saying 'help me'?

And my mother says: 'Don't you know that girl?'

My mother says: 'Didn't that girl go to St Helen's?'

My mother says: 'Wasn't that girl at your birthday party once?'

My mother says: 'Wasn't that girl at our house once?'

My mother says: 'Didn't you have a sleepover with that girl one time?'

My mother says: 'Isn't that one of your friends?'

Yes

Yes

Yes

Yes

Yes

Yes.

And we take to Facebook and we write tributes:

'We miss you Scarlett. Come back.'

'We miss your beautiful smile.'

'We miss your winning personality.'

'We miss your jokes.'

'If you're reading this, know that – '

And some of us are on TV

The man is interviewing us

And we tell the camera:

'Scarlett was our friend. We miss her.'

'We miss her beautiful smile.'

'We miss her winning personality.'

'We miss her jokes.'

'If you're watching this Scarlett – '

And we cry. For real.

And I feel like I'm gonna throw up

And I feel like I've been punched in the stomach

And I feel like I've been kicked in the face

Because the screen switches to live footage. At the river. It's dark and you can't see anything. But the newsreader in the suit erases any doubt. They've found a body.

Music. 'Slut Like You' by P!nk. Again the GIRLS *put on headphones. This time the dance is led by a* GIRL WITH SHOULDER PADS.

But this time they can't quite get into it. Something is wrong. They don't really sing or do the dance with commitment. Some don't do it at all. Eventually they all stop, but before the music does. Beat.

Then the music suddenly stops. The GIRLS *face away with their headphones.*

GIRL WITH SHOULDER PADS

Olivia is singing let's get physical. When she kicks I kick, when she punches I punch. And the afternoon is replaying in my mind which only makes me kick higher and my forehead sweat harder and my heart pound faster. It is 1985 and soon girls will run the world. Just wait till I tell the girls at school.

I have only worked at Pierce, Richards and Stanley for a week. My mother is nervous. They don't normally take on girls as young as me, but I want to be a lawyer so my mum has made some calls and got me this after-school gig a couple hours a week. I am what you call a 'runner' at the law firm. And runner is not a euphemism. From four to six p.m. I run between floors delivering mail, delivering coffee, delivering photocopies, delivering staples and paperclips, delivering memos and faxes from other floors. Lucky for me Olivia has got me in shape, cos some of the other girls who are a bit – well they just can't work as fast as me. Which is why I don't think they like me very much. 'I'm raising expectations' one of them has told me. And we're supposed to stick together. But I can't help doing my job well, can I? I even bought a new outfit, just for work. *Work.* How cool am I? The girls are like what are you doing after school? 'Oh you know, I'm just going to work. To my law firm.'

And the girls tell me to stay out of Stanley's way. Stanley is his first name and his last name which is the dumbest thing I've ever heard. Unless the girls are just saying that to trick me, but I don't care. And then today I've got these papers I gotta deliver to Mr Stanley's secretary. Only she's on break so I knock on his door. The first thing he says is: 'That's a pretty outfit.' See, it's important to dress for success. That's what my mum says. I don't tell him this obviously. I just say: 'Thank you sir.' And this is where it gets really good. As I'm handing him his papers, he puts his hand on my waist and he says: 'What an efficient young woman you are. You'll be put to good use here.'

'I want to be a lawyer, sir.'

And his hand has subtly slid further down my waist.

'Well this will certainly be a good experience for you then,' he says.

'I thought so too,' I tell him. 'But I'm not so sure. See you're supposed to be this amazing lawyer, but you seem not to know about any kind of employment law.'

He doesn't understand.

'See this, right here, would be considered sexual harassment in the workplace. And you seem not to know that. Either that or you've assumed that because I'm wearing a pretty skirt that somehow means that's an invitation or I'm too young or naive to know otherwise. Either way, if you don't remove your hand from my firmly toned arse right now I will scream this whole office down, and then I will recruit Pierce, or Richards to sue the pants off you, and then I will call your wife.'

Beat.

'I'm glad you like my skirt. I'll be sure to wear it again.'

On my way out I see his secretary is back. She pretends to be typing on her Commodore 64 but I can see she's smiling.

When my mother picks me up, she asks how work was. I tell her 'fine' and she doesn't ask anything more. I turn up the car radio, Hall & Oates are singing:

*She sings the last two lines of the third verse, and the
first two lines of the chorus of 'Maneater' by Hall &
Oates.*

Here she comes indeed.

She exits. The GIRLS *take off their headphones, turn
back to face us.*

GIRLS The news doesn't show any photos, they're not
allowed to. It might frighten us. We're only children
after all.

Besides the family haven't identified the body yet.

There are counsellors in school in case any of us wants
to talk. But the counsellors haven't got a clue.

We don't want to talk. What we want is to forget.

We are in history and we have brought candles. Miss
has given us permission to put aside the presentations
scheduled for today and instead do a kind of vigil.

And we stand in a circle holding candles, and we are
each going to say a few words.

Except no one does. Not one says any words.

And Miss says: 'Would someone like to say
something?'

Silence.

And then a girl's voice says

SCARLETT (*Appearing*.)
I would like to say something.

GIRLS And it's like a ghost. It's like we are nine years old with
the Ouija board. Because standing there is Scarlett.

I can see her.

I can see her too.

And it's like, by being together, the St Helen's girls, we
have brought forth the spirit of Scarlett into the room.

SCARLETT
　　　I would like to say something.

GIRLS　And it's like, it's almost like she's actually there...

　　　Because she is actually there.

　　　Beat.

　　　At about this same moment, Scarlett's parents have
　　　confirmed the body from the river is not that of their
　　　daughter. Later discoveries will confirm the body is
　　　that of a fourteen-year-old Latvian prostitute and an
　　　autopsy will reveal she died with a boot to her skull.

SCARLETT
　　　I have something to say.

GIRLS　And first I'm frightened, then I'm confused, then I'm
　　　relieved, then I'm actually angry. I feel like we've
　　　been duped.

　　　We have been tricked.

　　　We have shed tears, we have made tributes, we have lit
　　　candles, and for what?

SCARLETT
　　　I would like to do my presentation now.

GIRLS　And Miss is so bewildered that all she can say is:
　　　'Sure.'

SCARLETT (*Presentation notes in hand.*)
　　　You have asked us to research the history of women in
　　　our family. Which was not especially easy as my
　　　mother is not a sentimental. No photos or nothing. But
　　　through a combination of some old shoeboxes of stuff
　　　at my nan's house, and newspapers and books found in
　　　the British Library in London where I have spent the
　　　last couple days FYI, I can tell you all the following:

　　　My mother is one of only five female FTSE 100 chief
　　　executives. She did this, I imagine, by donning
　　　shoulder pads and body-checking any man who got in
　　　her way.

Her mother, my nan, was a teacher. Which doesn't tell
me much about history. But when she was about my
age, in the sixties, she marched with other women to
make abortion legal. Which was like, a big deal. And
she wore her hair in braids sometimes. And she had lots
of sex. And no one judged her for it. Except maybe her
mother. Were she alive. Because she, my great-
grandmother, died when British European Airways
flight 411 crashed on approach to Manchester from
Amsterdam. This is ironic because from 1944 to '45 my
grandmother worked as a pilot during the war delivering
planes that needed to be fixed. Which, is like, not that an
exciting job to have. She wasn't dropping bombs or
anything. But it was a big deal, because she was doing a
man's job. And men were bastards and didn't like girls
like my great-grandma doing their jobs. And her mum…
well she was a long time ago so I didn't find out much
but her name's mentioned in an article in the *Daily Mail*
from 1928 because she went to a scandalous pool party.
I'm not sure why it was so scandalous. But the man who
wrote it from the *Daily Mail* did not like that girls were
dancing to Negro music and drinking cocktails in
swimsuits. Which shows that some things don't change
since the *Daily Mail* still does not like girls drinking and
having fun but it does like photos of girls in swimsuits.
So maybe things do change.

I have basically learned that in my family history there
were always boys who were arseholes who made
things shit for the girls in my family. But things have
moved on for my generation. Because for me, it is not
so much that boys are arseholes – they are – but more
that the girls have become the arseholes the boys used
to be. (*Puts away notes.*)

I used to ask myself every night *why*?

Why?

What did I ever do to you?

And then I would imagine twenty-five years from now
coming to a school reunion and I'd be there in my

Armani suit with my beautiful husband and my
beautiful handbag and my beautiful children and when
you all said: 'Scarlett! Scarlett!' I'd say: 'I'm sorry. I
don't recognise you. I don't recognise any of you.' And
then I'd leave.

But as I sat on the packed Tube in London, no one
recognised me. No one pointed, no one whispered.
And I realised you are all nothing. There is a big bad
world out there where St Helen's means nothing. There
is a big bad world that is just ready to swallow you up.
But when it swallows up you lot, it will vomit you
back up. Because you are indigestible girls. That's the
kind of girls you are. You are food poisoning. And the
world will know you are girls like that. And you will
be all alone. Together, but alone. Do you see?

And I will forget you. I have forgotten you. Because
I am not a St Helen's girl. But you will not forget me.
After all, you have my photo to remember me by.

Exits.

GIRLS   A moment later we look around and realise we're still
standing in a circle, holding lit candles.

*Pause. No one knows what to do. Then they blow the
candles out.*

And the year is over. And now we must go our separate
ways.

Well not me. Me and four of the girls are going to the
same uni. We're going to be flatmates, which is like,
it's gonna be totally… it's gonna be…

Oh God, what have I agreed to?

It's gonna be like actually amazing. We're gonna like
see each other every morning when we wake up, when
we go to bed.

Oh God.

It's the last day of school and so we run around signing
messages on each other's school uniforms.

'Remember when'

'Remember when'

'Friends for ever'

'We'll always be'

I write 'We'll always be…' I'm meant to write
'friends', I'm meant to write 'Keep in touch'. But I…
can't. Because I know it isn't true. Like these girls,
running around with their marker pens are not, I
suddenly realise… are not my friends. And suddenly I
feel… so old. So very old. So I just leave it: 'We'll
always be.'

I don't go. For the whole last week since Scarlett – I
haven't gone in. I have a restlessness in my stomach
like I'm pregnant. Which I'm not. Which is
impossible. It is not the immaculate conception. Unless
it is. Unless I am being punished. Maybe she has put a
curse on me.

I write these emails where I – I don't actually send
them to her. But I. I write them. And it makes me feel
better. I am not a bad person. I am not Osama bin
Laden or Simon Cowell. I am just… a girl.

I have decided to move to Canada. My mother has
gone apeshit, thinks I've totally lost it. Not even like
city Canada. Like proper Canada. Like I'm going to go
live on a reserve with the indigenous people and go
ice-fishing and there's no internet and no phone
reception and I'm going to live in an igloo. 'What will
you do for money?' my mother wants to know. I won't
need money though because I'll trade in furs and I'll
hunt for my food. It's just something I need to do.

I've accidentally been assigned a flat with all boys
instead of girls for September. I explained to Mum that
I called and it's too late and there's nothing they can
do. So I can't change. But I never actually called.

I start crying. Out of nowhere just. And I don't know
why. Maybe I'm just sad to be leaving all the girls.

I start a Facebook group. For the St Helen's girls. No one else is allowed. So that we can stay in touch.

I lift up my shirt and take a photo of myself in the mirror. I don't know why. I just do it. And then delete it.

I commit suicide.
Oh sorry not, not like for real. I mean Facebook suicide. I delete my account, my photos. Everything.

One of my hens is dead. Fox got her. And it's weird cos she was like Mother Hen, the one in charge. But the fox obviously didn't give a toss about the pecking order. Which kind of just defeats the whole purpose, doesn't it?

Something has changed. I'm looking at the signatures on my shirt to figure out who still needs to sign and it's like I recognise the names, but I don't know them. Does that make sense? And when did everything change? I try to rewind, to find and replay that moment when it changed… but I don't know when it was. When it was that I decided I no longer want to hang around girls like that. I can't find it. The video has been deleted, or violated the user agreement. It doesn't exist.

And I want to take a photo. A group photo.

Oh yes, one final photo of us all together!

Gather round!

But we're suddenly temporarily distracted by a group of boys who go running across the field in their pants.

There is no logic to why they do this. To why a group of boys are laughing, screaming, jumping on each other in their underwear.

Us girls sign school shirts. The boys run around half-naked. It's in our DNA somewhere.

And it confirms for me what Miss left out in history lessons. That while girls have got more intelligent over generations, boys have become more stupid.

And I'm a bit jealous. I want to run around in my pants instead of standing here with a marker pen. I imagine doing it. Just do it. Right now. Strip off, run over and join the boys.
But they're too far. They're gone. And I've missed my chance.

A photo! Gather round!

The St Helen's girls.

My mother told me these girls are my friends for life.

One final photo. To use for the Facebook page.

A photo with smiles, and her arm round her waist

And her arm round her waist

And her arm round her waist

And her –

But someone is not here today with stomach cramps

And someone is walking away to the toilets

And someone says it's a stupid idea

And someone says she doesn't want to be in the photo, she'll take it

Which defeats the purpose because it has to be all of us

And someone says: 'Well it's not going to be all of us anyway.' And I don't know what she means by that. Like if she means it's my fault somehow. Like what does she mean by that?

Like would it kill her to be in a photo?

And those of us who are standing there with our arms round someone's waist just start looking kinda dumb, cos no one's taking the photo

So she takes her arm off her waist

And she takes her arm off her waist

And she

And the moment is gone, and there will not be a photo, which is actually really frustrating because we will look back on this moment and we won't remember it because we will not have a photo. And that's just a wasted opportunity, really

And I don't get why some of the girls have to spoil it for the rest of us

Why they can't just go along

Be a team player

There's always a couple who have to stand apart from the crowd just to prove a point. To feel individual. Which is pretty pathetic if you ask me

Girls like that ruin it for everyone

Bitches.

Sluts.

And so I just start snapping photos.

Flash

Flash

Flash.

But then

Crack.

Smash.

It falls.

It breaks.

Which is called pathetic fallacy. Or foreshadow. Or something. I dunno. All I know is I will never be with all the girls together again.

Change. Forty-five years old.

I am with all the girls together again.

We are in the dining hall.

Twenty five-year-olds are singing 'sleigh bells ring are you listening?'

We are forty-five years old. We are at St Helen's. They are tearing down the school, building a fresh new state-of-the-art all the bells and whistles blah blah.

And so all the former St Helen's girls are invited to come for a reunion of sorts.

There is about two hundred in all. Everyone from our year has made an appearance. And it's nice to see the old faces. Because over the years, despite our best intentions – well life gets in the way doesn't it.

And I'm not sure why I've come.

I can't believe I've come.

Maybe out of curiosity.

Maybe out of some weird twisted obligation.

Maybe I think I'm going to give her all the unsent emails I've written over the years.

Maybe to see her entrance. Like she promised.

And after the current reception class finishes singing we have some time to catch up. To reminisce about school shows when I was the lead.

And that boy we used to fancy… um Robert? Roger? Can't remember but one of the girls ran in to him and apparently he's fat and bald and works in IT.

And someone still sees Tyler, who used to have the parties, who has a much younger boyfriend who is a model. Go figure.

And it's like no time has passed at all. It's like we are sixteen again. Except that I *have* a sixteen-year-old. A daughter.

My daughter's ten.

Mine are six and eight.

Mine are twelve and thirteen, God help me. Can I fast-forward please?

My three are all boys. I still don't know what to do with them.

I had my tubes tied.

My girls are at the age where I say: how was school? And all I get is 'fine'. I've stopped trying to get more out of them. Futile.

And I look around for her. But she's not there. I don't think so anyway.

And as we're heading to the car park, I see the reception girls in the playground. But something's wrong.

One of them has built a snowman, but someone is trying to destroy it. A boy.

And I wonder if I should intervene. Should say something. But what would I say?

So we just watch.

And then suddenly without planning, without saying a word, the girls start to link arms. All twenty of them.

Making a barrier between the boy and the snowman.

Her arm in her arm

Her arm in her arm

Her arm in her arm

Her arm in her arm

Her arm in her arm

Her arm in her arm

Her arm in her arm

Her arm in her arm

Her arm in her arm

Her arm in her arm

Her arm in her arm

Her arm in her arm

Her arm in her arm

Her arm in her arm

Her arm in her arm

Her arm in her arm

Her arm in her arm

Her arm in her arm

Her arm in her arm

The GIRLS *stand at the front of the stage like at the start, facing the audience in a line – their arms linked.*

And then one of them speaks, the smallest of the group:

'Us girls stick together.
Think you can break through us, boy?
Go on. Just you try.'

End.

PRONOUN

For Danny

238

Author's Note

While the play was written for a cast of seven, with the same actors who play the main characters also playing the additional characters, larger casts could certainly have separate actors play these roles (or could increase the number of the Senior Management Team). So the play could have anywhere from seven up to any number of actors. In either case, there should be a heightened awareness with the latter characters that these are young actors playing adults – that this is performance: when they first appear, we watch an actor put on an apron to become Mum, an actor put on a doctor's coat, etc. But once they're 'dressed', they needn't worry about playing the gender or age of their character, merely the truth of that moment.

Dean is a transgender male – meaning Dean was born a girl, and is biologically female, but identifies as male, and in transition to becoming male. In the stage directions, Dean is referred to as *he* as this is the pronoun that Dean, if he were real and not in a play, would go by and identify with.

Set – it's imagined that somewhere on stage (or maybe the whole stage) is a closet/wardrobe/clothing rack... or maybe a dress-up chest. Somewhere from which the actors get items of clothing on stage to become the adult characters.

Also, on stage is a large poster of James Dean from *Rebel Without a Cause*.

The play takes place over thirteen months from May of one year to June of the following year.

Acknowledgements

Anthony Banks, Rob Watt, Lucy Deere, Paula Hamilton, Tom Lyons, and all the staff at the National Theatre. James Grieve and Michael Fentiman.

Tanya Tillett at The Agency.

The staff and young people at Gendered Intelligence. Also the brilliant resources on their website, particularly 'A Guide for Parents and Family Members of Trans People Living in the UK' and 'A Guide for Young Trans People in the UK'.

Jamie, for the insight, openness and anecdotes.

Rebel Without a Cause by Steward Stern, Irving Shulman and Nicholas Ray, from whom I have quoted lines. And the screenplay for *Breakfast at Tiffany's* by George Axelrod, based on the book by Truman Capote, for the same reason.

The many young people who took part in the premiere productions of this play. You give me hope for the future.

E.P.

Pronoun was commissioned as part of the 2014 National Theatre Connections Festival and premiered by youth theatres across the UK, including a performance at the National Theatre in July 2014.

Each year the National Theatre asks ten writers to create new plays to be performed by young theatre companies all over the country. From Scotland to Cornwall and Northern Ireland to Norfolk, Connections celebrates great new writing for the stage – and the energy, commitment and talent of young theatremakers.

www.nationaltheatre.org.uk/connections

Characters

A Note on Punctuation

A forward slash (/) denotes a line that is interrupted, and the point of interruption.

A dash (–) is a cut-off, sometimes of one's own thought with a different thought (not a pause or beat).

An ellipsis (…) is a loss or search for words.

A lack of punctuation at the end of a line means the next line comes right in.

Words in square brackets are not spoken, but there to clarify a line's meaning.

Scene One

AMY's bedroom. JOSH *wears a dress. He looks in a full-length mirror.*

KYLE. What the fuck?

JOSH. For nothing in the world.

KYLE. What?

JOSH. For nothing in the world, will I swear not to arm myself.

KYLE. What?

JOSH. Will I swear not to arm myself and put on a man's dress.

KYLE. Josh.

JOSH. Who said that?

KYLE. What?

JOSH. Who said that?

KYLE. Said what? Josh, why are you –

JOSH. For nothing in the world, will I swear not to arm myself and put on a man's dress. Who said it?

KYLE. Rihanna?

JOSH. Joan of Arc.

KYLE. …Okay.

JOSH. But in history, sir overlooked that bit, why she was actually condemned to death, y'know.

KYLE. Josh?

JOSH. Yeah?

KYLE. You're wearing a dress.

JOSH. Yeah.

KYLE. Okay.

JOSH. Yeah.

KYLE. So you're aware, you're aware, that you're wearing –
I thought maybe.

JOSH. No. I'm aware.

KYLE. Right.

JOSH. Amy rang when you were downstairs. They're out of
pineapple so she's replaced it with mushrooms, which in my
mind isn't really a comparable replacement, one's a fruit and
the other's – and she's got it without cheese, which actually
entirely defeats the purpose of ordering a pizza if you ask me.

KYLE. Dude, why the fuck are you wearing a dress?

JOSH. I dunno. I thought. Thought it would help. Understand,
y'know.

KYLE. And?

JOSH. Nothing.

KYLE. At least you look pretty.

JOSH. You think?

KYLE. Shows off your legs.

JOSH. Thought somehow, if I, like there'd be this moment, it
would just click, that I'd feel how she, how he… but I just
feel like a boy in a dress.

KYLE. You used to wear eyeliner and mascara.

JOSH. For like a week.

KYLE. Three as I recall.

JOSH. That's not the same.

KYLE. Your emo days.

JOSH. It's not the – this isn't how it was supposed to go. This
wasn't part of the plan.

KYLE. Every plan has variables, mate.

JOSH. You go away for a shitty two-week holiday for Easter
with your annoying family to some three-star shithole in
Benidorm, you expect to come home with a sunburn, you

expect to come home with diarrhoea, you expect to come home with a pen that has a picture of a woman on it whose clothes fall off every time you click it – what you do not expect when you come home is to find your sixteen-year-old best friend engaged and that your girlfriend is…

KYLE. Come here.

JOSH. No. What are you –

KYLE. It'll help. (*Puts eyeliner on* JOSH.)

JOSH. We were supposed to – there were so many things we were supposed to do, that we'd planned to do. After next year, gonna spend our gap year together. Travel Thailand.

KYLE. You still can. (*Gets lipstick, starts to put it on* JOSH.)

JOSH. How are we –

KYLE. Stop talking.

Push your lips together.

JOSH *looks in mirror.*

Anything?

JOSH. No.

KYLE *gets on one knee. Holds out a ring box.*

The fuck you doing?

KYLE. Joshua Robbins.

JOSH. Kyle.

KYLE. We've known each other a long time now.

JOSH. Kyle, get up.

KYLE. Ever since I first spotted you having pissed your pants by the sandpit in nursery, I knew. I knew then you were the one. Joshua Michael Robins, make me the happiest groom and be my best man? (*Opens box, it's a Haribo sweet.*)

JOSH *takes it, eats it.*

Is that a yes?

JOSH. I love you, man.

KYLE *picks* JOSH *up, spins him around, whooping.*

KYLE. It's gonna be ace. Here. (*Envelope.*)

JOSH. What's this?

KYLE. Your duties as best man. I've put a tick-list in.

JOSH.…Terrific.

JOSH *gets distracted by himself in the mirror again.*

KYLE. It'll be alright, man.

JOSH. It'll be great.

KYLE. I meant about.

JOSH. Oh.

KYLE. Josh?

JOSH. Yeah.

KYLE. Amy'll be back any minute, and [if] she finds you in her room she'll castrate you with her bare teeth. Trust me, I've got the teethmarks. It still hurts when I pee. (*Exits.*)

The song 'Everyday' by Buddy Holly begins to play.

JOSH *takes off the dress. On the other side of the mirror (somewhere else),* DEAN *enters in boxers and a sports bra/vest top. Faces himself in the mirror. The effect being that by this point* JOSH *too is in his underwear – the two of them looking at each other through the mirror.*

Beat.

JOSH *exits.*

Scene Two

Continuous from Scene One.

DEAN*'s bedroom. A large poster of* JAMES DEAN *from* Rebel Without a Cause *on the wall.*

DEAN *retrieves a needle. Fills it with liquid from a small tube. Squirts the end of the needle gently. And reaches round and confidently injects himself in his bum cheek.*

He then wraps a large roll of bandage around his chest, binding his breasts so they're flat. Puts a T-shirt on. Looks in mirror.

Puts another T-shirt over top of the first.

Gets a sock. Puts it in his underwear, adjusts it.

Puts on some skinny jeans and Converse.

Hair product in his short hair.

Douses himself in Lynx. The ritual is complete.

JAMES DEAN *appears. The music stops.*

JAMES DEAN. Hey, kid.

DEAN. I look crap.

JAMES DEAN. Take it easy.

DEAN. Do I look crap?

JAMES DEAN. You look swell.

DEAN. Fuck off swell.

JAMES DEAN. You look a bit like me, kid.

> DEAN *looks at the poster of* JAMES DEAN, *then at the* JAMES DEAN *standing there.*

DEAN. You're totally photoshopped.

JAMES DEAN. There was no such thing then. It's all me. C'mon. It's time for your jab, buddy.

> *Draping arm around him, the two looking in the mirror.*

> DEAN *throws off his arm, feeling insecure when looking at them both side by side.*

DEAN. I already took it. Buddy.

JAMES DEAN. Whoa. I'm not the enemy, Dean.

DEAN. No, you're just some dumb dead guy I talk to.

JAMES DEAN. No need to get personal 'bout it.

Shouting is heard.

What's that?

DEAN, *unhappy with his appearance, changes the T-shirt for a button-down shirt instead.*

DEAN. *That* is why no one should get married. *That* is why some people shouldn't be allowed to have children. *That* is the alien life forms also known as Mum and Dad.

JAMES DEAN. 'She, she says one thing, he says another, and everybody changes back again,' right?

DEAN. Some things haven't changed.

DEAN *looking at himself in profile again.*

JAMES DEAN. Too big.

DEAN. What do you know?

JAMES DEAN. Well I've got one for a start.

DEAN. You're not even here.

JAMES DEAN. You're the one talking to me.

DEAN. It's the T. It's messing with my head.

Beat.

Takes the sock out from his trousers.

JAMES DEAN. Told you.

DEAN (*throws it to him*). Put a sock in it will you.

JAMES DEAN. Touché.

DEAN *puts a smaller sock in.* JAMES DEAN *lights a cigarette.*

DEAN. Don't you know smoking can kill you?

JAMES DEAN *laughs.* [*I'm already dead.*]

Touché.

JAMES DEAN *joins him at the mirror. Both of them side by side checking themselves out in profile. Fixing their shirts.*

DANI *enters. She stands there for a moment watching before* DEAN *notices her.*

Beat. JAMES DEAN *watches the rest of the scene unseen by* DANI.

DANI. They're shouting as per usual.

'Once upon a time'

This is clearly a game they used to play/story they used to tell as kids.

DEAN. 'there were two kids who learned they were in fact royalty'

DANI. 'who were in fact abducted by the people they thought were Mum and Dad'

DEAN. 'so they left their screaming parents and went to live in the castle'

BOTH. 'and lived happily ever after.'

Beat. DANI *still lingers in the doorway.*

DEAN. You can come in.

DANI. Can I?

DEAN. You've always been –

DANI. It's different now.

DEAN. …No.

DANI. Yes.

DEAN. …Yes.

DANI. Looks good. The shirt.

DEAN. You think?

DANI. Matches your eyes.

DEAN. / Thanks

DANI. / Almost wouldn't know.

Almost.

Doesn't it bother you?

DEAN.…No.

DANI. No. You don't even know what I'm asking. *No.* Some things don't change. *No.* You were always scared of me. Meant to be the other way around. You're the older one. And even now.

DEAN. What do you want, Dani?

DANI. Doesn't it bother you? How everyone's chatting shit about you?

DEAN. No.

DANI. No?

DEAN. I couldn't give a damn.

DANI. *Couldn't give a damn.* You're so goddamn *American* sometimes.

DEAN. I don't care.

DANI. Well I do. I give a damn. You remember at primary. When people were chatting shit about you. Saying about you and what's his name, Brad, douchebag, saying how you'd, and I stood up for you. Even though you were the older one. When they were saying 'Hear your big sister's a right' – I stood up for you, fought for you. No one said nothing to me 'bout you after that, once I told 'em what's what, showed 'em what's what.

DEAN. Okay.

DANI. But now I can't say nothing. Cos this time the shit they're talking's true.

DEAN. I'm sorry that you're… I'd never want you to… because of me.

DANI....I know.

Pause.

Let's have a look at you then.

Are you happy?

DEAN. Yeah. I am. I'm. Getting there.

DANI. Okay. (*Goes to leave. Changes her mind. Turns back.*)

Dean?

DEAN. Yeah?

DANI. You can pretend all you want, but you'll never have a dick.

Scene Three

MUM *and* DAD *appear. We watch as a male actor puts one thing on from the closet – e.g. apron – to become* MUM, *and a female actor puts one thing on – e.g. tie or hat – to become* DAD. *They speak to the audience.*

MUM. Once upon a time there was a girl.

DAD. We'd read to her every night.

MUM. Once upon a time there was a little girl who lived in a house.

DAD. She'd cry all the time. Nights, days, you name it.

MUM. Isn't anything else to name. Nights and days. That's everything.

DAD. She cried all the time.

MUM. First day wouldn't stop crying, in the hospital. Nurse said, I remember, she said 'Think this is bad, wait till she's a teenager.'

DAD. Slamming doors.

MUM. You have hopes for your child.

DAD. Headphones attached to her ears.

MUM. Dreams for your child.

DAD. Don't even know what her ears look like any more.

MUM. Big plans for your child.

DAD. Weeks without saying a word to us.

MUM. And you plan for all that other stuff, the awkward years
they want nothing to do with you, but this.

DAD. Silence.

MUM. This you don't plan for. This is not in the handbook.

DAD. Can't remember the last time you actually saw her.

MUM. It's not even in the secondary reading.

DAD. Maybe she was never there.

MUM. After the incident. When she was thirteen. We went on
this course.

DAD. It was counselling.

MUM. To try to understand why she tried to... well...

Beat. This is uncomfortable for them.

DAD. We all went. The whole family. To Dr Learner.

MUM. She wasn't a doctor.

DAD. She had a PhD.

MUM. In anthropology.

DAD. Sociology.

MUM. She sent us on this course. They may as well have
called it the Centre for Failed Parents, the sorry lot of us,
doing role-plays.

DAD. As I recall you refused to take part.

MUM. I am forty years old – I think it's a bit ridiculous I should
have to prance around finding my inner teen. This is the best
part, they had these situations, and I had to play my

daughter, while some out-of-work actor gets trolleyed in to play me. Show me how to communicate with my child. Girl's half my age, can't even get a walk-on part in *Hollyoaks* and she's telling me how to be a mother.

DAD. The point is

MUM. The point is *this* was not covered on the course. Not even mentioned. I should go ask for a refund.

DAD. It's not like we knew then anyway that's what this was all about, why she – he, he. I find the pronouns so confusing. Spend half the day practising, in my head, so I don't get it wrong.

MUM. Once upon a time there was a girl. She was breastfed and burped and rocked to sleep and everything the manual tells you to do. And she grew up and became a princess.

DAD *gives her a look.*

What?

Scene Four

Glastonbury Festival. DEAN *and* LAURA *by a tent. Shorts, hoodies and wellies.* AMY *returns with beers. She wears leather boots.*

AMY. Think I just saw sir.

LAURA. Is that one of the bands? Are they cute?

AMY. As in Sir sir. As in Mr Woolner.

LAURA. Eww, isn't that like, isn't there like an age limit? To ban teachers' entry? It's not on seeing teachers in the summer hols. Glastonbury should be off-limits.

DEAN. How'd you get beers?

LAURA. Last thing I want to see in my hols is Mr Woolner putting on factor forty-five in a vest top.

AMY. Sister's ID. I think he's kinda cute.

LAURA (*fixes hair, looking round*). Who?

AMY. Mr Woolner.

DEAN. Gross.

LAURA. Mega-gross. And you're not allowed to say stuff like that – you're engaged.

AMY. He was wearing a motorbike jacket.

LAURA. Ew, literally mid-life crisis. When I reach middle-age, I'm going to embrace it. Start wearing polo necks, and my hair in a bun, and big pants.

AMY. God I'd rather die.

LAURA. No you wouldn't.

AMY. I would. Literally.

LAURA. No. Not literally.

AMY. Literally. I'm gonna die young, forever remembered like this, never age, like all the greats – Buddy Holly, Kurt Cobain, James Dean. Forever young and beautiful.

LAURA. Yeah, but those are all guys. Can you think of one famous girl who went young?

AMY. Amy Winehouse.

LAURA. Yeah, but do you really, I mean honestly, Amy Winehouse? Do you really wanna go out like her?

AMY. Thanks, Laura, now I'm now destined to a long unhappy future growing old. At least I'll age gracefully. No big pants for me.

LAURA. No, sorry. Men age like red wine. Women age like milk.

AMY. Did you actually just – you can't say things like that any more, this isn't 1950.

LAURA. Speaking of which we've thought of the perfect theme for your wedding.

DEAN. We have?

AMY. There's a theme?

LAURA. As your maids of honour

AMY. Maid and male of honour

LAURA. We thought that

DEAN. We haven't actually discussed this actually.

AMY. I don't know that I want a theme.

LAURA. You *have* to have a theme. Literally everyone has one. Everyone.

AMY. Maybe we should check with Kyle. The wedding's all kind of his thing, you know.

LAURA. But you're the bride – when will he be here?

DEAN. Kyle's coming?

AMY. Didn't I say? They got last-minute tickets.

DEAN. They? Who's they?

Pause.

Fuck you, Amy.

AMY. I could've sworn I told you.

DEAN. Fuck you, Amy.

AMY. Can't we all be grown-ups. I mean I'm getting married for God's sake.

DEAN. Good for you. You grow up then.

AMY. Shit. I'm getting married. Bit scary when you say it out loud.

DEAN. You could've warned me, Amy.

AMY. Shit.

LAURA. You literally haven't talked to each other in months. You gonna spend the last year of college ignoring each other? Speaking for myself, just me, it's a bit awkward for the rest of us, don't you think, Amy?

AMY. I'm gonna be a wife.

LAURA. I'm happy to be the mediator. My mum's a psychologist y'know.

DEAN. I remember. She came in to give us all counselling in Year 10 when the science teacher ran off with that Year 11 girl.

AMY. Whatever happened to her?

LAURA. She became a Scientologist. Had twins.

DEAN. How do you know this?

LAURA. My mum counselled the teacher.

AMY. I thought he's in prison.

LAURA. No, he's in Slough.

KYLE *and* JOSH *enter with bags of food.*

KYLE. If food be the music of love, eat on.

AMY. Thank God, I'm starving.

JOSH. We've got Tesco's finest breadsticks, falafel, and hummus.

LAURA. Didn't you bring any real food?

JOSH. Oh. Hi.

DEAN. Oh. Hi.

Awkward pause. AMY *has already dug into the hummus.*

AMY. Hummus anyone?

No?

LAURA. Did you bring any sausage rolls?

KYLE. Amy's a vegan.

AMY. Sweetie, I'm not *a* vegan. I'm vegan.

KYLE. Well yeah.

AMY. Well no. It's derogatory. You don't say *a* black, *a* gay.

KYLE. I do actually.

LAURA. Oh my God, the wedding's not going to be vegan is it?

AMY (*simultaneous*). Yes.

KYLE (*simultaneous*). No.

LAURA. It doesn't really fit with the theme though.

KYLE. What theme?

AMY. So, what, we're going to have dead animals on every table are we?

KYLE. My mum just wants roast chicken, you make it sound like we're gonna have some taxidermy centrepieces.

JOSH. That'd be pretty cool actually. (*Off* AMY*'s 'kill you' look*.) Or not.

LAURA. We were thinking it could be

DEAN. Again there's no we

LAURA. Like a *Grease* wedding.

JOSH. As in a fry-up?

LAURA. As in the musical.

KYLE. I hate musicals. There's just so much… singing.

LAURA. Well it could just be like a fifties theme.

AMY. You just want to wear that stupid poodle skirt you bought and can't wear.

LAURA. They were supposed to make a comeback.

DEAN. Fifties, I like it.

KYLE. We could get like a fifties band.

AMY. Or maybe you could just get some battery hens and force them to play the bongos with their broken beaks and I can wear a piglet-skin dress with leather shoes!

LAURA. You're actually wearing leather shoes. Literally. Like right now.

KYLE. You actually are though, babe.

AMY. I had them before, okay! God! I'm not marrying you! (*Stomps off.*)

KYLE. Wait. Was she being serious? Shit. Babes! (*Goes after her.*)

LAURA. I hope they're okay. The venue's non-refundable is all. And I've already cut the price tag off my skirt.

DEAN. People get married for less.

LAURA. I better go mediate. (*Exits.*)

JOSH *attempts to set up the tent. He quickly becomes exasperated with it and its lack of cooperation. Beats the tent with one of the poles.*

JOSH. Dumb-ass piece of… piece of… plastic, piece of carrier bag!

DEAN. Easy, cowboy, or someone's gonna call a hotline for victims of tent abuse.

JOSH. She was asking for it, your honour. She'd unzip the door to anyone.

Sorry, not funny.

DEAN. No.

It's inside out.

JOSH. How do you mean?

DEAN. The bit that's currently on the inside should be on the outside.

JOSH. Oh.

He begins to put it up. Still struggling. DEAN *wordlessly assists him, and together they quickly put it up.*

Thanks. I would have managed eventually y'know?

DEAN. No. You forget we've been camping before.

Beat.

JOSH. So you're talking to me?

DEAN. So you're talking to me?

JOSH. I never stopped talking to you.

DEAN. I never stopped talking to you.

JOSH. Then why weren't you talking to me?

DEAN. Cos you weren't talking to me.

JOSH. Only cos I thought you weren't talking to me.

DEAN. Why would you think that?

JOSH. Cos you sent a text and that was it.

DEAN. That was it cos you never wrote back.

JOSH. What was I meant to write?

Pause.

DEAN. You're staring. What?

JOSH. Spent the last few months avoiding eye contact that I've
not properly got to really... you've got the same eyes.

DEAN. No shit, Josh.

JOSH. The rest of you, it's you, but not. But you still look...
still look –

DEAN (*defensive*). *Look* what?

JOSH. Look fit. You still look fit. But as a boy. You're a fit boy.

Beat.

I'm not gay.

DEAN. I know.

JOSH. Just saying, cos don't want you to think

DEAN. I know, Josh. I know.

JOSH. I know you do.

I bloody hate festivals. Buncha smelly muddy pissheads in
wellies pretending to have a good time.

DEAN. So why'd you come?

Beat. [*Because I knew you'd be here.*]

Your tent's a bit crap. Sure it's gonna keep you dry?

JOSH. Got nowhere else to sleep. Do I?

He looks to his tent.

Is that you? Inside out? Outside in?

DEAN. Maybe.

JOSH. I'm trying here, Izz – Dean. I'm trying. Cos I don't, you don't just wake up one morning and…!

DEAN. I did. I did just wake up one morning and.

JOSH. Well that's that then.

DEAN. I don't have to explain myself to you.

JOSH. No. But you should. You should want to. As your, as your former

DEAN. As the artist formerly known as boyfriend.

JOSH. Do you always have to make a joke of everything? If you were gonna change something, couldn't it at least have been your sarcasm?

Why are you smiling? It's not funny.

DEAN. It is. Us. Here. This. I dunno.

JOSH. Right. Well you have a little laugh. I'm gonna join the others.

He goes to leave, but stops when DEAN *starts speaking.*

DEAN. I woke up.

I woke up. I showered.

I woke up. I showered. And then the mirror was just there. Suddenly there. Only it had always been there, but I'd, somehow, I'd managed to never look. To never really look. Little tricks to avoid myself. But this day, I was there reflecting back, naked. And it took a minute, prolly only seconds, but felt like ages before I realised it was me. My body. And without even thinking I crossed my arms, have you ever noticed – how I always do that? For as long as I can remember I've always been doing that. And I tried to make them go away. I tried to look away. Because I'd never really looked. But I couldn't. This was me. And I hated it. Because it wasn't me. Do you understand? My little cousin Adam, you met him at my aunt's wedding, and she's always complaining because Adam won't leave it alone – he's five and he won't stop playing with his willy. Always investigating. I never did. Never investigated my own body. Why? Why is that? I'm standing in front of this mirror, the steam fading away, making the image clearer and clearer, this girl, this woman staring back at me. And it was like everything clicked into place. People say your life flashes before your eyes before you die, well I wasn't dying but suddenly everything in my life was playing back.

MUM *and* DAD *appear, speak to audience. They can't be seen by* DEAN *or* JOSH.

MUM. My mother gave her a doll for her sixth birthday, the one, what's the one, everyone had it, everyone had it but it was hard to get, but my mother had gone all over town just to get one, and she opened it up and started screaming: 'I don't want a doll! I don't want a doll!' Threw it at Granny. It landed in the lasagne. We laughed about it the next day. But. Well, the lasagne was ruined.

DAD. When she was five, I took her to the toilets, at a fair, into the men's, cos Mum wasn't there. At first she tried to use the urinal. A week later she asked: 'Daddy, when am I going to grow a willy?'

MUM *and* DAD *disappear again.*

DEAN. And in the mirror it all just suddenly made sense. Why I'd always felt a bit… wrong. And suddenly in my head, everything was… right. I'd never investigated, because I knew I wouldn't like what I found.

Music can be heard distantly. JOSH *suddenly does an impromptu dance move – cartwheel, flip, weird dance?*

What was that?

JOSH. Dunno. Couldn't think of what to say…

DEAN. I can't believe they're getting married. Christ. They should be locked up.

JOSH. Both their parents are letting them.

DEAN. They should be locked up too.

JOSH. I'm still in love with you.

Pause.

Then thunder. It starts to piss it down.

Shit.

Each goes into their respective tents.

Shit, there's a – I'm getting – there's a bloody hole.

DEAN. It's just water.

JOSH. This is a new shirt. It's a bloody bathtub in here.

DEAN. If you're gonna be a girl about it. Just come here.

He goes and sits in DEAN*'s tent. They're close together. Their legs touching.*

JOSH. You've got leg hair. Is that the um, the hormones?

DEAN. I've always had leg hair, douchebag. I just used to shave it.

JOSH. Right. Yeah.

They watch the rain.

JOSH *watches* DEAN.

DEAN. What?

JOSH. I bloody hate festivals.

DEAN. Yeah. Me too.

Scene Five

*Some actors enter the stage. Put on suit jackets or ties or
something smart. This is the school's* SENIOR MANAGEMENT
TEAM. *Divide the lines amongst actors as desired.*

SMT. We the school

We the SMT of the school

must tell you

want to tell you

that we one hundred percent support you

one hundred percent of the way.

We the SMT

need to stress

want to stress

that we are a very tolerant school

meaning we will show no tolerance

for those who are not tolerant

meaning we're tolerant of everyone

except those who aren't tolerant.

Meaning we the SMT

and you

we're all going to go through this together.

It's a first for all of us.

We're all transitioning together.

Well not literally.

Not literally, no, we won't actually

my wife wouldn't...

Not actually

not literally

but in a manner of speaking.

What we mean

the key

yes the key. This is a key

to the staff toilets

should you

if you feel

if you'd like to use those

if it would make you more comfortable.

It's up to you.

Absolutely. We're not saying

we're definitely not saying you can't use the student loos

definitely not

meaning where you pee is up to you

where you pee is your business

pee where you like.

Within reason.

Within reason.

Pee wherever suits you.

Not literally. You can't actually start peeing in the corridor.

What it boils down to

what it comes down to is…

Ofsted are coming.

Literally.

Actually.

Some time in the next school year.

And there'll be an assembly for them.

Not *for*, just while they're here.

For the students, we don't do things just for Ofsted.

About diversity, and inclusivity, and tolerance.

And we, the SMT, would like you, Dean, to make a speech.

What do you say?

Scene Six

Boys' toilets at school. DEAN *pees at a urinal.* JOSH *watches.* DEAN *finishes, and turns around.*

DEAN. How long have you been standing there?

JOSH. Why are you avoiding me?

DEAN. Were you watching me? That's a bit –

JOSH. Been trying to speak to you all week, you haven't answered my texts, I have to follow you into the boys' toilets to actually get you to talk to me.

DEAN. That's a bit

JOSH. Determined.

DEAN. I was gonna go with stalkerish.

JOSH. Ever since the festival

DEAN. There's never any soap in here.

JOSH. I thought it was good, I thought we were

DEAN. Why is there never any soap?

JOSH. And then in the morning you went all

DEAN. You don't have any hand sanitiser, do you?

JOSH. Do you have to be such a dick about it?

You just gonna pretend nothing happened? That we didn't – ?

DEAN. Yes that's exactly what I'm going to do.

JOSH. I don't get you, Dean.

DEAN. Sometimes I don't get me either, alright.

Can you move please? I have class.

JOSH. No. Not until we – you don't get to just, just make all the decisions. You don't get to pretend it didn't happen. I, I am part of that decision.

DEAN. Josh, move.

JOSH. No.

DEAN. You gonna trap me in here?

JOSH. Yes. Yes that's exactly what I'm going to do. (*Stands in a pose as barrier, reposes to something tougher – hands on hips? – reposes again, can't quite get right.*)

DEAN *laughs*.

Don't laugh. This is serious. This is, this is kidnapping, this is illegal, this is this is, this is fucking *no one's leaving this fucking toilet till I get some answers*!

Beat. He realises how ridiculous he is.

Christ, I can't even pull off a takeover in the school toilets. How am I ever going to be a detective?

Your fly.

DEAN*'s fly is undone*.

DEAN. Thanks, Miss Marple.

(*Re: crotch/peeing.*) It's a tube thing before you ask. That's how.

JOSH. I wasn't going to ask.

DEAN. Yes you were.

JOSH. No.

DEAN. You were thinking it.

JOSH. I was thinking it, but I wasn't going to ask.

Beat. They smile.

DEAN *takes an audition poster off the wall/stall door.*

DEAN. The Year 9s are doing *Twelfth Night* again.

Woolner has a limited repertoire.

JOSH. Worked for us, didn't it?

'Want me to help you practise your lines?'

DEAN. You're such a cheeseball.

JOSH. Rehearsed it the whole night before. Couldn't even look at you. 'Want me to help you practise your lines?'

DEAN. You're an idiot.

JOSH.
> '…what a deal of scorn looks beautiful
> In the contempt and anger of his lip!'

DEAN.
> 'We men may say more, swear more,
> But indeed our shows are more than will; for still we
>   prove
> Much in our vows, but little in our love.'

JOSH. I thought we were good.

DEAN. Your acting was a bit ropey.

JOSH. At the festival. I thought we were back on track. When we

DEAN. I'd been drinking.

JOSH. You invited me to sleep in your tent.

DEAN. Yours had turned into a wading pool.

JOSH. You said, after, you said how we'd still go away gap year. 'Course' you said. Go to Thailand like we planned. Bum around on the beach, get shitfaced, bathe in the sea, go see the Lady Boys of Bangkok, / swim in the

DEAN. / I definitely never said anything about the Lady Boys of / Bangkok

JOSH. / and then we get back to school and you go all –

I won't just pretend it didn't happen. The festival.

DEAN. But you want to pretend it's the same as before. Like nothing's changed.

JOSH. That's not true.

DEAN. You're not gay, Josh. You said it yourself.

JOSH. So?

DEAN. So! What do you mean so?

JOSH. I mean so. Why do you have to put a label on everything? I want you. What does the rest of it matter?

DEAN. It just. It matters.

JOSH. What are you so afraid of?

DEAN. I don't know. I don't…

I hated *Twelfth Night* you know.

JOSH. What?

DEAN. I'm just saying.

Everyone all happy, getting married, just hated it. And that line. When Viola says: *Conceal me what I am*. I always thought it should be: *Conceal me what I'm not. Conceal me what I'm not*.

This is who I am, Josh. It can't be like before. I'm trying to protect you.

JOSH. From what?

DEAN. Me. Them. It'll be worse for you, Josh. Worse for you than me. They'll give you a harder time than me.

JOSH. Fuck 'em. Fuck 'em.

DEAN. And if it's not them, it'll be me. The hormones, they're, I'm moody, and tired, and my sex drive is out of control –

JOSH. I can cope with that.

DEAN. And I'm, emotionally, I'm on a fucking other planet, I'm a concrete wall, and when I'm not, I'm a goddamn waterfall, I just start, out of nowhere, and I've got like a hundred doctors, and my fucking parents, and my fucking sister, and the fucking school and their fucking equality policies they want *me* to update, and I'm a complete – like you said, I'm a complete dick. Okay? Right now, I'm just a, a complete fucking dick.

JOSH. Well be my fucking dick. Be my dick, Dean.

Beat. DEAN *takes* JOSH's *hands. They're back together.*

Some stories have a happy ending, Dean. You're allowed to give yourself a happy ending.

Scene Seven

MUM *and* DAD.

DAD. I bought lots of books.

MUM. I read her lots of books.

DAD. I like to read up on things to really understand, what's what – I'm a scientist, how my brain works.

MUM. You're not a – you work in computers.

DAD. Need to understand the logic. The whys and wherefores. Only no one really knows.

MUM. There's no science.

DAD. There are theories that it's the shape of the brain. The bed nucleus of the stria terminalis. Or could just be her environment. How she was nurtured.

MUM. No, we did everything by the book.

DAD. I've read every book on the subject. And you know what I learned in the end?

MUM. Once upon a time, there was a girl. The girl was given everything she was supposed to. Pretty dresses, and pretty toys, and pretty ballet slippers. And pink wallpaper.

DAD. Left her alone for a day, seven hours, she was ten. Walked to B&Q and back. We came home. She'd painted over all the wallpaper. She'd painted her room black.

MUM. Ballet class and gymnastics and horseback riding – we signed her up for everything, so don't give me your nurture bullshit. She sucked at my nipples for eighteen months. What the hell did you do?

DAD. There was a point I thought she might be – it crosses your mind as a parent – I thought she might be a lesbian.

MUM. We both did.

DAD. She was never a girly girl.

MUM. They were playing classics at the Picturehouse. She was thirteen, just after she – around the time of the counselling.

DAD. Dr Learner.

MUM. And so we made an effort. A family trip. *Rebel Without a Cause*. And she fell in love. Poster on her wall of James Dean. And I thought, yes, yes! Normal. This is what normal teenage girls do – they put posters on their wall.

DAD. Arrived one day. In the post. An A1 James Dean.

MUM. We followed the books and we succeeded.

DAD. Two months earlier she'd tried to kill herself. I think she'd self-harmed before, but we didn't know.

Pause.

MUM. Once upon a time…

Once upon…

There's a line in the film. *Rebel Without a Cause*. The dad of the girl says: 'All of a sudden she's a problem.' And she, the wife, says: 'She'll outgrow it dear, it's just the age. It's just the age where nothing fits.'

I've only seen the film once. But I still remember that line.

Scene Eight

DEAN*'s room and various doctors' offices. We watch three actors put on doctor's coats to become* MONROE, BOGART *and* BRANDO. *The scene should become more and more physical and surreal as it goes on. It should feel by the end that* DEAN *is engaged in a workout.*

MONROE. Diagnosis is important, to get access to treatment

BOGART. Transgender, Gender Dysphoria

BRANDO. Gender Identity Disorder

MONROE. Gender non-conformity.

BOGART. Assessments:

MONROE. Psychodiagnostic and psychiatric

BOGART. Social

BRANDO. Physical.

MONROE. To prepare you for

BOGART. Full transition

MONROE. Treatment

BRANDO. Surgery.

BOGART. Take a seat

MONROE. Take a seat

BRANDO. Take a seat.

JAMES DEAN. Look how you're sitting. Lean back. Like you own the place. More.

But don't slouch.

Put an arm on the back of the chair.

Let your wrist flop. Not that much.

Open your legs. Guys take up a lot of room.

Yeah. Sorta. Look, watch me, kid.

Your turn.

DEAN *copies his sit.*

You look like you're constipated.

DEAN. It's easy for you, alright. It's natural. You don't need to think about it.

JAMES DEAN. You think this is natural? It's all performance, kid. I learned it. Now try again.

MONROE. When did you first have dysphoric feelings?

BOGART. Will your parents be coming to any appointments? It would be useful to speak to them as well.

MONROE. Are you in a relationship? Girlfriend? Boyfriend?

BRANDO. I'll refer you to Dr Monroe

MONROE. I'll refer you to Dr Bogart

BOGART. I'll refer you to Dr Brando

BRANDO. It'll be just fine, Dean. Just breathe.

JAMES DEAN. Breathe deep. Gotta speak from the back of your throat, your chest.

Hum down, head down, then bring your head up.

Again.

Again.

Really open your throat.

MONROE. Need you to open up. Need to ask how it felt? How it feels?

JAMES DEAN. 'Boy if I had one day when I didn't have to be all confused and I didn't have to feel ashamed of everything. I felt that I belonged someplace, you know?'

DEAN. That's my favourite part of the film.

JAMES DEAN. Your turn.

DEAN (*American accent*). Boy if I had one day

JAMES DEAN. Not in my accent, crazy.

DEAN (*back in own accent*). Boy if I had one day

JAMES DEAN. Lower.

DEAN. Boy if I had one day

JAMES DEAN. Lower

DEAN. Boy if I had

JAMES DEAN. Guys got less inflection. More monotone.

DEAN. Boy if I had one day when I didn't have to be all confused and I didn't have to feel ashamed of everything. I felt that I belonged someplace, you know?

MONROE. I do. Yeah.

JAMES DEAN. Yeah. We're getting there.

MONROE. Dean. Can I ask about the scars on your arms?

DEAN *standing*. BRANDO *measures his chest*.

JAMES DEAN. What you doin' with your arms?

DEAN. I dunno!

JAMES DEAN. Monotone.

DEAN. I dunno.

JAMES DEAN. Well gotta put 'em somewhere. Put your hands in your pocket. Walk.

Not so straight, your hips'll sway. Imagine an invisible line.

DOCTORS *roll out the measuring tape on the floor*.

You wanna be walking a foot either side of that.

DEAN *does*.

BRANDO. Keep the partying to a minimum. Drugs, alcohol – they can mess with your testosterone.

JAMES DEAN. T-time.

Hands needle. DEAN *injects*.

BRANDO. Some of it's irreversible. You can expect

DOCTORS. Body-hair growth

   Scalpel hair loss

   Increased muscle mass

   Body-fat redistribution

   Skin oiliness

   Clitoral enlargement

JAMES DEAN. Lean back.

DOCTORS. Body-hair growth

JAMES DEAN. Hum down

DOCTORS. Scalpel hair loss

JAMES DEAN. Monotone

DOCTORS. Increased muscle mass

JAMES DEAN. Pocket

DOCTORS. Body-fat redistribution

JAMES DEAN. Invisible line

DOCTORS. Skin oiliness

JAMES DEAN. Lower

DOCTORS. Clitoral enlargement

JAMES DEAN. Again.

   Lean back

DOCTORS. Body-hair growth

JAMES DEAN. Hum down

DOCTORS. Scalpel hair loss

JAMES DEAN. Monotone

DOCTORS. Increased muscle mass

JAMES DEAN. Pocket

DOCTORS. Body-fat redistribution

JAMES DEAN. Invisible line

DOCTORS. Skin oiliness

JAMES DEAN. Lower

DOCTORS. Clitoral enlargement

JAMES DEAN. Again.

BOGART. Have you seen Dr Monroe yet?

> LAURA *and* JOSH *appear.*

JAMES DEAN (*keeps repeating underneath* LAURA, JOSH, *and* DOCTORS). Invisible, pocket, mono, lean, low, hum, T, again.

LAURA. Don't forget to bring a naughty parcel for the hen do. I've got her this hilarious penis-hat to wear all evening. It's gonna be a riot.

JOSH. Don't forget to bring booze for the stag. We've got him a naughty nurse's outfit he's got to wear all evening. And a fourteen-stone stripper. Gonna be brilliant.

BRANDO. For you it would be a bilateral mastectomy.

BOGART. Horizontal incisions across each breast.

MONROE. Peel skin

BRANDO. Remove mammary glands and fatty tissue

BOGART. Remove the areola, nipples

MONROE. Trim

BOGART. Then regraft them onto the chest in a male position

BRANDO. And you'll be home in time for supper.

MONROE. How does that sound?

JAMES DEAN *and* DOCTORS (*can be divided up or in unison*). Skin, trim, hair, T, lean, line, low, again.

> Skin, trim, hair, T, lean, low, again.

BRANDO. I can schedule the chest surgery for 12th of June.

DEAN. Perfect. I've got a wedding late June.

BRANDO. Haha. No, not this June. Two years' time.

DEAN. Two years?

BRANDO. See you then.

Things speed up.

JAMES DEAN, DOCTORS, LAURA *and* JOSH (*can be divided up, or in unison*). Skin, trim, hair, T, lean, line, low, penis-hat, stripper, again.

Skin, trim, hair, T, lean, line, low, penis-hat, stripper, again.

Again. Again. Again. Again. Again.

DEAN *emerges, stands calmly, collected. At ease with his male self.*

DEAN. I felt that I belonged someplace, you know?

Beat.

JAMES DEAN, DOCTORS, LAURA *and* JOSH *all disappear and are replaced with* MUM, DAD *and* PRIVATE DOCTOR.

MUM. We agreed to go along

DAD. Dean had found a doctor, a private doctor.

MUM. She was very nice. I don't know what I was expecting. Frankenstein or something.

PRIVATE DOCTOR. Lots of people go private for the same reason. Shorter wait times.

DAD. She explained the procedure.

MUM. She *was* very nice.

PRIVATE DOCTOR. August 30th of this year, okay, Dean?

Don't forget, you'll need to pay by the 29th.

Five thousand nine hundred twenty-five pounds.

MUM. Once upon a time there was a witch who could turn the princess into anything.

DAD. Photos. What it would look like after. Without...

MUM. And I'm sorry. If that's what she wants to do. If she wants to mutilate her – then that's her prerogative. But we're certainly not going to bankroll it. When Sharon's daughter got a tattoo, do you think she paid for it?

DAD. This isn't a tattoo.

MUM. No. It's worse.

DAD. And these photos. All these *after* photos. And I thought

MUM. I'm sorry.

DAD. All these daughters. All these. Not just ours.

Scene Nine

DEAN*'s room.* DANI *is in there.* DEAN *has just entered.*

DEAN. Dani.

DANI. They're fighting again.

DEAN. What are you doing?

DANI. Nothing. Just y'know. Looking.

DEAN. Don't look through my stuff, alright?

DANI. I'm your younger sister. I'm meant to look through your stuff. I've done it for years.

DEAN. Well stop.

DANI. I thought maybe I could have your old clothes.

DEAN. I got rid of them already.

DANI. I noticed.

DEAN. Well… can you get out of here then?

Beat.

DANI *holds up a pair of boxers.*

DANI. Where did you get these?

DEAN. It's weird you going through my underwear.

DANI. *I'm* weird?

DEAN. Don't go through my stuff.

DANI. Where'd you get them?

DEAN. Why?

DANI. Topman. Says so on the price tag.

Why'd you steal them?

DEAN. What?

DANI. Cos they're expensive these. Especially when you only get six fifty an hour at Tesco. Expensive when you're saving up for an operation that costs six grand. Heard Dad say. Should buy your underwear from M&S. Much better value for money. Then you wouldn't have to steal.

DEAN. I don't know what you're talking about.

DANI produces a security tag from her pocket.

DANI. The security tag was on it.

DEAN. What do you want?

DANI. Why'd you steal them?

DEAN. I didn't.

DANI. You used to tell me stuff. But now you…

Fine. I'll just tell Mum and Dad and you can tell them why. (*Goes to leave.*)

DEAN. I panicked. I just… panicked. I was going to the till, and all these young men behind with their biceps, and rolled-up sleeves with bits of armpit hair sticking out, and designer beards, and the line of hair below their belly button when they absently start scratching, the band of their own Calvin Kleins and what if I get up there to pay and they…

DANI. And they know.

Beat. DANI *hands* DEAN *the underwear.*

I stole a dress last month cos it was ridiculously overpriced and I just wanted to see if I could. My friend taught me how to get the security tag off. (*Hands* DEAN *the security tag.*) So we're not that different, you and me.

(*Of poster.*) You sort of look like him.

DEAN. You think?

DANI. Sort of. Not really.

You remember when we all went to see that film all together? Don't think we've done anything all together since. Don't think we've been happy since.

I found this hidden in your wardrobe. (*Photo album*). The trip to the South of France when I was nine. Spent every day swimming. Look. We even had matching swimsuits. Do you remember? Cos if Mum bought it for you, she had to buy it for me. Do you remember? (*Laughs.*) And those hideous polka-dot long-sleeve dresses. So we cut the sleeves off – Mum was so angry. (*Laughs harder.*) Remember?

Look.

DEAN. I don't want to.

DANI. We were happy then.

DEAN. I wasn't. I wasn't happy then.

DANI. You were.

DEAN. No.

DANI. I was there. There are pictures! Look! We're smiling.

DEAN. Still

DANI. Not still. I was there!

DEAN. It wasn't the same for me.

DANI. You can't just change everything! You can't just change history, Izzy.

DEAN. Don't call me that.

DANI. They're my memories too. It's my life too. You can't just say it wasn't what it was and that's that – it's not some fucking video game you can just start again, new character, like none of it ever happened.

DEAN. I'm not saying it didn't happen. I'm just saying it wasn't the same for me.

DANI. That's not fair.

DEAN. No. But it's true.

DANI. We had matching swimsuits. We were a pair. The Cheeky Girls we called ourselves. (*Sings*.) 'We are the cheeky girls, we are the cheeky girls, you are the' –

DEAN. I hated that swimsuit.

DANI. We cut the sleeves off our dresses. Mum was so

DEAN. I wished I could've cut the whole thing up.

DANI. No. No, Izzy.

DEAN. Stop calling me that.

DANI. I have pictures, Izzy. We're smiling.

DEAN. Don't call me that.

DANI. Izzy, Izzy, Dizzy Izzy, Isabella!

DEAN *grabs the photo album. Rips a page from it. Scrunches/rips it up.*

Stop it! Stop it!

But DEAN *is on a mission.*

DANI *grabs the* JAMES DEAN *poster. Rips it down the middle. Runs out.*

DEAN *stops himself crying by focusing on mantra.*

DEAN. Invisible. Pocket. Mono. Lean. Low. Hum. T. Again. (*Calmly gets some scissors and cuts Izzy out of one of the photos as he repeats his mantra.*) Invisible. Pocket. Mono. Lean. Low. Hum. T. Again.

Scene Ten

Later. JOSH *has just entered. Cut-up photos are all over the floor.*

DEAN. What's five thousand nine hundred and twenty-five divided by two?

JOSH. Why does it look like Instagram vomited all over your room? I got you something.

DEAN. That's like... that's like three thousand a month, which is...

JOSH. A present.

DEAN. Fifteen hundred a week.

JOSH. Here.

DEAN. Which is like, with my six fifty a Tesco-hour, that's like, that's like

JOSH. Over two hundred hours.

DEAN. Two hundred hours. How the hell am I gonna work two hundred hours a week?

JOSH. You're not. There aren't two hundred hours in a week.

DEAN. What the hell am I meant to do?

JOSH. Are you not going to open my present?

DEAN. I could buy Lottery tickets.

JOSH. Dean.

DEAN. No you're right, that's completely, the odds are against me. Something less risky.

I could rob a bank.

JOSH. That's a brilliant idea.

DEAN. I could start an online business, and sell, sell – I could sell my old underwear. People pay big money for that you know.

JOSH. Dean, that's weird. Would you just open

DEAN. Yes, yes, I'll open the damn –

JOSH. There's a card.

DEAN (*opens it*). *Happy Anniversary*. Shit. Sorry. Shit.

JOSH. I don't care.

DEAN. I've just been completely wrapped up in

JOSH. I know. Honestly, I don't care.

DEAN (*opens gift*). *Lonely Planet Thailand*.

Sorry I didn't… Sorry. I'm crap.

JOSH (*affectionately*). I know. But you're my crap.

Look, they've got a whole chapter just on beaches. I thought we could start planning, y'know. Make it like a thing. A date. Each week we read one of the chapters, plan stuff.

DEAN. That sounds great. Though at this rate I won't be going.

JOSH. What do you mean?

DEAN. Well the tiny bit I've saved so far now's gotta go to the surgery, right? And if I can't get the money together by August, might have to have the surgery in the autumn or the winter.

JOSH. But we're leaving September 1st. That was the plan.

DEAN. Plan might have to change.

JOSH. You can have the surgery when you get back.

DEAN. That's not an option.

JOSH. I don't get what the hurry is.

DEAN. The hurry is I've already spent more than seventeen years like this.

JOSH. So what's one more year?

DEAN.…what?

JOSH. Maybe there's a reason the other wait list is two years, maybe you should just wait, you're meant to wait, and when we come back then you can see if you still…

DEAN. Still what?

JOSH....there's nothing wrong with the way you are now.

DEAN. Oh my God. What you think – have you been hoping all this time I'd suddenly – what – that this is a phase or something?

JOSH. No.

DEAN. Oh I've seen sense, pass me the dress and make-up!

JOSH. No! That's not fair, Dean!

DEAN. What's not fair is having to wake up with these every day.

JOSH. I'm just saying how it is now is fine, you don't need to

DEAN. Fine for who?

JOSH. I'm trying here, Dean.

DEAN. Try harder.

JOSH. I have, I have, I have... well I've done loads haven't I? I'm here aren't I?

This affects both of us.

DEAN. This?

JOSH. And I'm sorry okay, but the thought of you, I'm okay with this, I love this, but the thought of you... mutilating your body... the thought of you without... it just, it just... freaks me out a bit.

Pause.

Dean.

DEAN. Get out.

JOSH. Don't be

DEAN. Get out, Josh.

JOSH. Let's talk about this. We'll figure something out.

DEAN. Stay away from me.

JOSH. I love you, Dean.

DEAN (*grabs scissors, holds out*). I said stay the fuck away from me.

Get out. (*Holds scissors to breasts.*) Or I'll cut them off myself.

JOSH *exits*.

DEAN *drops the scissors, starts crying. Sorts himself out in the mirror, repeating the mantra quietly to himself. Puts on some music. Buddy Holly's 'Everyday' like at the start. Gels his hair. Sprays some Lynx. Grabs a box/piggy bank. Takes a handful of cash from it.*

Scene Eleven

Voicemail.

SMT. Dean, we're just checking in

checking up really

making sure you're alright

making sure everything's alright

cos you've been absent for the past three weeks

so we wanted to make sure everything's okay…

And to inform you that the warning came

the call came

they're coming. Ofsted.

Which means the assembly

and you haven't given us your speech

which is fine

we totally trust you

absolutely

we just want to double-check you're still game

still on board

still alive and well.

And getting better.

Get well soon.

And if you could get better by Monday at 2 p.m. well then all the better.

Scene Twelve

DEAN*'s bedroom*. DEAN *looks a bit worse for wear. He's been partying hard the last couple of weeks*. LAURA*'s just entered*.

LAURA. What happened to your sick poster? I wanted to borrow it.

DEAN. What for?

LAURA. For the wedding. Would work brill-iant-ly with the decor. We could tape it.

DEAN. Um. Maybe.

LAURA. Who have you been out partying with?

DEAN. No one. I haven't.

LAURA. Sorry to just like, but I've left you like, literally a hundred messages. And no one's seen you. And you've missed a bunch of Tesco shifts.

DEAN. I've been here studying.

LAURA. Then why are you like dressed? Who have you been out with?

DEAN. I've been here.

LAURA. Dean.

DEAN. No one, Laura.

LAURA. Well you look a bit like a Pete Doherty Amy Winehouse love child.

So. Anyway. It's a bit awkward, but it's just best to come right out and say it. I'm a bit concerned about you and Josh.

DEAN. Oh. Thanks. But you don't need to be.

LAURA. But I do. Literally. Cos you're meant to be partners, walking back up the aisle after. And I'm concerned really, that your not talking could affect the dynamic.

DEAN. I'm not gonna get back together just for the sake of a wedding march.

LAURA. No. Course. That would be. Just. It might ruin the wedding. And I wouldn't want you to feel guilty, to feel responsible for ruining the most important day of their lives, that's all.

DEAN. I won't.

LAURA. Good, no. I just don't – like if it ends in divorce, don't want you to feel that you could've prevented it.

DEAN. Laura, I'm sure I can walk down the aisle with Josh, smiles and all.

LAURA. Good. Well that is a re-lief.

DEAN. Is that why you came over?

LAURA. No. I came. To show you… this! (*Pulls out poodle skirt and bow.*) What do you think?

DEAN. Yeah. You'll look great in it.

LAURA. Aww. Actually. It's not for me.

DEAN. Who's it for?

LAURA. Um. Well.

Pause.

Look, Dean. We all support you one hundred percent. Really. But this is their wedding day and I was chatting with Amy's mum and we both agree that, well, it could take the attention away from Amy and Kyle. Steal the limelight. You understand.

DEAN. I'm not wearing a skirt.

LAURA. It's just for one day.

DEAN. Do you know what you're asking me?

LAURA. Definitely. I definitely do. And I wouldn't if it were any other day.

DEAN. Does Amy know about this?

LAURA. She's got enough to worry about.

DEAN. I can't. No.

LAURA. Sure. I understand. It's just. Her mum said. Dean, you can't come to the wedding then. I'm really sorry.

I'll just. (*Leaves outfit.*) It's just one day, right? (*Exits.*)

DEAN *takes more money from his piggy bank/box.*

JAMES DEAN *appears.*

JAMES DEAN. I thought you were saving that money.

DEAN. I thought you were dead.

JAMES DEAN. Why? Cos she ripped the poster? I'm James Dean, buddy. I don't die. Not really.

Where are you going?

DEAN. I'm not.

JAMES DEAN. Who are you going with?

DEAN. What are you – my mum? If I'd wanted a mother figure I'd have dreamt up Audrey Hepburn or someone instead of you.

JAMES DEAN (*impersonating Hepburn*). 'I don't want to own anything until I find a place where me and things go together. I'm not sure where that is but I know what it is like. It's like Tiffany's.'

DEAN. You weren't even alive any more when that came out.

JAMES DEAN. Ouch. So why are you ignoring them? Your friends?

DEAN. I'm not ig– it's complicated. You wouldn't understand.

JAMES DEAN. Try me.

DEAN....

I just went in. I don't know what I was planning.

Sound/light from the bar/memory filters through, so it's like DEAN*'s there.*

To get shit-faced and forget him and snog some random maybe. But I... walked in, started talking to these young guys and they went to buy me a drink. And so I stood alone waiting in some crappy disco lights in a place that smelled of sweat and piss and farts, and I realised: they don't know anything about me. No one here does.

The disco light/sound goes, so we're back in the bedroom.

When I'm with them I feel like... I can forget.

JAMES DEAN. So you're just gonna cut off your friends? Forget them?

DEAN. But that's just it. Maybe they're not my friends. Maybe they're her friends.

Scene Thirteen

Men's toilets at a bar. DEAN *turns around from a urinal to find* KYLE *standing there.*

KYLE (*speaking into mobile phone as if it's a walkie-talkie*).
  Got him. Read: Subject has been located.

DEAN. Kyle, what are you doing here?

  AMY *enters.*

KYLE (*speaking into mobile*). Subject identified.

AMY. You don't need to talk into your phone, I'm right here.

DEAN. Amy? You know you're in the men's toilets.

AMY. You know you haven't returned my calls or texts.
  Literally not a single one.

DEAN. Sorry, I've been... busy.

AMY. Is it drugs? Alcohol?

DEAN. What?

AMY. Well there must be some teenage cliché going on, which
  has forced us to stage an intervention.

DEAN. Oh. Is that what this is? How'd you find me?

AMY. Let's just say we have our ways, we know people.

KYLE. Your dad told us. Maybe we should go outside.

AMY. I'm not letting him out of my sight.

KYLE. But we're not really supposed to be in here. It's a bar.

AMY. What kind of bar has board games by the way? People
  getting pissed playing Connect Four.

KYLE. Just, if we get caught... I mean we're (*Whispers.*)
  under-age.

AMY. We're GETTING MARRIED for God's sake.

KYLE. And if you're caught in the gents', you could get
  arrested.

AMY. Well at least if I'm in prison I can stop talking about
  bloody table decorations. (*To* DEAN.) What's going on,

Dean? You and Josh break up and then you stop talking to all of us, just disappear for like weeks and now Laura tells me you might not come to the wedding? We miss you, Dean.

DEAN. ....I miss you guys too.

KYLE. Great. Sorted. Can we go? We're meant to be at an hors d'oeuvres tasting in like five minutes. (*To* DEAN.) We've been here like an hour. Amy didn't want to cause a scene in front of your new friends. So I've been waiting in here ages. One guy even called the manager to say there was a perv just sitting eating crisps in the toilets.

AMY. So who are they? That guy in the coveralls –

DEAN. Bart.

AMY. – is he your boyfriend?

DEAN. I guess he's...

JOSH *jumps out of one of the stalls* (*or wherever he's hidden*).

JOSH. That hipster-douche is your boyfriend?

DEAN. What the hell?

AMY. How long have you been hiding in there?

Kyle?

KYLE. I wanted someone to keep me company. (*To* JOSH.) You promised not to come out, mate.

AMY. I cannot believe you. I actually cannot like literally look at you right now, Kyle.

KYLE. You are looking at me.

AMY. It's a mirror. It doesn't count.

JOSH. Bart? Bart? As in Simpson?

DEAN. As in the Apostle actually. Bartholomew.

JOSH. You dumped me for a guy in a farmer's dungarees!

DEAN. Just because I find someone who's funny and chilled out and nice to me and doesn't hide in toilets –

JOSH. Does he know?

DEAN. Does he know what?

JOSH. Think if I go and tell him he'll still be so nice and funny and chilled out?

DEAN. Do you always have to be such a douche? All of the time?

JOSH. *I'm* a douche? I was peering at that guy for like the last hour. *He's* the douche. The king of douchebags. The *apostle* of douchebags.

KYLE. We should probably go, Amy.

AMY. I said I'm not looking at you.

KYLE. Yeah, but you can still hear me right?

AMY. If I hear the words seat cover or party favours once more, I swear to God I will divorce you before the wedding. Dean, can I ring you tonight? Will you pick up?

DEAN. Yeah. Yeah.

KYLE. Later, guys.

AMY *and* KYLE *exit.*

JOSH. We should talk.

DEAN. Ever noticed how your talks always need to happen in toilets? A metaphor for how piss-poor your talking is and the crap that comes out of your mouth. You're one of those turds that just won't go down. No matter how many times I flush you away you magically keep reappearing.

JOSH. I still care about you, Dean.

DEAN. Well stop. Hiding? Spying on me? What is wrong with you?

JOSH. What is wrong with *you*? You don't even know this guy.

DEAN. It has nothing to do with you, Josh.

JOSH. He could be a… proper mental case, kill you in the night.

DEAN. Well he hasn't killed me in the night yet.

JOSH. You've spent the night with him?

DEAN. What do you want, Josh?

JOSH. He could be part of some crazy paedophile ring.

DEAN. He's fifteen!

JOSH. What kind of name is Bartholomew anyway? What is he, a pirate?

DEAN. Yeah he's a pirate.

JOSH. Really?

DEAN. No, Josh. Now please just go home and leave us alone.

JOSH. Us? So you're an us?

DEAN. You know what, I don't care, stay here. Stay in the toilets. Write poetry about your genitals on the wall. (*Goes to leave*.)

JOSH. The plane tickets came.

DEAN. What?

JOSH. Thailand. Ordered them months ago. Well they arrived.

DEAN. No, no, you don't get to – this is what you do. I sort things out, I finally get shit in my life together and then you come along and fuck everything up again.

JOSH. I haven't – I'm just telling you the tickets arrived. And I don't know what to do. Tell me what to do, Dean.

DEAN. Sometimes you need to figure out what to do for yourself.

JOSH. Yeah. Yeah. I know. So I researched, I went online, and they say… it's normal.

Beat.

That I'm normal…

DEAN. You're…?

JOSH. How I reacted. And they… I think you need to be more patient with me.

I was, I was, all things considered, quite patient with you. And you were quite… selfish. So.

Pause.

And I think I've been, all things considered, I was, I've been a really tolerant person. So… yeah.

Pause. DEAN moves slowly toward JOSH, stands close. Looks him in the eye. JOSH (and we) think DEAN might even hug him, or kiss him.

But then DEAN punches JOSH in the chest.

Ow.

DEAN *hits JOSH again.*

Dean, that really hurts.

DEAN *hits him again.*

DEAN. Hit me.

JOSH. What?

DEAN. You wanna sort this out? Is that why you came here?

JOSH. I guess I –

DEAN. Is it?

JOSH. I s'pose.

DEAN. Then let's sort this out. Hit me.

JOSH. I'm not gonna –

DEAN *hits JOSH again.*

DEAN. What? Not gonna fight back? Be a man, Josh.

Hits him again.

JOSH. Ow, I'm not gonna

DEAN *hits him again.*

DEAN. You wanna sort this out? Keep your *tolerance* and fight back.

Hits again.

Fight.

And again.

Back.

JOSH. Stop! I'm not gonna hit a…

DEAN. A what? A what, Josh?

Hits again.

Say it! Say it!

Hits again.

JOSH. Stop it!

DEAN. I dare you. Say it!

Hits again.

JOSH. Stop it!

DEAN. Or

Hits.

hit me!

Keeps hitting.

'I'm not gonna hit a' – say it!

JOSH. Stop it!

JOSH *punches* DEAN *in the face.* JOSH *is as shocked as* DEAN *is.*

Shit. Sorry, sorry.

Pause.

DEAN (*genuine*). Thank you.

JOSH *goes.*

Scene Fourteen

School assembly. DEAN *has a black eye.*

DEAN. Good afternoon, students, teachers, and visitors from Ofsted.

Our school prides itself on tolerance. You can be who you want to be and we will tolerate you. It says so in a policy document in a drawer somewhere.

We learn in history about a black woman who decided one day to sit where she wanted to on a bus.

We learn about another woman who chained herself to Parliament.

We learn about some angry drag queens in a bar who fought back one night.

We learn that to be tolerant of every person is what we should aspire to. A badge of honour we can wear. *I am a tolerant person.*

Fuck tolerance.

Those people – the black lady on the bus, the woman in chains, those men in heels. They weren't fighting for tolerance. To be tolerated.

Because tolerance is horseshit.

Tolerance is the emptiest word in the dictionary.

Tolerate is what you do when someone's playing their music loudly on the bus.

Tolerate is what you do when someone's texting next to you in the cinema.

I don't want to be tolerated.

I want to be admired.

I want to be envied.

I want to be… loved.

Love me.

And if that's too much to ask. Then hate me.

But don't tolerate me.

Because tolerance means sweet fuck-all.

Scene Fifteen

AMY*'s bedroom*. KYLE *wears a wedding dress*.

JOSH. What the fuck?

KYLE. The band cancelled. Lead singer's getting a hip replacement.

JOSH. You're wearing a dress.

KYLE. Yeah.

JOSH. Okay.

KYLE. Yeah. So we've had to get a new band.

JOSH. Guess that's what happens when you get a band who were actually playing in the 1950s.

KYLE. So we've had to get impersonators. Buddy Hollister and the Abercrombies. Who were only born in like 1992… so just not as authentic – like what will these kids actually know?

JOSH. Why are you wearing a wedding dress?

KYLE. I don't like surprises. Couldn't leave it to chance.

JOSH. Oh. But why'd you put it on?

KYLE. Not sure.

JOSH. I thought it's bad luck to see the dress before.

KYLE. No, bad luck to see the bride *in* the dress.

JOSH. Groom in the dress is alright then.

KYLE *puts on the veil*.

Amy could walk in any second.

KYLE. No, she's watching *Don't Tell the Bride*, analysing all the things that could go wrong.

JOSH. Gonna be perfect.

KYLE. No surprise punches.

JOSH. There won't be.

KYLE. I mean you and Dean. Walking down the aisle.

Lift up the veil for me.

He does.

Is it easy?

JOSH. What?

KYLE. The lifting. What if it gets stuck?

JOSH. It won't.

KYLE. Gets caught in my cufflink and I can't raise it up?

JOSH. It's gonna be perfect. (*Starts to cry.*)

KYLE. Save it for the day, mate. Tears look great on camera.

JOSH. I fucked up. I royally – I always thought we'd get married. One day. Maybe after Thailand, uni. Find a flat, move in together. Grow old together. That was the plan. And I fucked it up.

KYLE. If you have a plan, you could make it happen.

JOSH. Sorry to break it to you, Kyle, but sometimes plans don't go to plan. Sometimes no matter what you wish for or plan for, what you get… you just get a shit fifties knock-off band.

There are days when I'm like I can do this. It's all normal. It's just a pronoun. And then suddenly I think it's all – and I think about Izzy and what we – and I don't know if I can handle it.

DEAN *appears on the other side of the mirror.*

KYLE. Do you love him?

JOSH.… Yeah. Yeah.

KYLE. Then unfuck it up.

Beat as DEAN *and* JOSH *stare at each other through the mirror. Then* JOSH *and* KYLE *go.*

Scene Sixteen

DEAN*'s bedroom.*

DEAN *holds up the poodle skirt and bow in front of him in the mirror.* JAMES DEAN *appears.*

JAMES DEAN. You know that skirt is so last century, right?

DEAN (*in an American accent*). 'Y'know. I bet you're a real yoyo.'

JAMES DEAN. 'I love you too.'

I saw your little speech.

DEAN. What'd you think?

JAMES DEAN. You've got balls. I'm proud of you, kid.

DEAN. It just sorta came out… the words.

BOTH. But it felt… I felt… for the first time I was really… me.

JAMES DEAN. Gimme those.

DEAN. I haven't got anything else to wear to the wedding.

JAMES DEAN (*takes off his jacket*). Here.

DEAN. What will you wear?

JAMES DEAN (*takes skirt and bow*). These.

JAMES DEAN *puts on the skirt, puts the bow in his hair.* DEAN *puts on the jacket.*

DEAN. Are you coming?

JAMES DEAN. Think I'll pass.

DEAN. Will you be here when I get back?

Pause.

JAMES DEAN. You'll be alright, kid. I think you'll be just fine.

Goodbye, Dean.

DEAN. Goodbye, Izzy.

> DEAN *finds a dollar bill in the jacket pocket. Turns to give it to* JAMES DEAN *but he's gone. He puts the bill in his now empty piggy bank/box. A new start.*

Scene Seventeen

MUM *and* DAD.

DAD. Dani's not coping very well. So. She'll go live with her mother. She found a place not far. She didn't want the house.

MUM. She cut up all the photos. One night when everyone was sleeping. Cut herself out of all of them. If she was in the middle, if it was like a group photo, a family photo, she just cut out her head. Frame after frame after frame of... space. The space where my child used to be.

DAD. Book after book after book. And you know what I learned in the end?

MUM. But she missed one. (*Holds photo.*) Forgot to check my wallet. My baby. My baby girl.

DAD. I learned nothing. Cos no one has an explanation. But who needs an explanation? He's my... my...

MUM. My...

> *They switch clothes. So the female actor now plays* MUM, *the male actor* DAD.

DAD. My... I still struggle saying *son.* When she was pregnant, I hoped it was a boy. I know you're not supposed to say that. But I did.

MUM. Once upon a time there was a girl. And then there wasn't.

DAD. He's my child. And I love him.

MUM. The guidebooks don't –

When a child dies you mourn. They say losing a child is the hardest of all deaths. They describe the feeling as – the noun they use is loss. Mourning. And when a child goes missing and is never found, you feel you're never able to rest, to properly just live. The noun they use is restlessness.

(*Starts to cry softly.*) My daughter is not dead. My daughter is not missing. But she is gone. And so I don't have the language to describe what I'm feeling. It's not in any of the books. There's no noun for that.

DAD. We went out for dinner the other day, the two of us, and the waiter comes over and he says: 'What can I get you lads to drink?' Two lads. Out for a drink.

MUM. There's a line in the film when she says: 'She'll outgrow it dear. It's just the age when nothing fits.'

I think that's a lie. Cos sometimes you turn forty-one, and still nothing fits like it's supposed to.

I hope… I hope he does. I hope Dean… fits.

Scene Eighteen

Wedding reception. Everyone wears fifties outfits. DEAN *looks like* JAMES DEAN.

JOSH. Nice jacket.

DEAN. You think?

JOSH. I think.

DEAN. Amy's mum was giving me evils.

JOSH. No, it suits you. And the colour distracts from your eye.

DEAN. Is that meant to be funny?

JOSH. Yeah. No. I'm not sure.

DEAN. You're useless.

JOSH. I know. I'm sorry. 'Bout the eye.

DEAN. I asked for it. Literally.

JOSH. I'm still sorry. If it's any consolation, my chest still hurts like a bitch. That's some fist.

I liked your speech by the way.

DEAN. Laura wrote most of it. A speech to the tune of 'Summer Lovin' certainly wasn't my idea.

JOSH. I meant your speech at school.

DEAN. Oh. Got me two weeks' suspension.

JOSH. Still. It was kick-ass.

DEAN. Yeah.

JOSH. Bartholomew here? Or is he on a ship with a parrot looking for gold?

DEAN. I wouldn't know. Call me jean-ophobic but I just couldn't see a future with someone who wears dungarees.

JOSH. Here. (*Hands gift bag.*)

DEAN. Meant to get a gift for the bride and groom.

JOSH. Just open it.

DEAN *does. It's a McDonald's Happy Meal box.*

DEAN. Uhh… thanks… not sure weddings are really 'bring your own meal'.

JOSH. No, inside.

DEAN *opens the Happy Meal box. There's lots of money inside.*

DEAN.…

JOSH. Ever since that date we had at McDonald's, a couple years ago, when we first talked about spending our gap year together, I kept the box, to remind me. And whenever I

could, I'd put savings in there, for our trip. Took it out in
cash, put it under my bed, make sure I didn't spend it.
There's about three and a half grand. It's over two grand
short, but it's all I have.

DEAN. Josh.

JOSH. And before you even say it, you have to. Okay? You
have to take it. August 30th.

DEAN. But Thailand.

JOSH. Thailand can wait.

*Music lingers through from the dance floor. 'Teenager in
Love' by Dion & The Belmonts.*

DEAN. Josh, I don't know what to…

JOSH. One last dance?

DEAN. You're so melodramatic.

JOSH. Just shuttup and dance with me.

DEAN *approaches. They're unsure where to put their
hands… who's the boy in the dance? They try a couple things
out and dance.*

I always thought Olivia should've married Viola, and
Sebastian should've married Orsino… don't you think?

They keep dancing.

*The song comes to an end, and changes to some cheesy
wedding music.*

I fucking hate weddings.

DEAN. Me too.

They stand close. Are about to kiss. When AMY *runs on in
her wedding dress.*

AMY. Save me. If I have to smile for one more photo, I swear to
God I'm gonna be the first bride to go berserk and murder all
her guests on her wedding day. Kyle's made a spreadsheet of
every photo that needs to be taken today. And who thought it
would be a good idea to have a five-kilo wedding dress?

DEAN. At least you look beautiful.

AMY. I look like a Tinkerbell on steroids.

JOSH. Well at least you look better in it than Kyle.

AMY. What?

Are you eating McDonalds at my wedding?

KYLE *enters, with a clipboard.* LAURA *follows.*

KYLE. There you are. We're like eleven minutes behind. We're meant to have already cut the tofu cheesecake.

LAURA. And everyone's waiting for you to throw the bouquet.

AMY. I can barely lift my arms in this.

KYLE. Oh come on, my little soy chocolate button. I'll help you.

KYLE *leads her off,* AMY *mouths 'help' behind her.*

JOSH. I like your skirt, Laura.

LAURA. Thanks. You look good too. You both do. Really.

Don't want to miss the bouquet! (*Exits.*)

JOSH. Coming? It'll be fun.

DEAN. I'd rather spend eternity eating tofu cheesecake.

JOSH. Fair enough.

JOSH *exits. Pause.* DEAN *alone. Distant wedding sounds.*

DEAN. Once upon a time.

JOSH *runs back in.*

Josh.

Josh?

JOSH *grabs* DEAN. *Kisses him passionately.*

He runs back off. Before he's quite off:

Josh?

JOSH. Yes, Dean?

DEAN....

Catch that bouquet and I'll kill you.

JOSH *smiles. And exits.*

Once upon a time there was a boy.

End.